D0585229

Propagation of
Hardy Perennials

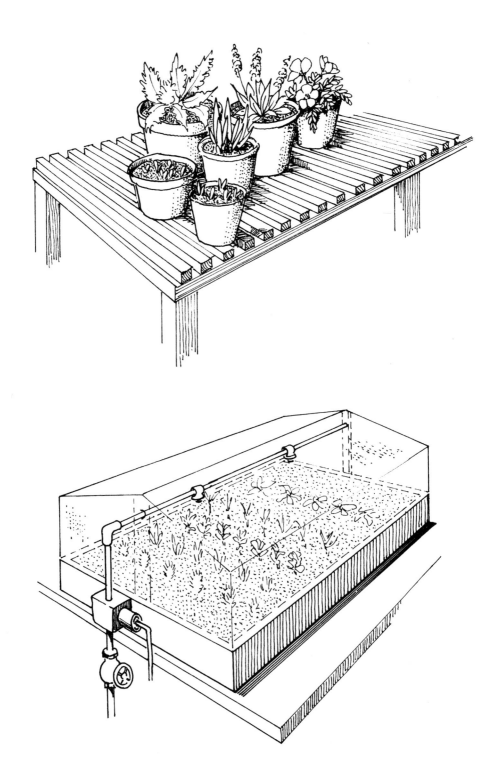

Propagation of Hardy Perennials

RICHARD BIRD

B. T. Batsford Ltd · London

For
Anne Stephney

First published 1993
© Richard Bird 1993

All rights reserved. No part of this
publication may be reproduced, in any
form or by any means, without
permission from the Publisher.

Typeset by Deltatype Ltd, Ellesmere Port,
Cheshire
and printed in Great Britain by Butler and
Tanner, Frome, Somerset

Published by

B. T. Batsford Ltd
4 Fitzhardinge Street
London W1H 0AH

A catalogue record for this book is
available from the British Library

ISBN 0 7134 7062 3

Contents

Colour Illustrations

Introduction

Plants and gardening can become an obsession. Many gardeners start innocently enough, perhaps merely as a means of tidying up the mess that can be seen from the house, but gradually something rather basic takes hold of them; the much clichéd 'return to the soil'. A great deal of pleasure and satisfaction can be had from growing plants well and having an attractive, well-stocked garden. Growing annuals and bedding plants bought from a local garden centre is often the starting point, but as interest grows, so does the scope of the garden and the means by which it is grown. The gardener turns to the common perennials that can be seen grown to perfection in so many gardens open to the public, such as Sissinghurst Castle. These gardens also contain many rarer and more difficult plants, and soon many gardeners are inspired to move beyond the limited bounds of the local garden centre.

From an early stage it is useful to be able to increase plants for personal use and for giving away, but once the realms of the more out-of-the-ordinary plants are reached, then it becomes essential to be able to propagate, as often the only way of acquiring certain plants is to raise them from seed or grow them from a couple of cuttings begged from a friend. Once stocks have been built up then the gardener, in turn, will be able to provide plants for the delight of others.

Propagation is one of the fundamental skills in gardening. Not all gardeners need to acquire it, many can happily get along by buying fresh plants, but most feel the urge to create something from seed no bigger than a speck of dust or from a cutting that looks no more than a scrap of vegetation. Gardening becomes more alive and satisfying when it is possible to grow your own plants and many gardeners take quiet pleasure in their skills.

This book aims to help the gardener who wishes to learn how to propagate a wide range of hardy plants for the flower garden. The first part deals with basic techniques, the second discusses the plants genus by genus. The latter part is probably the more important as, whilst the techniques have been written up before, there has never been a comprehensive listing of all the genera the gardener is likely to meet. This listing contains detailed information on how each genus can be propagated and any variations for individual species or cultivars.

On the one hand the listing deals with common plants that the first-time grower might come across and, on the other, it deals with far more obscure plants (many of which are on the fringes of hardiness) that the more experienced grower may discover or wish to acquire. It is surprising how often keen gardeners come across plants or seed that they have never heard of before and are uncertain how to cope with them. This book hopes to provide guidance so that they can make the most of these opportunities.

So little has been written about the propagation of individual plants and, yet, the accumulated knowledge of gardeners past and present is enormous. Alas, apart from that handed down by word of mouth, much is lost as gardeners lay down their tools for the last time, each new generation having to rediscover what is in effect quite common knowledge. This then is a distillation of a fraction of that knowledge, presented as a jumping-off point from which gardeners may gain more experience.

In the final analysis, there are no definitive ways of doing anything in gardening. One gardener will succeed in growing a plant in one way, while another will also succeed, but with quite opposed techniques. Conversely, a third will fail by using either method. Much depends on where the gardener lives, the kind of soil and the local weather conditions. Even gardeners' temperaments can affect the way they grow their plants and, certainly, the amount of time available has an important influence. To a certain extent depth of pocket can also alter things, but expensive propagators and other gadgets, although useful, are far from essential (I currently use no extra heating other than the sun in my propagating).

Any book on gardening, then, must only expect to be a guide, it can never hope to be definitive. The techniques expounded here are all based on experience, but there are bound to be others who have had different experiences and have successfully raised plants using different methods. I apologize for any omissions and, should there be any future editions, would hope to include any new or forgotten information.

The plants I have dealt with in this book are very wide ranging and I make no apology for including many shrubby, annual, and biennial plants not strictly considered as hardy perennials but which are frequently grown along beside them. The category a plant belongs to is irrelevant if you want information about it. Strict classification may have its place on the show bench or in the botanical garden, but matters little in the ordinary garden. Similarly, I have been a bit cavalier in my treatment of hardiness. I have included all the material likely to be hardy somewhere in the British Isles, even if it is only the Isles of Scilly. This may seem extreme to someone living in the colder areas but it is surprising what can be grown in certain parts of the country, especially in a sunny spot protected by a warm wall. It is well worth experimenting; *Agapanthus* were once considered impossible to grow outside and yet there are some wonderful stands at Harlow Carr in Yorkshire and many more in Scotland.

Gardeners are the most generous of people both through their gifts of plants and through the time they spend talking about their craft and their plants. Many have, wittingly or unwittingly, contributed to this book through years of friendship and conversations. To all these I extend my grateful thanks.

Richard Bird
Rogers Rough, Spring 1993

Getting Started

Propagation is one of the fundamental arts of gardening. It is not a difficult skill to acquire and many embark on it without a great deal of thought. A packet of seed purchased from a garden centre and scattered along a row or in a patch is propagation at its simplest. However, most packets of seed purchased over the counter are annuals or easy-to-grow perennials, and more thought and skill are required to cope with the less usual plants.

Skills can be improved by reading books but the only real method of learning is by actually doing the job, and in the case of gardening it means getting your hands dirty. Beginners should start by taking cuttings and divisions of plants that are quite easy to deal with. Thus they might try dividing a clump of *Aster novi-belgii* (Michaelmas daisy) into the smallest portions possible in order to see how many new plants can be made from it. They might also like to take cuttings from *Anthemis cupiana* or from *Penstemon*. Having gained confidence with these plants, move on to others. It may be surprising to find how easy the majority of plants are to cope with, it is only a relative few that need really special treatment and these problems will become a challenge rather than a barrier.

Often it is only a minor factor that changes a difficult plant into an easy plant and it is the purpose of this book to act as a guide to these details. For example, timing may be important. Many growers have great difficulty in germinating *Helleborus* and, yet, if the seed is sown fresh (as opposed to the following spring) then they will germinate like the proverbial mustard and cress. Similarly, cuttings of some plants will root more readily if taken in spring rather than in summer or autumn. Alternatively, as in the case of *Pulsatilla*, it is impossible to take normal cuttings from a plant but it is possible to take root cuttings. All this information is learnt from experiment and experience. So if you wish to propagate, do not hesitate, just go out there and do it, you will have your failures but you will also have an increasing number of successes.

10

WHERE TO PROPAGATE

The tools required are few beyond a number of pots and a sharp knife or scalpel, all of which will be returned to later. The first consideration is where propagation takes place. There are several possibilities. Out-of-doors can be pleasant and enjoyable for the gardener in sunny weather, but is the worst situation for plants as cuttings or roots can dry out very quickly if exposed to the sun and wind. They are much happier if it is raining, but then it is not so pleasant for the gardener.

The solution to this conundrum is to propagate inside if it is at all possible. For many people the only choice is the kitchen. There is nothing wrong with this if you are prepared to clear up the mess after you. However careful a propagator is, compost always seems to go flying into every corner of the room. Another disadvantage is that it is usually impossible to have composts, pots and your favourite tools always to hand.

Another option is to use a greenhouse, although they are expensive luxuries to most gardeners. Indeed, they are more for the gardener's comfort than for the plants. For nearly all practical purposes a cold-frame can be used as an alternative to a greenhouse: they are cheaper to buy or build and cheaper to heat. Their one big disadvantage is that you cannot walk into them or work in them in inclement weather. Working in a greenhouse, particularly in the late winter or early spring when there is a cold wind but enough sun to bring the temperature inside to that of the summer, can give the gardener a snug feeling. Greenhouses do have one or two disadvantages when used for propagating. One is that they are never big enough. Any area allocated as a workbench area will soon be required to be converted to staging to take all the extra plants that appear. Another is that I am not keen to bring in plants for division, for example, only to discover as I open them up that they contain vine weevils or some other pest that can easily be transferred to the healthy plants already in the house. The drying sun has already been mentioned in connection with the open air and inside a hot glass-sided house the problem of drying roots and flagging cuttings can be a serious one. Having said all this against greenhouses, it must be admitted that many very successful gardeners use them all the time for their propagating. The point is to realize their limitations and take steps to counteract them: build pull-out or flap up work-surfaces; check all plants for pests and remove all soil before taking them into the house; and use shading.

Old-fashioned though the concept may be, the ideal is to have a potting shed. This need not be too big, as big as the pocket allows in fact. It really needs to be somewhere where the gardener can work protected from the weather, surrounded by bags of compost, fertilizer, rooting powder and tools. It needs to have a bench or table, preferably under a window for good light, with space under it for your legs when sitting on a stool, plus any bags or bins of compost and waste plant material. Shelves can be attached to the walls to take containers, labels, small tools and countless other things that seem to accumulate. Space may also be provided for racks to take a variety of sizes of clean pots. I have also managed to accomodate an old stainless-steel sink unit in my shed so that it is possible to soak pots or trays of compost in the sink and then place them to drain on the draining board, all of which can be reached from the main potting bench without getting off the stool.

This kind of setup may seem sheer luxury to many but, apart from the initial cost of the shed many years ago, all the fittings have been made from odds and ends and have cost nothing. I cannot tell you how many happy hours I have spent in there sowing seed and preparing cuttings. All my propagation and potting is carried out in it, leaving the kitchen for cooking and the greenhouse for growing plants. But remember that although a potting shed is very useful it is not essential. Many, many gardeners have propagated successfully without and there is no reason to suppose that you cannot also do so.

There is a modern compromise that seems to embrace elements of all three and that is the conservatory, which has recently made a resurgence. Many people find this a very convenient place to pot and, as long as it is not too much part of the house, are prepared to leave tools and bags of compost lying around.

Any potting shed need not be in too conspicuous a position. Siting it under a tree is a good idea as this helps it keep cool, as long as you can stand the dripping from the branches when it is raining. Since it tends to have the same central relationship to the garden as the kitchen does to the house, make certain that it is easy to approach with decent paths, avoid having to stomp through the mud.

If you intend to propagate on a grand scale (and it is surprising how difficult it is to restrict yourself) then the area around the potting shed or greenhouse must also be carefully considered. It is extremely useful to have a flat, empty area, preferably concreted, on which to put things down. There will always be a movement of pots in and out of the shed, frames, and greenhouse. Many accidents have happened through lack of space where trays have been balanced on top of other things. It is a nuisance to have to repot plants that have fallen over, but it is a disaster if they are pots of newly sown seed as there is no way in which these can be resurrected. It is also useful to have a flat surface where pots can be stood temporarily while they are watered.

If large quantities of materials are used then brick bins to store peat, leafmould, loam, grit and used compost are useful, as is storage space for empty pots. This may seem excessive but even one bale of peat needs somewhere to be stored, and open bags of grit or compost can easily pick up stray weed-seed or become over-wet if not adequately stored.

FRAMES

Cold-frames and plunge beds (or standing areas) are indispensible to a propagator. Frames can be purchased or easily constructed. Basically they consist of four walls, the two opposite of which are sloping, and a lid consisting of a framework containing glass (known as a light). The walls can be made from timber (railway sleepers are excellent as they are stable and very warm), brick or some sort of composite block such as breeze or concrete. Some cold-frames consist of an aluminium framework covered with glass. These have the advantage of letting in more light but this is more than offset by the thinness of the walls, which quickly lets out the heat. It is a good idea to install some form of catch so that the lights can be fastened down if there is a strong wind in the offing.

Cold-frames can easily be insulated in winter by draping them with an old carpet or hessian. In really cold spells they can be covered with bales of straw, which will maintain the temperature inside above freezing. If heat is required then heating cables can be installed in a layer of sand in the base of the frame and another set, if necessary, can be installed around the sides of the frame. Both can be controlled by thermostats so that the temperature is maintained but electricity is not wasted.

The base of the frame can be concrete or packed earth covered with black polythene (in the case of the latter make certain that all perennial weeds have been removed from the soil). Pots can be stood directly on to this or on to a layer of sand. If this sand is kept moist it not only provides a little moisture for the plants through the bottom of the pots, but it also keeps the air moist, which is important for plants that are just becoming established. Gravel can be used as an alternative, but provides less moisture to the plants. It is, however, less attractive to algae and liverworts that quickly turn sand green.

Cold-frames are used mainly for storing plants after they have been propagated to give them a chance to settle down before being allowed out into the elements. With the lid on they provide a close atmosphere, which most plants require at this time. The type of plants placed here would be newly potted-up divisions, cuttings that have rooted and been potted up, and seedlings that have been pricked out. Store these in the cold-frame for a few days with the lid shut and, on sunny days, with a shade frame over the top. Gradually open the lid allowing more air to circulate. After ten days remove the lid completely. Move the plants to the plunge beds and clear the space for more plants that need hardening off.

Another use of cold-frames is to give plants a certain amount of winter protection. Often as not this is to prevent the plants from getting too much rain as to protect them from the cold. Pans of seedlings that have germinated in the open during a warm spell in winter often need to be put under cover in case the weather turns cold again.

13

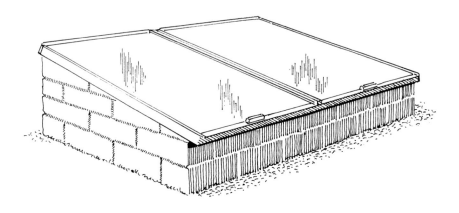

Fig. 1 *A simple home-made cold-frame made from concrete blocks or bricks.*

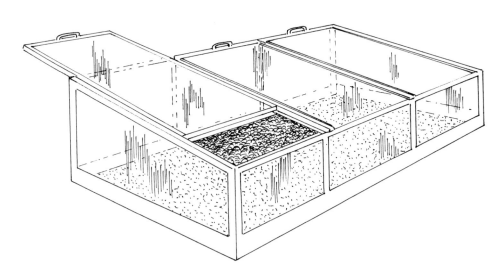

Fig. 2 *A ready-made frame of aluminium section and glass sides. These let in more light but are colder in winter.*

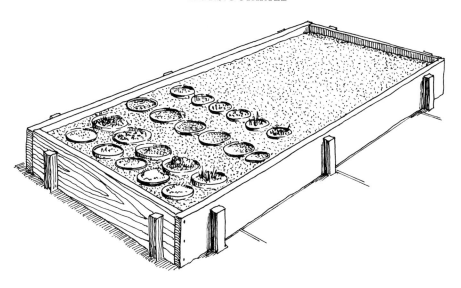

Fig. 3 *A plunge bed is an enclosure holding sand or ashes into which the pots are buried to their rims.*

Plunge beds or standing areas are similar to cold-frames except they do not have lids and because of this the walls are usually all horizontal. They are really just a neat and convenient way of storing pots of plants while they await planting out, being given away or otherwise disposed of. Plunge beds can also be used to store pans or pots sown with seed while they await germination. Most pots of hardy plant seed can be placed outside until they have germinated. In wet areas they may need covering to preclude excess rain, in which case a cold frame might be better. Plunge frames for seed pots are best sited in a shady area or provided with shade frames to keep off the drying sun.

More information about both these frames will be given as the various propagation techniques are discussed.

GREENHOUSES

Although to many gardeners the greenhouse might not be the ideal place to carry out propagation, it is, of course, the place where the results of the propagating activities are likely to end up. For propagation purposes any greenhouse is suitable. However, I would suggest that most greenhouses, as sold, do not have enough ventilation and extra opening windows or louvres should be made or bought at the time of purchase.

Staging or benching in a greenhouse is essential. Whatever it is made of or whatever form it takes, it must be strong. A whole bench full of pots, heavy with compost and water, weighs a tremendous amount and the legs should be strong enough to support this plus the weight of the gardener leaning on it. The simplest form of staging is a slatted wooden one. This has the advantage of allowing the air to circulate, but the uneven surface often allows smaller pots to tip over and it gives no warmth in winter or moisture in summer. An aluminum-tray bench is a better bet. If this has a lip all the way round, this will allow 2.5 cm (1 in) of sand or gravel to be spread over it, providing a good surface on which to stand pots. If this is kept damp, then there will be a more moist atmosphere around the pots and a small amount of water will also percolate up through the drainage holes of the pots, helping to prevent them from drying out.

Fig. 4 *Slatted wooden staging, which allows the air to circulate around the pots freely. It is cold in winter.*

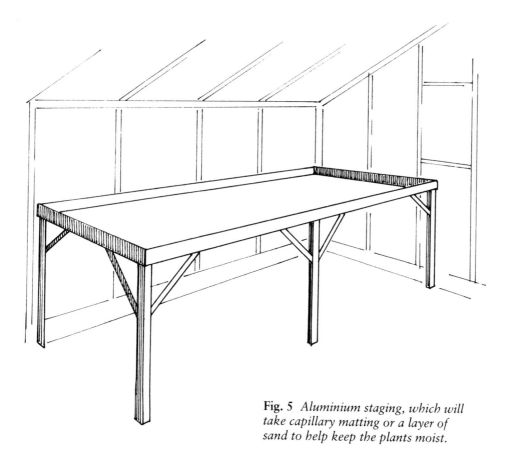

Fig. 5 *Aluminium staging, which will take capillary matting or a layer of sand to help keep the plants moist.*

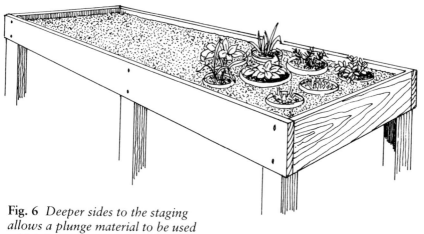

Fig. 6 *Deeper sides to the staging allows a plunge material to be used which keeps the contents of the pots moist and warm.*

Fig. 7 *Sliding, hinged or spanning boards that make ideal demountable work surfaces in the greenhouse.*

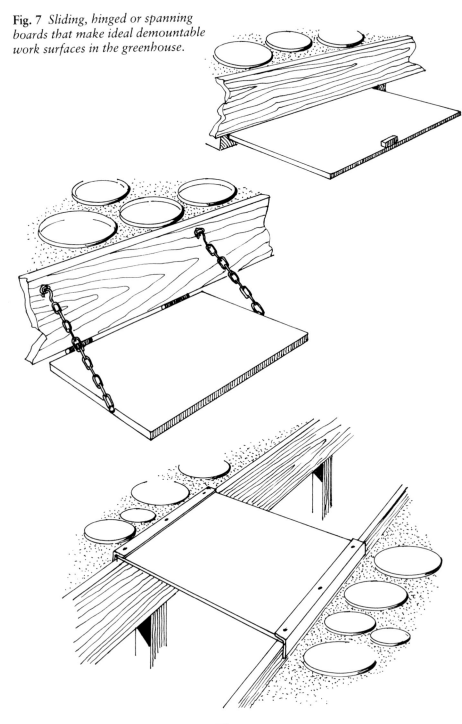

In colder areas (or in alpine houses where the pots are kept permanently in the greenhouse) a deeper bench can be used so that sand can be at least 15 cm (6 in) deep. This allows the pots to be plunged up to their rims, creating insulation that helps prevent them being frozen solid in cold conditions. This is a refinement rarely needed in most greenhouses.

There are one or two modifications that can be made which should make life easier. If work is to be undertaken in the greenhouse itself then a demountable bench will save wasting valuable staging area. This can be in the form of a flap that lifts up to a convenient height or a board that slides in under the main staging. It is also possible to have a loose piece of board that spans the gangway and simply rests on the staging on either side. The greenhouse may be the only place that will accomodate a propagating case of some sort. I will deal with these in more detail later, but for the moment let it be said that they can be installed either on top of the staging or, with a bit of ingenuity, beneath the bench where they will not waste any space but still perform their function very well.

PROPAGATORS

Some form of propagating frame is useful but, again, not essential. Many gardeners manage perfectly well to strike cuttings by placing them in pots and covering then with a polythene bag. An alternative is to cover the pot with a plastic sweet jar with the neck cut off. These are available free from sweet shops and have the advantage over plastic bags in that they are rigid.

The simplest form of frame, and one that I use, is just four pieces of wood, 15 cm (6 in) wide nailed together to make a hollow square, and a sheet of glass laid on the top. The length of the sides is immaterial and can be determined by the size of any glass that you may have available. I stand this frame on a tray of sharp sand, which forms a seal around the bottom and into which I can place cuttings directly if I so wish. A more sophisticated version can be made with two opposite sides sloping and a proper hinged lid. The sloping sides have the advantage that they allow any condensation on the inside of the lid to run down and fall off at the bottom of the frame as opposed to dripping onto the cuttings. With the single sheet of glass laid horizontally on the frame above, I just reverse the glass at least once a day.

To improve further still on this model, heating wires can be laid in the bed of sand in the base of the frame and a further set attached around the side of the frame to maintain an even air temperature. Both can be controlled by rod thermostats.

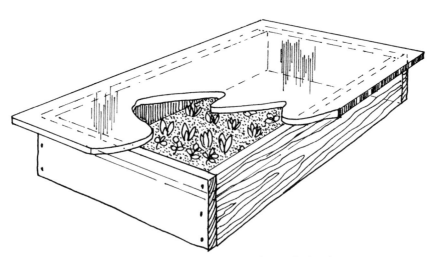

Fig. 8 *A simple propagator consisting of wooden sides with a sheet of glass over the top.*

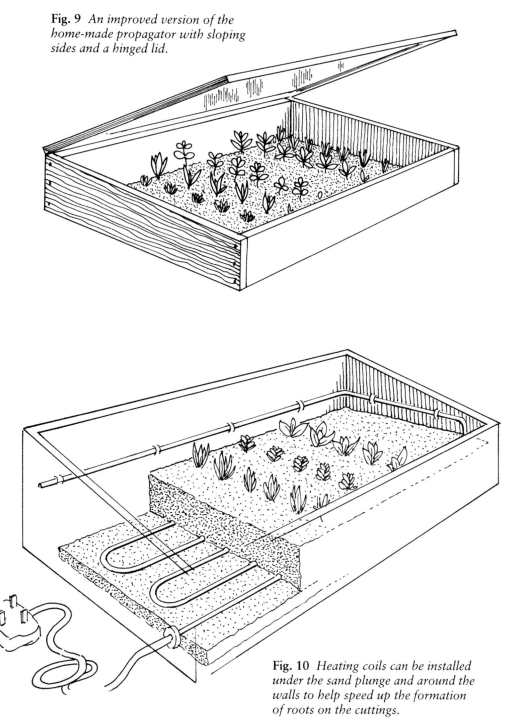

Fig. 9 *An improved version of the home-made propagator with sloping sides and a hinged lid.*

Fig. 10 *Heating coils can be installed under the sand plunge and around the walls to help speed up the formation of roots on the cuttings.*

This type of frame can be built on top of a bench or even under the bench if the greenhouse has glass sides right down to the floor. If used under the bench it is possible to build the frame into the ground. This will help maintain the heat and will also allow a larger amount of light to reach the cuttings as there will be more glass between the frame and the bench above. Such a frame is best sited in the corner of the greenhouse where it will receive light from two glass sides and the open gangway. Whether it is on or below the bench, if a hinged lid is used it is advisable to fit a catch or strut to support the lid so that both hands are free for working inside the frame.

So far I have only looked at home-made propagators. There are, of course, a large range of commercially produced alternatives. The simplest is just a seed tray with a plastic cover. The more sophisticated are still based on the same principle but are just built larger, usually with an aluminium frame and plastic or glass side panels and roof. Access can be through the top or sliding sides. Again heating may be accommodated in the base or sides.

The pros and cons of using propagating frames will be discussed later under the various propagation techniques.

TOOLS

Tools are a matter of personal choice. The one thing that is essential is a good sharp knife or a scalpel for the preparation of cuttings and possibly for cutting through divisions of plants. Knives should be kept sharp on a small oil stone and the difficulty or tediousness of this may make many people prefer surgical scalpels, which are readily available from chemists and model shops. These have replaceable blades and therefore can always be razor sharp. A razor-blade is a good alternative but the traditional double-sided ones can be dangerous to use.

When pricking out seedlings it can be useful to have a widger, which is really just a small spatula. Most people make their own or just use a plant label. It is used for digging out a seedling and then transferring it to a hole in the tray or pot into which it is to be planted. The hole itself can be made with a dibber (sometimes incorporated into the other end of the widger) which can be a round piece of dowel, a pencil, or that ever-present tool, a finger.

Compost in pots and trays should never be compressed and normally a sharp tap on the bench is sufficient to settle it, although some gardeners prefer to gently flatten the top with a piece of wood. A series of round discs, each with a knob to hold it, can be made to fit the common sizes of pot. A similar rectangular piece can be used for trays.

POTS AND TRAYS

The controversy over the use of either plastic or clay pots used to be a heated one, but good sense and experience has prevailed and now most gardeners will acknowledge that both have their place and uses, although for convenience many use just the plastic ones.

Clay pots are heavy, expensive, difficult to obtain, and not a standard size (although both these last two situations are now improving). They also dry out quickly, break easily and need cleaning. They have the advantage that it is virtually impossible to over-water a plant (the cause of a surprising number of plant deaths). They are cool in summer and warm in winter, and are more aesthetically pleasing. Plastic pots have the disadvantages that plants are easily over-watered, they deform when picked up (thus disturbing or breaking new roots), and are cold in winter and hot in summer. Their advantages are that they are comparatively cheap, light, easy to clean (or discard and replace), are a standard size, and easily obtainable.

From the propagation point of view, most gardeners now nearly always use plastic. Neither cutting compost nor seed compost should be allowed to dry out and it is easier to prevent this with plastic, especially if the gardener is out at work all day. (Care must be taken, however, not to over-water.) There are some situations where it is imperative not to over-water and then clays can be used. Once the plants have been established there are categories that are better grown in clays than in plastic, but this applies more to those that spend their lives in pots, for example, many alpines, and need not concern the grower of hardy plants, whose sole intention is to get them out into the border.

The heated debate about clay versus plastic has now moved on to square versus round pots. Some claim that the former are detrimental to plants as the extra space in the corner of the pots is not used by the roots straightaway, thus leaving pockets of stagnant moisture that can become sour and introduce rots. Square pots stack more easily into trays and the closeness wastes less space and, possibly, being closer together they do retain more heat. There are several other arguments and counter-arguments but they are not worth going into now. For most practical purposes it does not really matter, either way, use whatever you can get or which ever you feel best for your own purposes. I use both!

A range of sizes is useful. A 7.5 cm (3 in) pot is a good size for sowing small quantities of seed, taking a limited number of cuttings, and for potting up small plants. A 9 cm (3.5 in) pot is one of the most useful general-purpose sizes and it is just possible to get by with these alone. Once most plants have been potted in these they are ready to be moved into the open garden, but there are some plants that need larger pots right from the start and these are some of those that make larger divisions. There is also the occasional need to hold onto plants and these may need potting on to

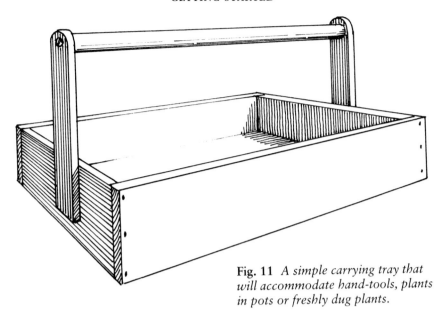

Fig. 11 *A simple carrying tray that will accommodate hand-tools, plants in pots or freshly dug plants.*

larger pots. It is, therefore, worthwhile getting a number of larger sizes. Some of the tap rooted plants, such as *Eryngium*, need to have deep pots if they are to remain in them for any length of time. The traditional deep clay pots were called 'long toms' and a plastic equivalent can be bought. I always have a number available for use. Once you have acquired a basic stock of various sizes, they can be used over and over again as long as they are washed out (a tedious job) between uses.

Be wary of using yoghurt cartons and other similar containers, although there is nothing intrinsically wrong with this. As long as the pots have holes cut, drilled or melted in the bottom for drainage, then plants will grow in them quite happily, oblivious to what is written on the outside or to their previous inhabitants. However, for some reason plants always look so miserable in such containers, especially if there is lettering or other designs on them. One reason for their dejected appearance is that there is not much root space and plants quickly become starved and, unless you have time to pot on plants a couple of weeks after they have first been pricked out, they soon become thin and undernourished. A look at plants in such containers at plant sales soon shows how retarded they appear compared with those in proper pots. When starting up as a propagator so many pots are required that it can become expensive and as a short term expedient use yoghurt pots by all means, but try and convert to proper ones as soon as possible.

Another alternative is the polypots, which are essentially bags of thin black polythene and are used a great deal by commercial growers. They are obviously much cheaper than pots, particularly if bought in bulk. However, their cheapness is somewhat offset by the large amount of compost they take. Because it is tubular and not a flat bottomed cone, a 9 cm (3.5 in) polybag will take nearly twice as much compost as the equivalent diameter pot. Another disadvantage is that they are not so easy to carry and the soil, and consequently the roots, are very easily disturbed by the distortions of the bag when it is picked up. One advantage (apart from cheapness) is that they pack together, making maximum use of space and they do keep each other warm. I recall once growing a dozen tomato seedlings in pots and the same number in polybags, not by way of experiment, but as far as I remember simply because that was what was available. All the seedlings in the bags forged well ahead of those in the pots and, since the compost and treatments were the same, I assumed that the extra warmth generated by the black polythene bags being squashed together in a tray with no air gaps between was the cause of the dissimilarity.

Propagating trays are traditionally used by most gardeners both for sowing seed and pricking out seedlings. Several points need to be raised here. Trays are fine for annuals and vegetables where seedlings are wanted in large quantities but, unless you are working on a commercial scale, only a few plants of each species or variety are required. Even if you want a couple of dozen plants then a 9 cm (3.5 in) or even 7.5 cm (3 in) pot will accommodate more than enough seedlings for your needs. Sowing a whole or half tray will not only be a waste of seed, compost and space, but a waste of energy potting up more plants than you need. If space is limited, it is much more worth while growing six of four different plants than two dozen of the same simply because you had masses of seedlings in the tray. Most of us learn the hard way that it is very difficult to throw excess seedlings away and, I am sure, have all ended up with so many plants that there has been nowhere to put them and, ultimately, nobody to give them to. The seedlings eventually finished their short lives as an expensive addition to the compost heap. Try to keep a sense of proportion and use pots instead of trays unless growing bedding plants.

Trays are not a good idea for pricking out perennial plants, which are better placed straight into individual pots. One of the big disadvantages of the modern seed tray as opposed to the old-fashioned seed boxes is that they are far too shallow and there is hardly any room for root development except sideways. They may be all right for annuals that only stay in the tray for a short time (and one wonders if this is really true) but are worthless for perennials. If you wish to use trays then either buy deeper ones or make them out of wood.

Increasingly you see people at plant sales carrying plastic tool trays into which they put their purchases. This type of carrier is ideal for moving pots around the garden. For many years I have been using a similar idea based on the wooden carrying trays that you often see at old fashioned nurseries. Mine are made from the more substantial tomato trays, although you could quickly knock up the equivalent in better quality wood. Two vertical pieces of wood are attached to the centre of the shorter side of the tray. These in turn are connected by a horizontal bar which forms the handle. These trays are cheap and can be made from scraps of wood so that making half a dozen or more is not expensive. The benefit of having such a number will soon be appreciated by anyone who is potting up even a small number of plants into pots as there are always plants to be moved from the shed to the frames and vice versa, and pots to put to one side to go somewhere else, and before long all six trays are in use.

If the carrying trays have gaps or holes in the bottom, a tray of pots can be stood in a water bath for bottom watering (after potting on, for example) and can save a lot of time moving pots about. Such trays are also useful for holding a selection of small hand tools, gloves, string, spare labels, etc. that are useful to have on hand when working over a border. They can also be used for storing envelopes or paper bags when you are doing the rounds collecting seed.

LABELS AND RECORDS

It is absolutely vital that every pot and tray of seed, seedling, cuttings or whatever is labelled. Every gardener at sometime or other has put a pot to one side meaning to label it later, only to forget and then not have a clue as to what it contains. Much of the incorrectly named seed in the seed exchanges is due to people forgetting to label pots and plants and then making a guess as to what it is.

At the propagation stage there is no need to make labels that are to remain with the plants throughout their lifetime as you might need to do in the open garden. It is quite satisfactory to use the cheap plastic labels. In the open garden these become brittle and useless after a year or so, but in the propagating area they usually last until they are no longer required.

On each should be written the full name of the plant and any other information that may be of use to the sower. I always include the date of sowing and the source of the seed. If it is from a seed exchange, I usually put the reference number on it in case something extraordinary happens and I want to trace the seed back to its source. When I prick out the seedlings I usually include this date as well.

Many growers who do a lot of propagation also keep a sowing book or a cuttings book. This is divided up into columns and contains all the details given above for labels. It also contains extra information that can be useful, particularly if the grower is experimenting with seed that has not been sown before or cuttings that have never been tried. This extra information might include the type of compost used, the temperature, and details of when and what percentage of the seed germinated. If the seed fails then another attempt can be made varying the procedure to see if more congenial conditions can be found.

Fig. 12 *Some of the information that can be written on the front and reverse of a label.*

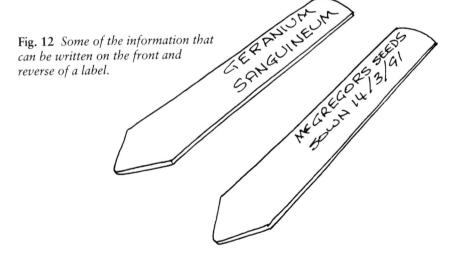

These records build up in to very important documents containing valuable material to any grower. I try to contain all the information on the label as I have failed to keep up a record book. But I have often cursed my lassitude when I have wanted information about a particular species long forgotten.

Records can be kept in a book with each sowing or batch of cuttings given a running number or they can be kept on index cards in alphabetical order of the plant names. The modern alternative is to keep all records on computer. This can make organizing the entries easier but the manual processes have got the big advantage that they can be carried out in the potting shed or greenhouse as the propagation procedures take place. If adding the information is left until you go into the house, it is soon forgotten and records become very bitty and ultimately useless.

WATERING

Some readers may be surprised at the need to mention this basic technique, but there are one or two things that must be said with regard to propagation. In the first place there are two methods of watering: from above and from below. Both have their advocates. Watering from above is normally carried out with a watering can. If not done carefully it can compact the soil, thus impairing the drainage and reducing the air spaces. Once the soil has become compacted, water poured from above often runs to the side of the pot, leaving the centre completely dry. Watering from above is useful in settling the seed into the compost or the compost around roots of the seedling. It should be undertaken with a fine-rosed watering can. Even with this fine rose the initial rush of water can be heavy, so start watering away from the pots and sweep the spray of water onto and across the pots, finishing away from them so that the final drips do not pit or compact the soil.

The other method is watering from below. The advantage of this is that the water percolates up through the compost, thoroughly wetting all of it but at the same time not compacting it. It also has the advantage of not knocking flat newly transplanted seedlings. It is accomplished by standing the pots in a bowl or tray of water. When the compost has taken up sufficient moisture its surface will change colour, indicating that it is time to remove the pot from the water. As well as a sink in the potting shed, which takes just a few pots, I have a galvanized iron tray about 45 cm (18 in) wide, 90 cm (3 ft) long and about 7.5 cm (3 in) deep. This stands on a level concrete area outside the shed and I can stand individual pots or whole trays of pots in it.

Watering from below is time consuming but in the initial stages has got much to recommend it. Once the plants are established then overhead watering from a can becomes the regime.

COMPOSTS

Individual types of composts needed will be discussed under the various types of propagation but there are a few general points to be considered. There is no doubt that a proper compost, whether it be a sowing, cutting or potting compost, will produce better plants than earth used straight from the garden. There are two ways of acquiring it, either buying it or making up your own. Many growers compromise: they buy in a basic potting compost and use this as a basis, modifying it to their own requirement.

The composition of composts is relatively straightforward, although many growers, especially specialists who concentrate on one type of plant such as chrysanthemums or auriculas, make up magic concoctions that even make witches' brews look quite innocent. It was not uncommon in the last century, and in some cases still today, to include things like bull's blood and sheep's urine. Certainly some gardeners will still argue the varying merits of sheep's, pig's, cow's, horse's or chicken's dung. And in truth there may well be scientific reasons, due to their chemical makeup, that would set out one against another in certain circumstances, but they should not detain us here.

There are two basic types of compost: loam-based and soil-less. Of the former the commonest is based on formulae produced by the John Innes Institution. Using compost of various mixes they worked out, by practical growing tests, which were the best for different circumstances. These are now used as the standards for most soil-based composts sold in Britain. Basically they consist of loam, which provides the body and nutrients to the compost, sand or grit, which provides drainage so that no stagnant water remains after watering, and peat, which acts as a storage medium so that water is available for the roots. The last two are complimentary and not contradictory as they may at first appear. Roots obviously must have water for the plant to survive, but on the other hand too much water will kill it off, especially a young plant, so the right mixture of peat and sharp sand will ensure that there is sufficient water but not too much. Added to these basic ingredients are various chemicals (lime and fertilizers) plants need in differing quantities.

The soil-less composts are almost entirely composed of a sterile medium, normally peat, but increasingly contain other materials such as coconut fibres. Here the peat acts as storage for water, as before, but also as the body of the compost or the medium through which the roots grow and which prevents the plant from falling over. Added to this is sand, to improve the drainage, and chemicals, which are important as they provide the entire nutritional needs of the plants (in the loam-based compost the loam provides a significant amount).

Each type of compost has its devotees. I personally always use soil-based composts because I find them more controllable. Peat-based ones are easy to overwater but, on the other hand, once they have dried out they are the devil to rewet and by then it is too late anyway, the plant is usually dead. Where I do use the peat-based mixtures is for ericaceous plants but more of that later. Growers should experiment and find the one in which they grow the best plants.

Whatever you decide, the compost will probably need modifying. In spite of compost being prepared to a standard formula there is rarely enough drainage material incorporated and so additional sharp sand or grit is nearly always required. Experience will soon tell you whether a bag you have just bought will need anything added to it. For the beginner, a way of testing a compost is to fill a pot with it and compress it slightly. Water it with a watering can and, if the water passes straight through without any accumulation on the top of the pot, then all is fine. If the water hangs about and takes time to percolate through, more drainage material is definitely required.

Another modification that is sometimes useful is the addition of further leaf-mould or peat to the compost if the plants involved are woodlanders that like a cool, moist, leafy soil, but this is only really necessary if the plants are to remain in their pots for any length of time.

There is no reason why composts should not be made at home. Good loam may be available from the garden or it may have to be purchased. Old turves stacked face down make a wonderful loam once the grass has rotted down.

If possible, the soil and leaf-mould should be sterilized (peat should already be sterile unless it has been open to the air for any length of time). Sterile soil can be bought by the bag (or lorry-load if you need a lot) or it can be prepared at home. An electric sterilizer is useful and the most convenient way if a lot of material needs processing. When sterilizing leaf-mould be certain that it has been shredded sufficiently to pass through a 0.6 cm (¼ in) mesh sieve, otherwise there is the possibility of it igniting in an electric sterilizer if the contents become too dry. For small quantities can be done in the kitchen oven or microwave. The idea is to raise the temperature of the loam to 82°C (180°F) and let it stay at that temperature for ten minutes before rapidly cooling it. In an oven it can be placed on a tray and covered with aluminium foil and a meat thermometer stuck into the centre of the soil to ensure that it reaches temperature right through to the middle. Only small quantities can be sterilized in a microwave and should be given, on average, 15 minutes of radiation time.

I should mention that there are those who recommend that soil should not be sterilized at all as it kills the good as well as the bad organisms, so if you want to prepare your own composts and do not want to go to the expense and trouble of buying sterilized soil or sterilizing it yourself, it might be worth experimenting with ordinary garden soil. One point that must be noted though is that it should be as free of weed-seed as possible otherwise the competition in the pots will be fierce. All loam that is to be used should be put through a 1 cm (⅜ in) sieve to remove stones and large lumps of soil.

Peat is the second ingredient. The best for this is a sphagnum moss peat, which does not need sterilizing but should be passed through a 1 cm (⅜ in) sieve to remove any large lumps or pieces or twig or bark. Leaf-mould can be used as an alternative. It has the same ability to hold water, but also adds some nutrients to the compost. Other ingredients, such as shredded coconut fibre, are coming on the market as an alternative to peat, but many are too coarse in composts that, for example, are to be used for sowing seed.

The third ingredient is the drainage material, which can be sharp sand (sometimes sold as screeding sand) or grit of less than 3 mm (⅛ in). Ordinary builders sand will not do, indeed it will cause water retention rather than the reverse. The sand or grit should be clean and have been washed to remove silt and any other impurities. It should not want sterilizing.

For the basic John Innes Potting Compost these ingredients should be mixed in the following proportions: seven parts of sterilized loam, three parts of peat, and two parts of sand or grit. The parts are all by volume and can be measured out in a flower pot or bucket depending on the amount to be mixed. Large quantities can be mixed on a clean concrete floor or drive, smaller quantities on the potting bench, a table or in a washing-up bowl or bucket.

Add lime and fertilizers to this. The latter can be purchased as a John Innes base fertilizer. The lime or chalk is added at 0.5 grams per litre (¾ ounces per bushel or 8 gallons) for JI No. 1. The quantity is doubled for No. 2 and trebled for No. 3. If ericaceous plants or other lime-haters are being grown, drop the lime from the formulation. The fertilizers are also applied at different rates. JI No. 1 contains 3 grams per litre (4 ounces per bushel or 8 gallons) and again doubled and trebled for Nos. 2 and 3. From these formulations it can be seen that the different John Innes Potting Composts are similar in make-up except that they vary in the lime content and nutritional strengths. If you want to make your own base fertilizer then the quantities (by weight) are: two parts of hoof and horn, two parts of superphosphate, and one part of sulphate of potash. This represents a nitrogen/phosporus/potash (NKP) of 5.1 : 7.2 : 9.7.

There is no reason why you should not prepare your own soil-less composts as well. These are not so fiddly as there is no sterilization to bother about. A general formula for most purposes would be (by volume): three parts of peat, and one part of sharp sand, although this may not be found sharp enough and some more sand or grit added. This compost would not of course contain any nutrition at all and so a complicated cocktail of ingredients is required. Fortunately these can be purchased as base fertilizers and added at the required rates according to the instructions on the packet.

All this can become a bit too technical and for many growers the simplest way (and a way with perfectly good results) is to go down to the nearest garden centre and buy a bag of potting compost. If you do, try and ensure that it has been freshly prepared. Stale compost has little advantage.

What has been mentioned here is a basic potting compost. Variations on this and other composts will be given as they are required under the different propagation techniques.

Propagation Techniques

CHOOSING THE METHOD

As most gardeners are aware, there are several ways of propagating or increasing a plant. Nature's most obvious way is through seed, but plants can also be reproduced vegetatively, that is by taking a part of the plant, a cutting or a division, for example and growing a new plant from this. These methods are also part of a plant's natural method of increase, although it might not seem as obvious as the use of seed. Parts of plants are often carried by water, wind and gravity (sliding or falling down mountains or lesser heights) to take root where they come to rest.

Gardeners have found it easier to increase some plants by one method rather than another, and the basis of this book is to show which can be propagated in what way. There are one or two major principles that help in deciding the method.

VEGETATIVE VERSUS SEED

The main principle concerns seed versus vegetative reproduction. If a vegetative method (cuttings, division, layering etc.) of increase is chosen, then all the new plants will be indistinguishable from their parent; they will be identical clones. Thus if you find a flowering plant in the garden with a particularly attractive colour, the only way that you can be absolutely certain of reproducing that colour in another plant is by taking cuttings or by dividing or some other vegetative means.

Plants grown from seed, on the other hand, are likely to exhibit variation. This might be only slight and to all intents and purposes they might be identical to the parents, but it is still the progeny of two different plants and therefore cannot be said to be the same plant as either. For most of our purposes this does not matter, as gardeners are prepared to put up with any variation or even positively like the diversity. But it does have practical implications in that, if you sow seed produced by most cultivars, you are unlikely to get plants that resemble their parents.

Examine any seed-sown population of one species in the wild and you will see quite a lot of variation. In the garden we tend to either like them as they are with this natural variation or select out those that have certain similar characteristics (colour, height, bushiness, colour of the leaves, etc.). It may be possible that these characteristics come through in the seed. If seed is sown and those plants that do not conform are weeded out, then it is possible to eventually arrive at a strain that has the characteristics we want. Strains are the bread and butter of seed merchants. If, however, an itinerant bee brings in pollen from a different strain from over the fence, the characteristics could be drastically changed and thus open pollination (i.e. plants pollinated by bees as opposed to hand pollination, which is controlled) can produce a range of characteristics and even involve the hybridization of different species.

This may seem a disadvantage, but it is often the reverse as it allows the gardener to raise new and better forms (hybridization) simply by selecting the parents and then hand pollinating them. From Nature's point of view, cross pollination keeps new genetic material entering the system and thus keeps the species alive and vital. Plants that are constantly increased by vegetative means can lose this vitality and can eventually refuse to increase and die out. Another important factor of seed propagation is that it cannot transmit viral or the many other diseases that effect some of our plant stocks, but which are passed from plant to plant when they are increased vegetatively.

If stored correctly, seed does not lose its viability for some time, in some cases many years. Therefore, if you are given some seed, you can, within limits, sow it in your own time. On the other hand, if you are given some cuttings or a division then you will have to do something about it straight away.

The method you choose will be determined by different factors: some methods are easier than others, some are quicker (seed can take up to seven years or more in some plants to produce a flowering plant), some produce plants that are identical to the original plant, some produce plants that vary from the original, some give a plant free of disease, and, finally, there are some which do not make much difference which method you choose. In the A–Z section the method mentioned first is usually considered the best or normal method to employ.

Surprisingly, you will often hear gardeners say that they never bother with seed or cuttings. This is extremely limiting, particularly as neither technique is particularly difficult to master. There will always be some plants that are difficult to germinate or difficult to raise from cuttings but the majority are comparatively easy and it will limit the number of plants that you grow if you turn a blind eye to some of the available techniques.

SEED

Basic Seed-Sowing

Seed-sowing can be as easy or as complicated as you wish to make it. In the first instance, there are very simple methods that will ensure germination in the majority of cases and, in the second, there are refinements that will help with the rest. I intend first of all to outline the basic way of sowing seed and then go on to discuss the mechanics of seed germination and the more sophisticated methods needed to overcome such things as dormancy.

The majority of seed will germinate given moisture and an average spring-time temperature. In the initial stages all the food that the seedling requires is stored within the seed case. The compost is there to hold the moisture and to give the roots something to grip so that the plant stands upright and does not fall over. This being the case, all the seed-sower requires is some compost, a pot to put it in and a packet of seed.

Compost is placed in the pot, which is then tapped on the bench to settle the contents so that the surface is level with the bottom of the pot's lip. The compost may need packing down lightly to make certain that the surface is level, but it should not be compressed. The seed is sown thinly on the surface of the compost. Seed that is known to germinate poorly should be sown more thickly. Traditionally books at this stage then tell you to cover the seed with sieved compost to half the depth of the seed, but most of the best growers have long abandoned this and cover the seed with 1.25 cm (½ in) of fine grit. I will go in to details as to why this is done later.

An important process at this stage is to label the pan. All gardeners must have experienced the frustration of leaving the labelling to later only to find they have forgotten what pot is what.

The pot can now be watered either from above with a watering can or from below by standing the pot in a water-bath, up to about half the depth of the pot. The pot should now be stood outside in a shady place and left to the mercy of the weather. If the weather turns really wet then it should be protected with a polythene or glass light; if the weather becomes dry then water it, ensuring that it never dries out.

If treated in this manner the majority of hardy plant seed will germinate. If it needs a frost or chilling it may take more than one year to germinate, but if the seed is kept moist and not exposed to the heat of the sun, you will eventually be rewarded with plants (assuming, of course, that the seed is viable). If germination takes place in the middle of winter during a warm spell, then put the pan of seedlings either into a greenhouse or a covered cold-frame to protect them from any ensuing frosts or wet spells that may rot them.

That then is the basic method. If you do not want to, you need not pursue the matter any further and you will still get very good results.

However, gardeners very rarely want to let any matter rest, particularly when there is the chance of getting closer to perfection, and so I will go into the matter in more detail.

Acquiring Seed

The simplest way of getting seed is from seed merchants, either direct via their catalogues and mail order departments, or through sales displays at garden centres and other outlets. The range of hardy perennial plants is quite limited but has been increasing over recent years. Exaggerated claims are sometimes made for the contents, often giving them a cultivar or similar name when in fact they are more or less straight forward species. Cultivars cannot be grown from seed, although they sometimes produce offspring quite close to the original. What seed merchants generally stock are strains, which are plants of similar habit, but with variations of colour within a limited range. Many seed merchants are very old-fashioned in the names they give to their plants, so what may seem a new plant to you may be a familiar one given an early name.

Seed sold by these commercial sources comes from all over the world, mainly specially grown by seed farmers. Sometimes they stock smaller quantities of rarer plants that have been grown and harvested by gardeners. The majority of seed is correctly named, but open pollination can play havoc and occasionally strange things turn up. When the seed is received by the seed merchants they usually test it for germination to ensure it is viable and then store it under optimum conditions to ensure this viability is retained. When packeted, many of the varieties are put into foil packs, which retain the best conditions of humidity. What cannot be controlled is the temperature once the seed leaves the merchant. If it comes by post direct from the controlled conditions of the warehouse, then all is likely to be well, but if it has been stored in a garden centre on a rack in full sun then the temperature within the foil pack will have been way above what it should have been and the seed is likely to have lost all viability. Seed firms usually send out their catalogues in the autumn and seed becomes available soon after that.

A greater range of seed, particularly in terms of species, is available from the seed exchanges attached to the main societies, for example, the Royal Horticultural Society, the Hardy Plant Society or the American Rock Garden Society. This seed is either collected in the garden or from plants in the wild by members and sent in to whoever manages the scheme. The seed is available only to members of the individual societies, some of which charge a nominal sum for each packet, while others only charge the postage.

The variety of plants represented on the seed exchange lists is large. The Alpine Garden Society, for example, listed 5,646 different taxa in its 1992 list, far more than any commercial firm could offer. The subjects offered usually reflect the Society, thus the Cyclamen Society only list *Cyclamen* seed, but some of the bigger societies offer a large range, for example, The Alpine Garden Society, which, although the majority of plants offered are alpines, also lists hardy perennials or trees and shrubs. Similarly, the Hardy Plant Society's list includes alpines.

To the beginner a list of over 5,000 plants all listed under their Latin names with no descriptions can be a daunting sight, but the lists contain material that cannot otherwise be obtained and gives the gardener a chance to grow a range of plants that would otherwise just be a pipe dream.

However, there are problems. One of the biggest is that the naming is not always as accurate as it should be. This is not through any deliberate misnaming but through simple human error. Sometimes labels are missing and the collector makes a guess at the name, or perhaps does not look at the label as it is a familiar plant and puts down the wrong name while distracted by something else. Often plants are acquired as one species when it is in fact another. This first plant is grown on and seed sent into the exchange, the donor using the name given. Further plants are raised from this seed, some of which continue the cycle with the wrong name, while the name of others may be rectified by their more knowledgeable recipients.

A good (or bad) example of misnaming was the introduction many years ago of seed of *Geranium rubescens* into the exchanges as *G. palmatum*. This was bad enough, but at the same time seed of *G. palmatum* was sent in as *G. maderense*. The resulting confusion has still not been sorted out and one still sees these plants incorrectly labelled in gardens and mislabelled seed still finds its way into the exchanges. None of this was deliberate or malicious, but you can see the kind of mess that can result from an innocent mistake.

There is another aspect of misnaming and that is that most seed sent into the exchanges is open pollinated and therefore the chances of it being pure is very variable. Promiscuous plants such as *Aquilegia* cannot be guaranteed to be true unless they have been isolated beyond the travelling distance of a bee and there is no way of telling with exchange seed whether this has happened or not. In some cases interesting new forms and hybrids can result.

Another problem with the exchanges is that the seed is not distributed until late winter, making it difficult to germinate that seed that needs to be sown fresh.

These criticisms are not to deny the usefulness of the exchanges, they are just a warning that the resulting plants may not be what you expected and that any seed you donate yourself should be accurately labelled. Most donors are very conscientious and a great deal of valuable seed is on offer. If used intelligently, the exchanges can provide a wealth of exciting and unusual plants.

Another way of acquiring seed is to collect your own. This does rather limit the gardener to growing plants already possessed, but is an important source of renewal, which must be constantly attended to in any garden. It allows the grower to sow seed at the optimum time as it can be sown at any time from when it leaves the pod. Allied to this of course, is getting seed from friends' gardens. Collecting seed will be dealt with at the end of this chapter.

A final way of obtaining seed is by taking shares in a seed collecting expedition. This is a fascinating and often exciting process as the plants concerned may be new to cultivation or are re-collections of material that has dried out or been bred out of all recognition. The going rate for shares is about £50 in Britain and $100 in the US, which may sound a lot but this may result in as many as 100 packets of seed, which makes it better value than most seed merchants can produce. In recent times the share system has changed and some collectors now issue lists and you choose what you want from these, paying by the packet. This works out more expensive and, since the choice is yours, you get none of the surprises of unknown plants that are likely to crop up, especially if collected by somebody like John Watson, who has a very good eye for a plant. These seed collecting trips and their lists are usually advertised in the RHS journal *The Garden*, the Alpine Garden Society's *Bulletin* or the American Rock Garden Society's *Journal*.

Timing

One of the great worries of beginners to serious seed sowing is when they should sow. I say 'serious seed sowing' because the average person who buys a packet of seed is unaware that there may be an optimum time as most seed is bought and sown in spring. However, once growers start to grow more unusual plants they are bound to come across references to sowing 'fresh' or 'in autumn' when they look the plant up in books. There are some seeds that need to be sown fresh (i.e. as soon as they are ripe) as either they have a short-lived viability or they have a dormancy factor (see later) that comes into play, which means that germination will take a long time or become erratic. Several familiar examples of this can be given. *Helleborus* and *Pulsatilla* from the buttercup family (Ranunculaceae) and *Cyclamen* from the Primulaceae all have a reputation of being hard to germinate but, if they are sown as soon as they are ripe, they will come up like the proverbial mustard and cress. The misconceptions over the ease of germination are mainly based on experience with commercial and exchange seed that is old by the time it is received and therefore much more difficult to cope with.

In nature most seed is scattered soon after it is ripe. In some cases it germinates straight away, while in others it remains until the return of favourable conditions in the following year (*see* p. 45). Some growers take

41

this to heart and sow everything fresh or as soon as they get it. Others sow the seed that needs to be freshly sown, but store the rest until the spring, rather than letting it lie in damp pots over winter when it may be prone to disease or to pests. In warm spells it may germinate prematurely and then be killed off by an ensuing cold spell.

Spring itself is, of course, rather a vague term and in the context of seed sowing it can mean any time between late winter and late spring. Late winter sowing is ideal for seed sown under heated glass or for seed needing a period of chilling provided by the frosts. If the pans of seed are to be placed outside, then the temperature may not rise sufficiently to allow germination until spring, in which case sowing can be delayed until the temperature rises. This then lessens the chances of seed being destroyed by pests or disease.

I have habitually sown most of my spring seed as soon as I have received it in late winter (February) sometimes taking until early spring (March) but one year I did not receive an allocation from a seed exchange until late spring (May). Thinking it far too late to be sowing seed I still went ahead and to my amazement I had a tremendous germination almost straight away, and the curious thing was that there were several members of the Ranunculaceae, all of which germinated in profusion within a week or so.

The moral must be that if you are not using artificial heat then a late sowing when the ambient temperature has risen produces a quicker and a better rate of germination. However, there are still those plants that need a pre-chilling before they will germinate and these are either better sown early or put in a refrigerator for artificial pre-chilling (*see* p. 46).

It is not always possible to know what seed needs to be sown fresh or what treatment it should be given in spring. In the A–Z section of this book there is a recommendation for all the plants mentioned and this can be used as a guide. With new and unknown plants the method most growers adopt is to sow half the packet in the autumn (assuming it is available then) while the seed is still fresh and the rest in the spring. If you are ever unsure of whether to go for autumn or spring, go for both.

Seed Composts

Seed composts, like all composts, are a matter of individual preference. As mentioned earlier, they are basically supportive mediums, the seedling getting its nourishment from within the seed itself. (Most gardeners will have seen seed sprouting on kitchen paper, mustard and cress for example, or, as a child, grown beans in a glass jar supported by a ring of wet blotting paper.) However if the seedling is to remain in the pot for some time, as is the case with many bulbs, for example, then there will be the need for a food supply in the compost and a more careful formulation is therefore required.

One of the best growers I have known, who is capable of germinating seed of high alpine plants, which are the most difficult in the world to cope with, does so simply by taking old potting compost, sweepings off the bench if necessary, and simply using that as his sowing medium. Most propagators would be horrified at this, but the results prove that it works with a very high level of success. I would not recommend this to beginners but it does prove the point that the medium is not too important, but the way you use it is.

More conventional wisdom requires that the ingredients of the compost should be sterilized and fresh. The fresher the sterilization, the better the germination. The basic mixture worked out by the John Innes Institute for its standard loam-based seed compost (by volume) is: two parts of sterilized loam, one part of peat, and one part of sharp sand or fine grit. To this they recommend the addition of 42 grams per 36 litres (1½ ounces per bushel (8 gallons)) of superphosphate and 21 grams per 36 litres (¾ ounces per bushel (8 gallons)) of ground limestone. Other proprietary base mixes can be used instead, in proportions as shown on the packets. Many would argue that if the seedlings are to be transplanted as soon as possible then the addition of the superphosphate is unnecessary. Lime should be omitted for ericaceous and other lime-hating plants.

One of the main modifications some growers make to this basic formula is to add further grit if they feel the drainage is inadequate, or to add more peat (and usually grit as well) if the plants require a more woodland type of soil. These kind of modifications are left up to the individual gardener as the variations are as infinite as the number of growers. A basic soil-less compost is usually (by volume): one part of peat, and one part of sand.

Nutrition is best added as the appropriate base fertilizer at the rate shown on the pack. For those wanting to compose their own the recommended rates are: superphosphates, 28–56 grams per 36 litres (1–2 ounces per bushel (8 gallons)), potassium nitrate, 14 grams per 36 litres (½ ounce per bushel (8 gallons)), and ground limestone, 112–168 grams per 36 litres (4–6 ounces per bushel (8 gallons)). Again, omit the limestone for ericaceous and other lime-hating plants.

The most vital aspect of a seed compost, especially if it is to stand outside in all weathers, is that it should have adequate drainage and it is vital that peat-based composts have enough grit in them. It is also very important that they are not allowed to dry out as the surface layer can become like a crust once dried and any water will simply pour off and down the sides.

A technique originally pioneered by Alex Duguid and championed by James Cobb involves the use of a sphagnum compost. Sphagnum moss is collected, dried, and rubbed through a fine sieve. The advantage of sphagnum is that it holds both air and moisture presenting the seed with constant, humid conditions perfect for germination. This is ideal for growing *Primula* and *Meconopsis* in particular. James Cobb has found that three layers of differing composts should be used. The bottom layer of the pan should contain a seed compost with added nutrients, the next a mixture of sieved leaf-mould grit and sphagnum, and the top layer (about 1 cm ($^2/_5$ in)) of a mixture of five parts sphagnum and one part rich compost. A thin layer of finely sieved sphagnum covers this. It is into this top dressing that the seed is sown. The water from a fine-rose watering can will wash the seed in. With larger seed it might be necessary to give another fine dusting of sphagnum.

Lilies have been found to germinate extremely well on a pan of sphagnum. As there are no nutrients in the sphagnum, once seed leaves have appeared, a weak (a third of the recommended dosage) feed of tomato fertilizer is required once a week until the plants are potted up or planted out.

This then is one of the special composts developed to suit certain plants and their individual growing conditions. There is still a lot to learn and much room for experiment.

Top Dressing

In the outlined sowing technique given at the beginning of the section on seed, I mentioned that the seed should be covered with 1.25 cm (½ in) of grit. There are several reasons for this. It helps to keep the seed in place when watered from above (i.e. it does not all get washed down to one corner), it stops the surface panning (i.e. becoming hard and impenetrable to water, so that it all runs off down the sides), and it keeps the surface of the compost moist (i.e. it acts as a mulch). Conversely, it provides a well-drained area around the neck of young seedlings, which is the most vulnerable part of new plants and good drainage can help prevent them rotting off. The layer of grit helps to keep the plant warm in winter and cool in summer. Liverwort and algae are less likely to grow on the grit than they are on moist compost and if they do or if weeds germinate, they can be readily removed as the whole layer of grit can easily be taken off and replaced. This is particularly important if the pans are kept moist and standing in a shady spot for any length of time. If the grower enjoys the aesthetics of growing plants, a pan of seedlings is always well set off against a background of grit, a trivial but a pleasurable point.

One point that worries some growers is that this amount of grit will prevent light getting to the seed. In fact, seed that needs light only needs a very small amount and enough will percolate through the grit, although in some cases it might pay to have a thinner layer. Some growers have found that with very fine seed it is often advantageous to place the grit on the compost and then sow the seed on top of this, watering it in with a fine-rosed watering can.

Gravel is becoming available at some garden centres but the size and cleanliness seems to vary considerably. The grit used for top dressing can easily be purchased from agricultural merchants or some of the larger pet shops as chick grit, which is sold in bags and fed to young chicks to help them grind up their food. A larger size is supplied for chickens, which is useful for adding to composts and a third size, turkey grit, is too big for most uses except dressing raised beds (but there are cheaper methods of doing this and this grit should be left to the turkeys).

Dormancy

Something that worries many growers is the concept of dormancy and what they should do about it. There are two ways of dealing with it. The first is simple: ignore it and it will eventually go away by itself. The second is to break it so that the seed germinates more quickly. But why and how does dormancy occur?

Seed is dispersed into a competitive and hostile world and while it cannot interfere with the things that create these, it can alter itself to achieve the best possible timing. The simplest way of achieving this is to produce masses of seed, some of which will get buried and re-emerge at a later date so that if the bulk of the seed met unfavourable conditions and all perished, some of the later germinations may be successful. Others have chemical inhibitors built into them so that a set of preconditions must come into play before the seed germinates. Everybody has seen a newly-felled wood covered with foxgloves, the seed of which has responded to a sudden increase in the availability of light. Another common example that most gardeners have come across is chipping the hard shell of a sweet pea seed to allow water in, without which germination cannot begin.

One of the commonest requirements to break dormancy is warmth; once winter has passed and the earth begins to warm, the seed knows that it is time to germinate because spring is now here. Many annuals and perennials can be brought into early growth in winter or early spring by giving them heated conditions. If left until the real spring they would germinate without the need for heat, but the plants will be late developing and might not even flower that year. Some seeds sow themselves in autumn when the earth is still warm and would germinate straight away, thus having to face the traumas of a winter as a seedling, except that they have a built-in inhibitor that prevents them germinating until they have had a period of cold (i.e. winter) before the returning warmth (i.e. spring) starts them into growth. The problem with this type of seed is that if it is sown in spring it will not get the cold period it requires and so the seed will lie dormant for another twelve months until it does experience a cold spell before launching itself.

Seed of this type can be fooled into thinking that it has had a winter by placing it in a refrigerator for a few weeks. This pre-chilling saves a year on the germination time. The seed is sown in the normal way and then the pot, wrapped in a polythene bag, is placed in a domestic refrigerator for six to eight weeks. There is no need to freeze the seed, a period of chilling is sufficient. Once the pan is taken out it can be treated as any other freshly sown pan of seed.

Seed from drier parts of the world respond to the coming of the wet season and need water to germinate. A modicum of moisture, as might be deposited by dew, is not enough to trigger the mechanism; it needs enough to wash the chemical inhibitor from the coat or to soften it to allow the moisture to get inside. If cyclamen seed is not sown fresh, then an overnight soaking in warm water will plump them up and accelerate germination. (A tip here is to add one drop of washing up liquid to the water as this breaks the surface tension between the water and the seed-coat, speeding up the ingress of the water.) Mechanical abrasion will also help this passage of water and a well-known example here are legumes, in particular sweet peas and lupins. An overnight soaking in water may be sufficient, but some of the harder cases may need to be chipped with a knife (a procedure not to be recommended for safety reasons) or scored by a file first. The easiest method is to place the seed in a jar along with some coarse sand and shake the lot vigorously or, alternatively, rub the seed between sheets of sandpaper.

Some seed benefits from the actions of enzymes in the gut of a bird or animal as it passes through. Any gardener who has experienced the ready way blackberry or ivy seedlings sprout up after the seed has been left by blackbirds in their droppings will need no convincing of this. The action of the bird's stomach removes the flesh, which often contains an inhibitor, and also breaks down the tough case of the seed. In the past some gardeners have recommended the use of concentrated acids as an equivalent means of breaking through the case, but this can be extremely dangerous and has little to recommend it as pouring boiling water over the seed will often remove any chemical inhibitors and mechanical abrasion will usually suffice to break down the coat.

There are other forms of dormancy but none that should affect the grower of hardy plants. Where it is necessary or desirable to break the dormancy, it is mentioned under the individual genera in the A–Z section of this book. Breaking dormancy will speed up the germination but it is no means essential.

If you have no desire to get involved with this procedure, sow the seed and leave the pan outside until the seed germinates. This may take a year or more longer than treated seed, but if seed of different species is sown each year then the wait will not be so apparent as you will have plenty with which to deal. Do not throw away ungerminated seed pans for at least three years as the seed may still be waiting for ideal conditions.

Apparent Delayed Germination

Another reason for holding on to your seed pans for several years is that some plants do not appear to be germinating when in fact they have put out roots in their first year, but will not make any visible sign of growth above ground until the second. A good example of this are Liliaceae including *Lilium* itself and other members such as *Erythronium*. Warnings have been given in the A–Z where this occurs.

Pricking Out

Once seedlings have reached the stage where their first two true leaves have emerged (the first leaves to appear are the seed leaves or cotyledons, the second pair of leaves are the first true leaves) they are ready to be pricked out. Most hardy perennials should be pricked out into a 9 cm (3.5 in) pot in a John Innes Potting Compost (*see* p. 33). If they are only spending a short while in these pots before either being moved on to a bigger size (and thus fresh compost) or being planted out then, a JI No. 2 will be sufficient. On the other hand if the plant is slow growing and is likely to remain in the pot until the next season, then a JI No. 3 will be more appropriate.

Set the seedling in the centre of the pot with its neck the same height above the surface of the soil as it was in the seed pan. I like again to top dress all my pots with grit or gravel for many of the same reasons as given above, but this is a matter of taste and economy and many gardeners prefer to forgo it. Do not forget to label the pot.

Never over-pot a plant, i.e. use too big a pot. If there is a lot of unoccupied damp soil the roots will not be able to take up all the available moisture and there will be constant damp, sour soil round the edge of the pot, which can promote rotting and other diseases. Only pot up the plant into a bigger pot when it requires it. Many hardy perennials can be planted straight out from the 9 cm (3.5 in) size pot.

Once the seedling, or plant if potting on, has been potted, stand it in a water bath or water from above. Place in a closed atmosphere, such as a cold frame, for a few days so that the plant can become established and than gradually hardened off. Once this has been done the plant can be left in an open cold frame or put into a plunge frame. Make certain that the pot does not dry out. Plants in an open frame need more frequent watering than plants in the open garden. In hot sunny weather it may be necessary to place shade frames made of green netting over the plants to protect them. This is particularly important for woodland and other shade plants.

Sowing Seed Outside

Not all seed needs to be sown in pans. Many of the more robust perennials, such as lupins and delphiniums, can be sown outside in rows in a reserve bed or vegetable patch. This is normally done later than if sown in pans, usually at the end of spring when the soil is beginning to warm up. Once the plants have reached sufficient size they can be transplanted to their final positions. Some plants that have tap roots or otherwise resent disturbance, such as some of the *Papaver*, can be sown directly where they are to flower and then thinned out when the ensuing seedlings are large enough to handle.

Many plants will happily self-sow themselves providing ample offspring for use in the garden and giving away to friends. If they need moving, do so as soon as possible, especially if they are tap rooted. Garden-grown plants often develop large root-systems, which makes them difficult to pot up if allowed to get too big. You cannot always expect self-sown seedlings to come true, i.e. be the same as their parents, and it may be essential to rogue out inferior or different colour forms. If this is done each year the chances are that the population may eventually come true. It is often possible to tell a white form of a plant before it flowers, sometimes at seedling stage. They may well be a paler green or, as in the case of *Digitalis purpurea*, the foxglove, the leaf-stalks are flushed with red or purple for the usually purple-flowered plants, and are green for the white flowered. It may be necessary to move some of the self-sown seedlings into a nursery bed if they are in a situation where they will be swamped and either drawn or killed by the larger plants around them.

Seed Collecting

It is important to collect seed from your own plants, particularly if they are rare. It is always useful to be able to produce reserve plants in case your own die. Some plants need renewing after two or three years anyway, and it is also useful to be able to supply other people and seed exchanges with material.

Seed collecting is a very simple procedure, although one that can be time consuming. The basic requirements are some paper bags and a pencil, and something to carry them, such as in a basket or carrying tray (*see* p. 27). The plants that are being collected should be examined every day and the ripe seed pods placed in a paper bag, which should be labelled immediately, otherwise they will get muddled up however good you think your memory is.

Experience will soon teach you when the seed is ready for collecting. Some, such as the Ranunculaceae (e.g. *Ranunculus, Anemone* and *Pulsatilla*) come away easily from the seed head when they are gently rubbed between thumb and finger. Others indicate their readiness by changing the colour of either the seed and/or the seed pod, usually from green to brown. Seed collecting starts surprisingly early in the year with *Helleborus* and *Hepatica*, for example, ripening in May. Some may take a long time between flowering and the seed being ready. *Cyclamen* can take almost a year and I have often seen flowers and seed pods on the same plant.

A greater problem is dealing with those plants that have an explosive method of seed dispersal, *Geranium* and *Euphorbia* being good examples. In both cases it is essential to watch the plants and determine the stage at which the seed becomes ripe, and when it is likely to be dispersed, making it possible to pick the seed heads just before they explode and pop them into a paper bag. Bags are usually left open to the air to allow the seed to dry, but in these cases they must be closed, otherwise the seed will be thrown well out of the bag.

Store the bags of seed temporarily in a dry airy place, but make sure that it is not exposed to the sun. When the seed is dry, it should be cleaned by removing all the dust and debris. The larger pieces can be removed by the fingers. Much of the chaff can be gently blown away; at first some seed will also get blown away but experience will soon refine the technique. Finally the seed can be introduced to a series of kitchen sieves. The finer mesh allows the dust to pass through and the seed to remain and the larger ones allows the seed through and the debris to remain. Final cleaning can be achieved by pouring the seed on a plate and pushing the seed to one side leaving any remaining debris behind. The main reason for removing debris is that the pieces from the old plant can still be carrying mildew and other disease, which may be passed on to the new seedlings.

Storing Seed

Once collected and cleaned, seed not to be sown straightaway should be stored. It should be put into a clearly labelled envelope and this in turn placed in a cool place away from mice or any other pests. A good method of storage is to put all the packets in a sealed polythene box in a domestic refrigerator and leave it there until the seed is required. This cold, but not freezing, temperature is ideal.

DIVISION

One of the easiest and quickest methods of securing new plants is to divide existing ones. This means splitting or cutting the plant up into a number of divisions, which are then either planted straight back into the ground or potted up. Since each part of the plant has its own roots and leaves with which to photosynthesize, the plant quickly recovers and reaches maturity much sooner than other alternative means of propagation.

Different plants need different treatment. The simplest and crudest is to lift the plant to be divided from the ground and cut it into portions with a sharp spade. Not far below in the scale of crudity is the much advised use of two garden forks as levers back to back, forcing the plant into pieces. Both of these methods are widely advocated and yet are far from satisfactory. They are only suitable for the toughest of clump-forming plants such as *Aster* or *Helenium*, but even here greater success will be achieved by taking more care. Having said all that, I must admit that faced with a shortage of time or lack of strength many gardeners do use this method on some of the more thuggish plants.

Plants sliced or hacked to pieces will inevitably contain cut and torn stems and roots, which will rot away and may let diseases into the plant. Plants treated in this way usually contain a lot of dead and congested material, by simply dividing them up you are putting all this back. Using proper techniques you only put back the young growths and then in a non-congested form so that a better plant will be formed and one that will last longer before it again needs redividing. Furthermore, by hacking a plant about you are wasting a great deal of propagating material. A large clump of Michaelmas daisies can be divided into up to a hundred pieces instead of being chopped up into four or five.

These crude methods do sometimes have their place. For example, it is sometimes possible to dig off a portion of a plant that resents disturbance without moving the bulk of the plant, but the section chopped off should then be divided up in the normal way.

Any plant that needs dividing should be watered the day before so that it has taken up its fill but the soil has had a chance to dry out a little so that it is not muddy or messy to work with. Dig up the clump and take it to the propagating area. Fingers are the most important tool for dividing plants. It is surprising how many will fall apart with just a gentle easing from the fingers. It helps if the plant is shaken during the process so that earth falls away from the roots. Hold a piece of the plant with a crown between each finger and thumb, shake and gently pull apart, and like magic they usually suddenly seem to float apart. Carry on doing this until all the crowns have been separated. Dig up a clump of *Primula* and try it.

With the more stubborn plants the earth should all be shaken free or washed free with a hose pipe. A bucket or bowl of water is a surprisingly

Fig. 13 *When dividing a plant by hand, shake free as much earth as possible and the plant will often just fall apart.*

useful aid. If a knotted clump of *Kniphofia,* for example, is manipulated under water all the individual crowns seem to float apart as the fingers gently prize through the tangles. In some plants the individual portions do not naturally separate and it may be necessary to cut through some of the roots or stolons using a sharp knife and leaving a clean cut.

Some clumps are too big to be manipulated in this way and need to be chopped up into manageable portions. This is wasteful but with a large clump there is usually plenty of propagating material anyway. With more mature plants the centre of the clump may be old and woody. This type of material should be discarded and the young growths around the edge used.

This type of manipulation may seem long-winded and fiddly compared with bashing away with a spade, but the results will repay the effort. On top of this there is a tremendous feeling of achievement as the crowns suddenly float apart in your fingers, the kind of satisfaction that one feels with any gardening process that is done well. It is not as difficult as it sounds and after a few attempts it will become second nature. One advantage of using your fingers is that you handle the plant and look at it, unconsciously learning all the time about the growth processes of individual species.

Not all species lend themselves to delicate manipulation. Anyone who has attempted to dig out a mature *Gunnera manicata* and divide it with their finger tips will immediately appreciate the problem. In such a case it is easier to dig round part of the plant and cut a piece off *in situ*. There are also plants that send out underground stolons so that suckers appear at a distance, short or large, away from the plant. These stolons can be severed, the sucker dug up and transplanted as a new plant. Similarly, new plants may be formed on runners above ground, strawberries being a familiar example. These plantlets can also be severed from the parent plant and replanted or potted up.

The timing of this operation is not crucial. The two best times of year are in spring and autumn but there are some plants that need to be dealt with immediately after flowering, which may well be in the summer. Generally speaking, divide up spring-flowering plants in autumn. In cold, wet areas leave most of the dividing until spring to avoid the damaged plants having to sit around in cold wet soil for three or four months before growth can restart, giving infection time to kill off the plant. The timings for individual plants are given in the A–Z section of this book.

Divisions can be either replanted directly back where they are to flower or in nursery rows. Care should be taken to ensure that they do not dry out until they are established. If drying winds or strong sun is forecast, then some form of shading might be necessary. Divisions can also be potted up individually either to be used later or to give away. They can be put in a closed frame for a few days to allow them to settle in. In many cases just covering the frame with a shade frame of netting will be sufficient as this gives them protection but at the same time allows air to circulate.

CUTTINGS

While most gardeners are not averse to pulling a plant apart to get divisions, many are frightened of attempting to take cuttings. Although there is often thought to be a mystical quality about the process, and 'green fingers' are always mentioned, there is nothing intrinsically difficult about taking cuttings. As with all propagation there are always some plants that are more difficult than others, but in the end these become a challenge rather than a problem.

Most people associate cuttings more with shrubby plants than hardy perennials, but a surprising number can be increased in this way, particularly if they are taken as basal cuttings. What you are attempting to do is to remove a shoot from the plant and to persuade it to put out roots and thus become a new plant. Most plants that will root (but not all) seem happiest to send out shoots around the node i.e. the swelling where the leaves or leaf stalks are attached to the stem.

Composts

As with seed composts, cutting composts are really only a support medium, i.e. something to contain the necessary moisture and something to keep the cutting upright. Traditionally, therefore, cutting composts have consisted of an inert mixture of one part sifted peat and one part sharp sand. Some growers just use coarse sand but this is obviously not so moisture retentive and needs more watering.

For the majority of cuttings it is not essential to make up this special compost and for the beginner who does not have the ingredients to hand, a well-drained potting compost will suffice.

Equipment

Propagating frames have already been dealt with (see p. 20) but brief mention of them must be made here. Most perennial cuttings are of softwood and these need to be kept in a moist atmosphere to prevent them from wilting and dying. This atmosphere can be obtained in one of two ways: by using a closed environment in which the base material (i.e. cutting compost) is kept moist, or by creating an artificial mist around the cuttings by using a mist unit.

If you require just a few plants then there is no need to go to all the expense of a proper frame, a jar or polythene bag over a pot will do. But if you want larger quantities and more reliable or quicker results, then a full-sized frame with bottom heat will be an advantage.

Mist units simply comprise a bench with a sharp sand base and a device that dispenses a very fine spray over the whole area. This is not left on

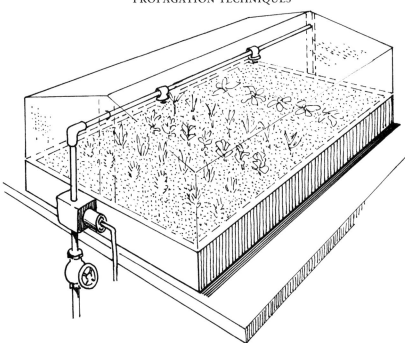

Fig. 14 *Mist units are invaluable for rooting cuttings and are now available to the amateur grower.*

permanently but is controlled by a metal 'leaf' that, when it dries out, switches on the mist. Originally these were only used by commercial growers but units are now quite cheaply available for the home propagator. There is no doubt that the use of these units increases the chances of cuttings taking root and the speed at which they do so. However, they are not so suitable for silver- and furry-leaved plants.

Cuttings can be placed in pots or trays, or directly into the sharp sand base of the propagator. The disadvantage of the latter is that you have to deal with one frame-full at a time and all the plants must root at the same time otherwise you will be reducing temperature and hardening off one batch of rooted cuttings before the others have got roots. Obviously, if one batch is in a pot or tray it can be taken out of the propagator and hardened off elsewhere, leaving others to continue rooting.

The only other piece of equipment required is a sharp knife or scalpel. This should be kept clean and very sharp. In order that virus infections are not spread, sterilize the blade in methylated spirits between cuttings from different plants.

Selecting Cuttings

Only choose cuttings from good, sound plants, which should be disease free and vigorous. Having said that, there are times when it may be necessary to rescue a dying plant and the only way is by cuttings. For example, a plant may have had all its roots chewed off by vine weevils and overnight it collapses. With luck a few cuttings can be taken and may revive sufficiently to root and thus perpetuate the plant. Be careful though if a plant is dying through a transmittable pest (e.g. eelworm) or virus as it is then not worth doing and could well effect other plants in the propagation area.

As well as being healthy, the cuttings should be vigorous. They should not be too drawn, nor should they be flowering or contain flower buds. Occasionally a plant is so floriferous that there is no way of getting a non-flowering shoot. In such a case remove any buds that are already there and any that develop while the cutting is in the frame. The best way to promote good healthy growth free from flowers is to shear the plant over about ten days before cuttings are required. New growth of just the right type will then develop. A good specimen to practice this on is something like *Viola cornuta* or *Aubrieta*. The other alternative is to take cuttings in the spring, while the growth is still young and vigorous and long before flowering is due. If the ground is dry and the plant flagging, give it a good soaking 24 hours before the cuttings are taken.

Stem Cuttings

Cuttings should be snipped from the plant with a pair of scissors or secateurs, or cut with a sharp knife. They should be longer than the final cuttings. In some cases, *Penstemon* for example, a whole stem can be taken as most of this can be used. In others it is sufficient just to take the top 7.5–10 cm (3–4 in) of the softer growth. This may either be the top of the stem or one or more of the lateral side shoots. The softer material feels more flexible to the touch and is usually a paler green than the harder, previous season's growth. Experience will soon help the gardener decide the best part to root.

The cuttings should be placed immediately in a polythene bag, which should be sealed and kept in a cool place out of the sun. Some plants will remain remarkably fresh in these conditions, which is particularly useful if you are collecting cuttings from a friend's garden and cannot deal with them for several hours. If they do go limp, they can be revived by standing in water before they are prepared.

For the final cutting, use a clean, preferably sterile, blade to cut neatly through the stem just below a node (i.e. where the leaves join the stem) at about 2.5–5 cm (1–2 in) below the top of the cutting, depending on the subject. Generally speaking, the larger the plant the larger the cutting, but

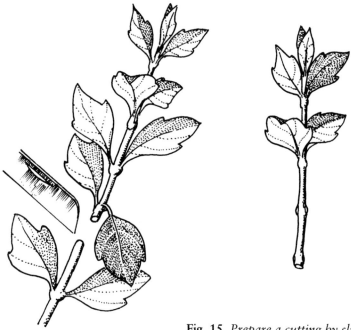

Fig. 15 *Prepare a cutting by slicing it through beneath a node and by cleanly removing the lower leaves.*

there is rarely any need to go much above 7.5 cm (3 in). With some plants, *Penstemon* for example, several cuttings can be made from the same stem, each being cut below a node at the lower end and above one at the upper.

Next, remove all those leaves that will be below or in contact with the soil. These should be cut off cleanly with a scalpel with no snags or pieces of stem remaining. This is important otherwise rot may set in. In leafy subjects it may be necessary to reduce the number of leaves or the leaf area so that the transpiration rate is reduced. If there are too many leaves more moisture will be evaporating from them than the non-rooted stem can pick up and the cutting will wilt. By reducing the area of leaves and by creating a moist atmosphere the transpiration rate is reduced sufficiently to maintain a balance. It is usual to remove all the leaves apart from the top pair (except where the leaves are small when more should be left). If the leaves are large then it might be necessary to cut each in half.

Before putting the cutting into the compost dip the cut end into a rooting powder or liquid to the depth of 1.25–2.5 cm (½–1 in). This is mainly intended to help with the development of roots, but many hardy perennials root very easily and the real advantage of using the powder is that it contains a fungicide that helps prevent the cutting rotting off in the damp compost and atmosphere.

Make a hole in the compost with a dibber (a pencil will do, but do not suck it if it has come into contact with the rooting powder). Place the cutting so that its base is in contact with the bottom of the hole and then firm round the edge so that there are no air gaps around the underground part of the stem. About 2.5 cm (1 in) should be below ground, less for smaller cuttings and more for larger ones. Observation and common sense will soon dictate the best planting depths for the different types of cuttings. Some growers simply push the cutting into the sand. This has two disadvantages. The first is that the stem can be damaged by the scarifying action of the compost as it is pushed in, and the second is that the rooting powder is pushed off.

If you are putting the cuttings into a pot, place them all round the edge. For some reason this seems to promote a quicker and more vigorous root system. On average you should be able to get about a dozen cuttings in a 9 cm (3.5 in) pot. Try to make certain that the leaves of the cuttings neither touch one another nor the sides of the propagator. If a polythene bag is used then wire or wooden hoops may be needed to keep it away from the cuttings.

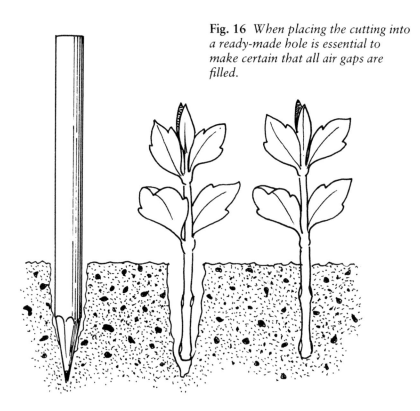

Fig. 16 *When placing the cutting into a ready-made hole is essential to make certain that all air gaps are filled.*

The compost should be moist when the cuttings are inserted and should be kept moist all the time they are in the propagator. This moisture will usually also be enough to keep the air in the propagator moist. In a mist propagator there is no lid, the mist nozzle keeping the air moist. Follow the instructions for the setting up of the mist unit, otherwise everything else is the same as with any other propagator. A gentle bottom heat is beneficial and will certainly speed things up, but is not essential. If used, it should be kept on until the cuttings have rooted.

Rooting is normally indicated by fresh growth and new leaves appearing on the cutting. It can be checked by digging up one of them and seeing if roots have developed. Another, more brutal method, is to give the cutting a gentle tug. If it does not yield then it has rooted. However, if the roots are just forming they can be damaged by this method, so only adopt it if you have plenty of spare cuttings. Once roots have developed the cuttings can be potted up (*see* p. 60).

In short the secrets for successful rooting cuttings are: good hygiene, plenty of light but not direct sunlight, a moist atmosphere and compost, and possibly a bit of bottom warmth. Having said that, however, I must admit that one of the top commercial propagators in the country uses a technique never recommended in books. He simply snips off the cutting and inserts it straight into his cutting compost, leaves and all. His argument is that the leaves below ground are less likely to cause rot than the wound made in removing them. He is a commercial grower and in a business where results count, so obviously it works.

Basal Cuttings

These are essentially the same as stem cuttings except that they are taken from the young growth at the base of the plant. This is a very good method of increasing a large number of hardy perennials, especially Compositae and many labiates They are usually taken in the spring when the new growth is appearing, but can be taken at any time that new growth appears. This can be created artificially by shearing over the whole or part of the plant. The cutting is removed as close as possible to the crown of the parent plant. Once taken they can be treated as the softwood cuttings.

Occasionally, particularly late in the season, it is possible to take basal cuttings with a few roots already formed where the shoot was in contact with the soil. These are known as 'Irishman's cuttings' and can be treated in exactly the same way as any other cuttings. They have the advantage of making a mature plant more quickly.

Fig. 17 *Basal cuttings are taken from the young growth around the base of the plant. This is generally done in spring.*

Fig. 18 *Using pipings is a specialized method for pinks where the cutting is gently pulled out of the stem.*

Pipings

This is a special type of cutting sometimes used for increasing pinks (*Dianthus*). Instead of cutting through the stem below a node, the stem is gently pulled so that it pulls out of the node as if it were coming out of a socket. No further preparation is required as it is then stuck straight into the compost up to the first pair of leaves.

Potting Up

Once the cuttings have grown roots they require potting up. If the plants are to go out into the garden as soon as they are big enough then a John Innes Potting Compost No. 2 will be strong enough. However if they are to remain in their pots for any length of time then the stronger No. 3 would be preferable. Partly fill a pot, either a 7.5 cm (3 in) or 9 cm (3.5 in) depending on the size of the cutting and the root ball, with compost and suspend the cutting between finger and thumb over the centre of the pot. Gently fill the remaining space up to the bottom of the rim of the pot. Make certain that the neck of the cutting is in the same position with regard to the surface of the compost as it was to the surface of the cutting compost. Tap the pot on the bench to settle the compost and top up if necessary. Stand the pot in a water bath or water from above, whichever you prefer. If the plant is to remain in the pot for any length of time I prefer to top dress with grit (*see* p. 44). Place the newly potted up plants into a closed cold frame, shading it if necessary from the sun. After a week the process of hardening off can begin.

ROOT CUTTINGS

There are a surprising number of plants that can be increased by taking cuttings from the roots. At first this seems a strange idea to many gardeners but you only have to remember what happens if you dig up a dandelion and miss a piece of the root. Similarly, most gardeners will have experienced the problems of leaving only a fragment of couch grass, bindweed or ground elder behind and seeing them sprout up into new plants in next to no time. Not all plants do this but many of the thicker rooted plants can be increased in this way. It is not, however, restricted to thick roots, some of the finer rooted *Linum*, for example, will grow from a very small section of root.

One advantage of taking cuttings from the root is that diseases found in the stems of many plants, such as eelworm in *Phlox*, are not transmitted to the new plant if root rather than stem cuttings are used. Normally cuttings are taken when the plant is in a dormant state, which for most plants means in winter. Any time, except when the weather is very cold, will do and many growers like to do it in the early winter.

To prepare root cuttings dig up the plant and wash the soil from the roots. Select one or more thick roots that are in good condition and have not been damaged in the process of being dug up. Cut these off and return the plant to the soil. Cut the roots into 5 cm (2 in) sections with the cut at the top of the root (i.e. that nearest the crown) being straight across and the one at the bottom on a slant. This in no way improves the quality of the cutting, it is simply an indication of which is the top and which is the bottom! It is not always necessary to remove the plant from the ground. Careful excavation down one side should reveal enough root for several new plants. This can be cut off and the soil replaced, leaving the rest of the roots undisturbed.

Fill a pot with cutting compost and plant several cuttings into it. They should be placed vertically with the flat end at the top. Cover with about 1.25 cm (½ in) of compost and then topdress with grit. An alternative that many growers prefer is to plant them horizontally in trays, again covering with soil and grit. The latter method is particularly suitable for the thinner roots. The method you choose is up to you and is really a matter of convenience. Place the pot or tray into a coldframe. Shoots and leaves will begin to appear in spring. Once roots are well established, pot up individually or plant straight out into open ground. Some of the thicker roots have sufficient stored energy to put up leaves before they establish roots, so do not automatically assume that roots have been formed.

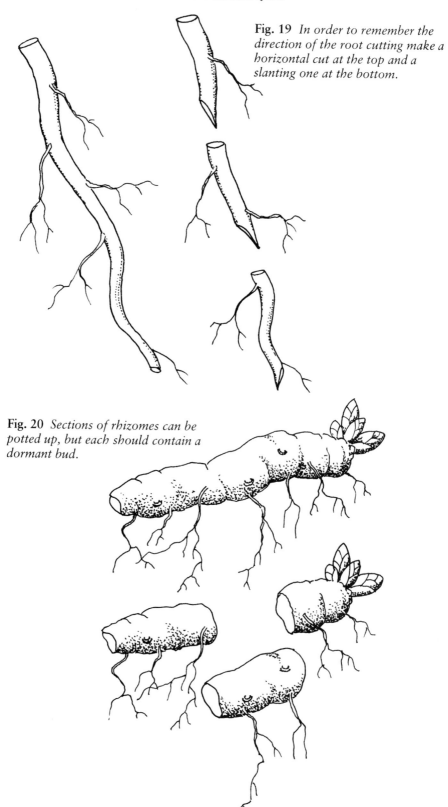

Fig. 19 *In order to remember the direction of the root cutting make a horizontal cut at the top and a slanting one at the bottom.*

Fig. 20 *Sections of rhizomes can be potted up, but each should contain a dormant bud.*

Rhizome Cuttings

A similar technique can be employed with plants that form thick fleshy rhizomes. Dig up a plant and wash off all the soil. Cut the rhizome up into sections about 2.5 cm (1 in) long. Each piece should contain a dormant bud that can often be seen lurking below a brownish scale. After being cut, the sections can be treated as root cuttings and laid horizontally in a pot or tray with the bud uppermost and any roots below. Quite a number of plants can be treated in this way including *Acorus*, *Bergenia*, *Dracaunculus* and *Canna*.

LAYERING

This technique is used more when dealing with shrubby plants but it can be a useful additional technique when dealing with herbaceous plants. Its best known use is for *Dianthus* but quite a number of other plants can be induced to throw out shoots from pegged-down stems and it can be a painless way of always ensuring that there are a few spare plants around. It is a simple method, the basic idea being to weigh or peg down a branch or stem so that it is in contact with the soil. It then puts out roots and a new plant is formed on the stem, a bit in the manner of a new strawberry plant on a runner.

The soil at the point of contact should always be kept moist and it may therefore help to enrich it or replace it with a potting compost. Some

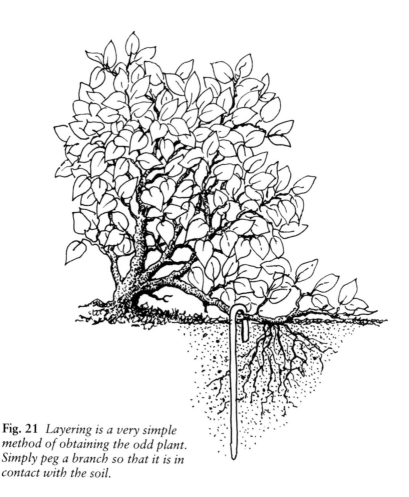

Fig. 21 *Layering is a very simple method of obtaining the odd plant. Simply peg a branch so that it is in contact with the soil.*

growers like to dig out the soil and insert a pot of compost so that when the plant is eventually severed from its parent it can be removed without disturbing the new roots. Before pegging the shoot down, the stem can be split a short way, which is claimed to help to speed up root development. Use a wire pin, wooden peg or heavy stone to keep the point of contact steady in the ground. The advantage of a stone is that it will help keep the soil moist.

This is a slow method of increase and in woody subjects it can take several years before the new plant can be cut free. With hardy perennials, roots are usually formed within the season but they are not necessarily as quickly as, for example, with cuttings. Once roots have been established the plant can be severed from its parent and moved to its permanent site.

A method akin to this can be used for heathers. If a peaty compost is poured into the centre of the plant so that only the extremities of the stems are visible, then roots are put down by the covered portions. When the roots have been formed, the whole plant can be lifted and divided up with each rooted stem being potted individually. This method may be applicable to other plants. As I am working through the borders I occasionally throw a couple of handfuls of earth across a straying stem from a spreading plant in the hope that it might root, giving me a spare plant to give away if any visitor should take a liking to it. This is a rather informal and not very scientific method, but it does not matter if it does not work, as I use more productive methods if I really want more plants.

MICROPROPAGATION

As far as the majority of gardeners are concerned, micropropagation is a technique that takes us into the realms of science fiction as new plants are grown from just a few cells under laboratory conditions. Unknowingly most gardeners have probably brought plants produced in this way, but it is not a method that need concern us here in detail as it is (at the moment) a technique that is only carried out on a commercial scale. Having said that, there are one or two gardeners, with a scientific bent of mind, who are already experimenting with some success, usually in specific fields such as lilies.

Essentially micropropagation is the removal of a few cells from the tip of a shoot under a microscope. The cells are placed in a culture medium in a tube and kept under ideal conditions of heat and light where they form plantlets that are eventually planted into ordinary composts and weaned. Everything must be undertaken under extreme sterile conditions, even the cutting under the microscope is accompanied by a stream of sterilized air.

One big advantage of propagation using this method, apart from the large number of plants that can be obtained from one plant, is that it is the only method that can be used for obtaining virus-free plants and is often used for 'cleaning up' plants that have become diseased to the point where they are likely to die out in cultivation. The method is sometimes referred to as tissue culture or meristem culture.

Special Groups
of Plants

BULBS

Bulbs are normally thought of as a group of plants distinct from hardy perennials, but they are often grown in association with each other and it seems invidious to omit information simply on the grounds of artificial groupings. Besides, it is often difficult to say where hardy perennials stop and bulbs begin. *Iris*, for example, contains both, and what about plants like *Crocosmia*, which definitely are bulbs but are nearly always the province of the hardy planter rather than the bulb enthusiast?

The basic methods of propagation are in fact the same as with other types of plants. Seed can be sown in the same way and divisions can be made. The latter is usually a simple matter of lifting the plant and removing the offsets that have formed around the parent bulb. There are, however, a few methods that are almost unique to bulbs.

The first is the use of bulbils. The best examples of this is in some species of *Lilium* and *Allium*. Here miniature bulbs are formed in the axils of the leaves (i.e. where the leaf or leafstalk joins the stem) or in the seed head. These can be removed and 'sown' in the open ground or in pots as one would with seed. Although they can be stored for short periods, they are best dealt with straight away. Normally they would drop to the ground and then root to form a new plant, but sometimes they form roots while they are still airborne on the parent plant. This premature root formation in no way hinders their subsequent growth. Unlike seed, these bulbils are a vegetative means of reproduction so they produce identical plants to the parents. Some herbaceous plants, *Cardamine bulbifera* for example, employ a similar mechanism.

The second method, which is again mainly relevant to *Lilium*, is scaling. The lily bulb is made up of layers of scales (an examination of a bulb will quickly show exactly what they look like). These scales are removed, dusted with fungicide, and placed vertically in trays of potting compost with their tips showing. Small bulblets will form along the basal edge of the scale and, when large enough, these can be potted up and grown

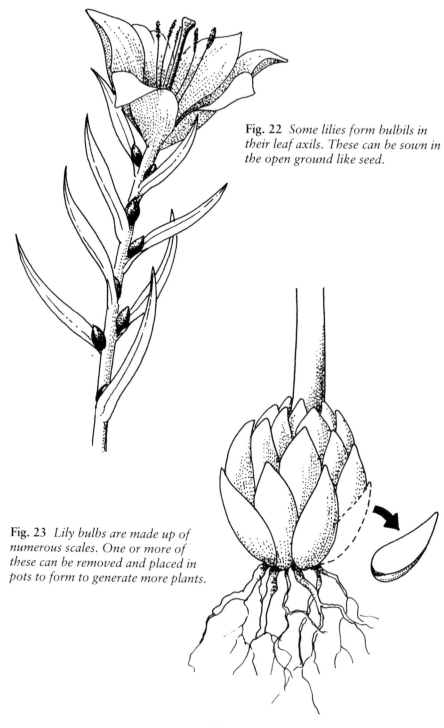

Fig. 22 *Some lilies form bulbils in their leaf axils. These can be sown in the open ground like seed.*

Fig. 23 *Lily bulbs are made up of numerous scales. One or more of these can be removed and placed in pots to form to generate more plants.*

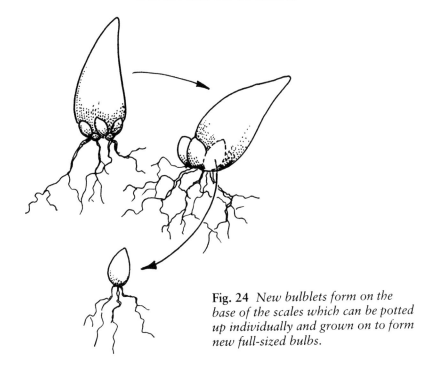

Fig. 24 *New bulblets form on the base of the scales which can be potted up individually and grown on to form new full-sized bulbs.*

on. The scales should be snapped off as close to the base as possible and should be in a healthy condition. Either one or two scales can be removed and then the parent bulb replanted, or the whole bulb can be taken apart to produce large quantities of new ones. This process can be undertaken at any time of the year, with different growers each having their own preferences; some prefer just after flowering, while others recommending the spring.

Another method is called 'twin scaling'. This involves cutting the bulb into sections, each with a part of the basal plate (i.e. the area from where the roots grow). The bulbs are dusted with fungicide and placed in trays of compost. This method is suitable for any bulbs with concentric rings such as *Galanthus*, *Narcissus* and *Tulipa*.

Another useful method is to score across the base of some bulbs to induce them to produce a larger number of small bulblets. One or more cuts are made across the basal plate, destroying the growing bud. Dust the cuts with fungicide and either place in a tray of compost in an upside-down position or in a similar position in a polythene bag with some moist peat. In both cases the bulbs should be kept in a warm place until the bulblets are formed and become large enough to pot on. *Amaryllis* and *Hyacinthus* are two subjects commonly treated in this way.

FERNS

Ferns must be treated as a separate category – at least as far as sexual reproduction is concerned – as they are unlike any other group of hardy plants in that they have a two stage process.

A fern produces sporangia, which contain a very fine dust-like spore, on the underside of its fronds. All ferns produce these asexually as there is no process equivalent to pollination involved. The spore can be collected and stored temporarily in paper bags. They can be stored for longer periods but are best used fresh.

Everything concerning germination of ferns must be kept absolutely sterile. Clean the pot thoroughly and then pour boiling water over it. Fill it with a peat-based compost. Put a piece of kitchen towel over this and, again, pour boiling water over it. Once it has cooled, remove the paper and dust the spore onto the surface. Place the pot on a tray of water and put it into a polythene bag, which is sealed tight. Place in a warm, light position, but not in direct sun.

After some weeks the spore will germinate and a green slime will appear on the surface, which will be the scale-like prothalli. These are not baby ferns but an intermediate step and it is at this stage that sexual reproduction takes place. The prothallus contains both male and female organs and it is only after fertilization that a true fern begins to develop. The compost needs to be kept moist (watered from the tray below) so that male cells can swim across to the female. When the egg is fertilized, a small fern emerges. It is only at this stage that the polythene bag is opened as the plants are slowly hardened off. They are transplanted while still small and the best way of accomplishing this is to scoop out a spoonful of young plants and place them into a similar depression formed by the spoon in a pot of peat-based compost.

The other main method of increasing ferns is to divide them as one would other hardy plants, although this method cannot be used on all ferns.

A specialized method used with some ferns, such as *Polystichium setiferum*, is to increase them from the bulbils that can be found on some fronds at the base of the pinnae (leaflets). These fronds are pegged down onto a peat-based compost and kept moist until the bulbils develop roots and begin to send up their own fronds. Pot up when large enough to handle. Room to pin down several fronds in each tray can be achieved by shortening the length of the pinnae.

Propagation of Individual Plants

INTRODUCTION

Plants included

This list is not confined to herbaceous perennial plants, it also includes a few honorary members from the shrubs, bulbs, annuals and biennials. In other words, it tries to cover all the plants normally found in a modern border that is predominantly herbaceous. It also contains a few low-growing plants often considered alpines, but which are excellent plants for the front of the border. Some plants may be considered tender by some gardeners, but have been included for those lucky enough to live in milder areas or those with courage to try them in warmer positions in the garden.

Family names

Families are given for all genera listed. In some cases more than one family has been given because some authorities now maintain that the genus in question should be reclassified. This is particularly true of the Liliaceae, which has now been split up into a number of new families. The Royal Botanic Gardens, Kew have accepted this change, but many botanists and gardeners are still using the older classification.

Seed sources

Some indication is given as to the availability of seed. It is impossible to name individual commercial seed merchants as the seed they offer naturally varies from year to year. *Commercial sources* refer to the commercial seed companies and means that the seed is generally available, usually through retail outlets such as garden centres. *Specialist commercial sources* refer to those companies that have an extensive range of seed on offer, including many of the rarer plants. Increasingly there are firms that specialize in seed of native plants. This is particularly so in the United States

71

where many of the wild flowers are now available as seed from one source or another. Some specialist nurseries sell seed of the plants they supply; thus one specializing in auriculas may well sell auricula seed, usually of a type not available elsewhere.

The seed exchanges are run by various gardening societies. *HPS* refers to the Hardy Plant Society. *RHS* refers to the Royal Horticultural Society. Other exchanges are too numerous to be listed. *Alpine seed exchanges* include those of The Alpine Garden Society, the Scottish Rock Garden Club, the American Rock Garden Society, the New Zealand Alpine Garden Society and the Alpine Club of British Columbia, amongst others. There are also many other specialist exchanges run by individual societies, for example the Iris Society, the Cyclamen Society and the RHS Lily Group, and these have been mentioned where relevant.

Reference to seed in this list means that seed has been available in the recent past, but it might not be available in the current year. It will be necessary to join the specialist groups in order to obtain seed from their exchanges. If seed is rare or not obviously available, then the availability of plants has been indicated, this at least allows gardeners to obtain one or more plants from which to propagate their own stock.

A–Z

Abutilon (Malvaceae). Propagate from cuttings in late summer or spring, or from hardwood cuttings at any time. They can also be raised from fresh seed. Named forms need to be vegetatively propagated. Plant out in spring in a sunny position. (Seed available HPS and other exchanges, and commercial catalogues.)

Acaena (Rosaceae). A genus of carpeting plants that can be divided in spring or autumn. They are not always happy with division and may not recover. Cuttings taken in summer or autumn may be easier. They can also be increased from seed sown in the spring. Although spiny, the seed-heads easily break up when ripe, the hooked spines contributing to the seeds' dispersal by becoming attached to clothing or animal fur. Some readily self-sow but any such plants should be moved when still young to their final positions. Plant out in spring or autumn in a sunny or lightly shaded position. (Seed from some specialist commercial sources and the seed exchanges, especially New Zealand ones.)

Acanthus (Acanthaceae). Bear's Breeches. Root cuttings taken in early winter provide a very easy method of propagating this genus. Any roots left in the ground after a plant is removed will automatically produce new plants (as many gardeners have discovered to their cost). They will also come readily from seed sown in the autumn. Self-sowing is a likelihood and any resulting seedlings should be moved while still young if required. Older plants can also be divided in spring but are slow to settle down. *A. dioscorides* can be reproduced from the suckers it throws out. Acanthus can become invasive. Plant out in spring in any well-drained garden soil, preferably in a sunny position, although they will tolerate some shade. (Seed available HPS and other exchanges, and commercial catalogues.)

Aceriphyllum (Saxifragaceae). See ***Mukdenia***

Achillea (Compositae). Yarrow. Propagate by division in autumn or spring. Many, particularly short-lived ones such as *A. clypeolata*, need lifting and dividing every three or four years. May also be increased by taking basal cuttings from young growth in the spring, particularly for some of the woodier forms, such as *A. taygetea* and *A.* 'Moonshine'. Can also be grown from fresh seed, but named forms are likely to produce inferior seedlings. Some named forms and new coloured strains are offered by seed merchants, but these should be ruthlessly culled for poor forms. Where derived from a cultivar they are given an ex-name e.g. 'ex-Cloth of Gold' to distinguish them from the true clones. Plant out into a sunny position in a moisture-retentive soil. (Seed available HPS and other seed exchanges, and from most commercial seed merchants.)

Achlys (Berberidaceae). Deerfoot, Vanilla Leaf. A genus of one or two species (depending on which taxonomist you follow). Rhizomatous woodland plants that can easily be increased by division of the rhizomes. They can also be propagated from seed sown either fresh or in the spring. They need shady woodland soil when planted out. (Seed available from HPS and alpine seed exchanges, and at least one specialist commercial seed merchant.)

Aciphylla (Umbelliferae). Speargrass. Tap-rooted plants that can only be propagated from seed. Sow freshly ripened seeds for the best results. Plant out in spring in a sunny, well-drained position. Wear tough leather gloves when collecting seed as the plants are, as their vernacular name implies, very spiky. (Seed available from HPS and alpine seed exchanges, and from some specialist commercial sources.)

Aconitum (Ranunculaceae). Monkshood. Most species are likely to come readily from seed if sown fresh. If sown in spring they may take longer, possibly over a year, although a pre-chilling may speed things up. *A. anthora*, from southern Europe, is one of the most difficult and erratic to germinate. Most have tuberous rootstock, which can be easily divided in autumn (particularly those that start into early growth in the late winter or early spring) or early spring. They require dividing every four or five years to prevent them becoming congested. Dividing is important for named clones, which need to be vegetatively reproduced. Seed and tubers are poisonous, so wash hands carefully after handling. Plant out into a sunny or lightly shaded position in a moisture-retentive soil. (Seed available from HPS and other seed exchanges, and from specialist commercial catalogues).

Acorus (Araceae). Sweet Flag. Two species only, both of which can be increased by division of the creeping rootstock in the spring. Can also be increased by rhizome cuttings, with each cutting bearing a nodal point indicated by a leaf or the papery remains of a withered leaf. Can be grown from seed, but other methods are preferable. Stand pots of divisions, cuttings or seeds in a bowl of water in order to keep the compost wet. Plant out in spring or autumn into a moist or boggy soil in sun or light shade. (Seed occasionally available from alpine exchanges, plants generally available from commercial and other sources.)

Actaea (Ranunculaceae). Baneberries. Division in spring or autumn provides an easy method of reproduction. They will also come easily from seed sown when fresh, having first been removed from the fleshy berry. Dried seed or that planted in the spring can take one or two years to germinate, although pre-chilling for two months may help to reduce this. Plant out in autumn or spring into a part-shaded position with a woodland soil. Berries and roots are very poisonous, so wash hands carefully after planting. (Seed available from HPS and other seed exchanges, and from specialist commercial catalogues.)

Actinotus (Umbelliferae). Flannel flower. Perennials that can be treated as annuals in colder areas. They come readily from seed sown, and cuttings taken in spring or division carried out at the same time of year. Plant out in a sunny position in well-drained soil. (Seed not common but available from some specialist commercial sources, and occasionally from seed exchanges. Plants commercially available.)

Adenophora (Campanulaceae). Ladybells. These are normally propagated from seed sown in the spring as with any other campanula. It is possible to take basal cuttings in the spring. They can also be increased by careful division, but the fleshy roots resent disturbance and the other methods present a better chance of success. Plant out into any fertile soil in a sunny position, although they will take a light shade. (Seed is available from HPS and alpine seed exchanges, and the more specialist commercial sources).

Adiantum (Adiantaceae). Maidenhair Ferns. Propagation is easily achieved by dividing the rhizomes if you can bear to split up the beautiful, slowly increasing clumps. They can also be propagated by sowing the spore, preferably fresh. Plant out into a moist soil in a shady position. (Spores may be available from pteridological societies and some specialist commercial sources.)

Adlumia (Papaveraceae). A monospecific genus consisting of *A. fungosa*, a biennial grown from seed. It self-sows providing sufficient seedlings for most uses. It prefers a woodland position in a moist soil. (Seed available from HPS and other seed exchanges, and the more specialist commercial sources.)

Adonis (Ranunculaceae). Pheasant's Eye. All can be increased from seed sown as soon as it is harvested. Seed obtained from exchanges or commercial sources is unlikely to be fresh and will be slow to germinate (possibly taking a year or more). They can also be propagated by careful division in autumn or early spring, although division is often quite difficult and it can take several years before the divisions establish themselves. Replant them in pots rather than the open ground. Double varieties can only be propagated by division. Plant out in autumn or early spring in a moisture retentive soil in full sun or a light shade. (Seed available from all seed exchanges and commercial sources).

Aeonium (Crassulaceae). Succulents tender in colder regions. These are succulents that can be easily increased from cuttings taken in the spring. They will also come readily from seed, but do have a tendency to hybridize, making it difficult to get true plants from this method. Some are monocarpic and die after flowering and seeding. Plant out in very well-drained soil in a sunny position. (Seed not commonly available but can be obtained from some specialist commercial sources and occasionally from seed exchanges. Plants available commercially.)

Aethionema (Cruciferae). These come readily from seed and will often self sow. They can also be increased from tip cuttings taken in spring before the plant comes into flower. They are not long lived so propagate regularly to maintain a stock. Plant out in a well-drained soil in full sun. (Seeds available from specialist commercial sources and from seed exchanges, particularly alpine ones.)

Agapanthus (Alliaceae/Liliaceae). African Lilies. Increase is normally achieved by division in spring. The fleshy roots are fragile and the plant should be dug up and handled carefully. Watering should be kept to a minimum as new roots will not be formed until early summer, which leaves time for the plants to rot if they are standing in excess moisture. Many consider that the best time to divide is when the plant is in full growth, when a better success rate can be achieved as new roots form much more readily. They can also be grown easily from seed sown in the spring, but will take several years to reach flowering size. Since agapanthus is late-flowering, the seed does not always ripen before the weather becomes unsympathetic for such processes, and it may be necessary in cold, wet autumns to cut the unripe stems and keep them in water until the seed fills out and turns black. Plant out in the spring two years after germinating in a well-drained, sunny position. Named clones will need to be propagated by division to keep the colours true. (Seed is available from all seed exchanges and commercial sources.)

Agastache (Labiatae). Mexican Bergamot. Propagation presents no problems and can be from seed sown in the spring or division taken at the same time of year. It seems likely that basal cuttings could be taken, as an alternative vegetative method, from the young growth in spring. Plant out into fertile, well-drained soil in a sheltered, sunny position. (Seed available from HPS, RHS or alpine seed exchanges, and some specialist commercial sources.)

Agave (Amaryllidaceae). Century Plant. A large genus of mainly tender plants needing glasshouse conditions, but a few, *A. americana* in particular, can survive outside in warmer areas. Many are monocarpic and must be perpetuated from seed or by detaching offsets or suckers that can form around the plant. There may be problems with seed-set and some species may need hand-pollination. Some species produce rhizomes and can be divided, while others have bulbils in the leaf axils, which can be potted up. Plant out in well-drained soil in a sunny, protected position. (Seed available from American Rock Garden seed exchange and some commercial sources.)

Ajuga (Labiatae). Bugle. Ground cover plants that form large carpets. Some do this by sending out runners forming masses of individual plants, which can easily be separated from their parents. Others form large rhizomatous mats, which can also very easily be divided. Both can be divided at any time between autumn and spring. Most forms seen in gardens are grown for the colouration of the leaves and to perpetuate this vegetative propagation is obviously necessary, but there are 40 species altogether and any of these can be grown directly from seed sown in the spring. Several species, *AA. genevensis, pyramidalis* and *reptans* for example, hybridize readily. If need be, some can be propagated from soft cuttings taken in late summer. Plant out in any moisture-retentive soil in sun or partial shade; the purple forms preferring sun and the variegated ones shade. (Seed of species available from alpine seed exchanges, and from the more specialized seed merchants, especially those dealing with wild flowers.)

Alcea (Malvaceae). Hollyhock. (*AA. ficifolia* and *rosea* are still sometimes listed under *Althea*). These are easily grown from seed sown fresh in the autumn or in the spring. Seed can be sown directly into the open soil in late spring. They should be planted in their final position when large enough to transplant, where they will flower in the following summer. Although perennial, they are better treated as biennials and renewed after flowering as they soon become exhausted, often breaking away from the woody base. Rust can also compound their problems. There are quite a number of colour strains that will come true, but open pollinated seed in the garden will generally produce seedlings with a variety of colours. The double forms produce seed and seedlings from these are generally more reliably coloured the same as their parents. Special colour forms can be increased by taking cuttings of young basal shoots in spring. Seed is normally abundant and they can usually be relied upon to self-sow. Any soil will do for planting out, but preferably in a sunny, wind-free position. (Seed readily available from seed exchanges and commercial sources.)

Alchemilla (Rosaceae). Lady's Mantle. Very effective self-seeding plant, at least in *A. mollis*, which self-sows itself everywhere unless deadheaded after flowering. Most, particularly the low-growing, mat-forming species such as *A. conjuncta*, can be easily divided at any time between autumn and spring. Plant out in any reasonable garden soil in sun or light shade; looks particularly well beside water. (Seed available from most sources, HPS and alpine exchanges having the greatest variety.)

Aldrovanda (Droseraceae). A monotypic, floating carnivorous plant. Simply divide in late spring or early summer and refloat in a shady area of pond or stream. (Difficult to find.)

Alisma (Alismataceae). Water Plantain. Increase from freshly sown seed. Place the pans or trays permanently in water or, better still, totally submerge. When seedlings appear, prick out into pots, keeping them just submerged, with the seedling sticking out of the water. Add water as the seedling grows. Plant out in shallow water either direct in the bed of the pond or in baskets. *A. ranunculoides* see *Baldellia*. (Seed available from seed exchanges and occasionally from commercial sources.)

Allium (Alliaceae/Liliaceae). Onions. A very large genus containing species very easy to propagate. All produce seed in quantity that germinates well when either sown fresh in autumn or in the spring. Self-sown seedlings are produced by many species. Most also increase from offsets, some more prolifically than others. Clump-forming species, such as *AA. schoenoprasum* and *tuberosum*, can be easily increased by dividing these offsets. A few such as *A. sphaerocephalum* can also be reproduced by 'sowing' the bulbils produced in the flower heads. Plant out in full sun, preferable in reasonably well-drained soil. Many alliums are invasive through self-sowing, or the overzealous dispersal of bulblets or bulbils. (Seed from HPS and other exchanges, including RHS Lily Group, and from commercial catalogues).

Aloe (Aloeaceae/Liliaceae). A large genus of mainly tender plants, of which only one, *A. aristata*, is likely to be grown outside glasshouse conditions, and then only in milder districts. They can be propagated from separating off rooted offsets or taking cuttings from young growth. Many are grown solely as foliage plants, but when available seed should be sown in gentle heat (about 70°F (21°C)). There is a strong tendency towards hybridization, so seed might not be pure. (Seed available from American Rock Garden seed exchange and some commercial sources.)

Alonsoa (Scrophulariaceae). Perennial plants usually treated as annuals in Britain as they are rather tender. They can be grown in the first place from seed sown in the spring under gentle heat. Once established, cuttings can be taken, as with their close relation *Diascia*, at any time during the growth season. Final cuttings should be taken in autumn so that there are a few plants to overwinter under glass in the colder areas. Plant out in a well-drained soil in full sun. (Seed commercially available and in seed exchanges.)

Alpinia (Zingiberaceae). Ginger Lily. These tender species are cut back by frosts but will often survive to shoot again. They can be propagated by simple division in spring or by sowing seed at the same time of year. Plant out in a rich, moist soil in full sun or light shade. (Seed not easily found, but plants commercially available.)

Alstroemeria (Alstromeriaceae). Peruvian Lily. The easiest method to propagate this genus is from seed. The seed pods of the alstroemeria are very explosive, scattering the seed far and wide, and will happily self-sow themselves around the garden. Collect the pods as they are turning brown and keep in a sealed paper bag until they have safely exploded. Ignore the darker brown or black seed and only sow the lighter orange-brown seed. Not all species are easy to germinate and can be helped by the following process: (ignore erroneous suggestions of soaking in warm water) sow seed and keep at a high temperature (25°C or 77°F by day and 15°C or 59°F by night) for four weeks, and then keep at 10°C (50°F) or below until they have germinated. A further aid for some of the more difficult species is to remove a small piece of tissue just above the embryo, where there is a brown spot. The fleshy roots are very fragile, which makes propagation from division difficult. With care this can be done for named cultivars. One way is to carefully split off a part of a large clump without disturbing the soil holding the roots. Because they come early into growth, this is best accomplished in autumn or early spring. Plant out into a sunny position in a well-drained soil. Beware of slugs. (Seed available from seed exchanges and most commercial sources.)

Althaea (Malvaceae). Hollyhocks. (*AA. ficifolia* and *rosea* have now been moved back to the genus *Alcea*.) The same principles apply to this genus as to the closely allied *Alcea*. Seed is by far the easiest form of increase. Sow when fresh in the autumn, or in spring. Plant out in their flowering positions when large enough, normally in the autumn, for flowering the following summer. Although perennial, they are short lived and should be resown every or every other year. Abundant seed is set. When planting out any good soil will do, preferably in a sunny position. Will self-sow. (Seed available from HPS and other seed exchanges.)

Alyssoides (Cruciferae). A small genus closely related to *Alyssum*, of which *Alyssoides utriculatum* is the only one generally seen in cultivation. It is similar to the wallflower and is grown in the same way. Increase is easily achieved from seed, which are abundantly stocked in the inflated seed pods, which are one of the attractions of the plant. If necessary, it can also be increased from cuttings taken early in the summer. This is not a long-lived plant and should be resown every two years or so. Plant out in any well-drained soil, in a sunny position. (Seed available from HPS and other seed exchanges.)

Alyssum (Cruciferae). These will come readily from seed when freshly sown, before the dormancy sets in. Seed sown in spring will need pre-chilling. Light and gentle heat at 15–20°C (59–68°F) increases the germination rate. There are several different colour strains of *A. saxatile* of which some will come reasonably true from seed, but these and special forms of other species can be easily taken as cuttings in early summer. They will often self-sow. Plant out in a well-drained soil in a sunny position. (Seed available from HPS and other seed exchanges, as well as commercial sources.)

Amaryllis (Amaryllidaceae). Monospecific genus. *A. belladonna* can be increased by seed sown as soon as it is ripe, using gentle heat if possible. Plants from seed can take up to eight years to reach flowering size. It can also be propagated by dividing up the thick mass of bulbs, which should be done around midsummer when the leaves turn yellow. It is also possible to increase by twin-scaling: the division of a bulb (*see* p. 69) or by scoring the base (*see* p. 69). (Seed not commonly available, but occasionally occurs in some seed exchanges.)

Amicia (Leguminosae). A small genus of quite tender plants, suitable for warmer districts. Increase from seed sown in spring or cuttings taken at the same time of year. Plant out in full sun and any good soil. (Seed is difficult to come by, but plants are commercially available.)

Amsonia (Apocynaceae). Only one of this genus (*A. tabernaemontana*) is normally grown. It can be propagated from either seed or division during the spring. It can be sown in pots or in rows in open ground. Plant out in full sun in any good soil. (Although not common, seed is available from the HPS and other seed exchanges.)

Anacyclus (Compositae). Daisies. These can be easily propagated from seed, preferably sown fresh, but it can still be sown in the spring. They can also be increased by taking cuttings from young side shoots in early spring. Plant out in a well-drained soil in full sun. (Seed available commercially and from seed exchanges.)

Anaphalis (Compositae). Pearl Everlasting. Clump formers easily divided in spring. For most purposes this is the best way of propagation, but they can be grown from seed, preferably sown fresh in autumn to get the best germination rate. Plant out in spring in full sun, although they will take some shade. The soil can be any garden soil as long as it is free-draining. (Seed from specialist commercial sources and all seed exchanges.)

Anarrhinum (Scrophularaceae). Several species of this genus are grown, but most are tender except in warmer areas. Easily propagated from seed sown in the spring, or by cuttings taken at the same time. Plant out in any good soil in full sun. (Seed difficult to find, but occasionally offered in seed exchanges.)

Anchusa (Boraginaceae). The easiest way of increasing the named forms of these plants is by taking root cuttings in late autumn or early winter, planting out in the following autumn. Can also be increased by careful division or from seed, although the latter will not come true for named forms. Sowing is in autumn or spring, but germination can be erratic and some inferior forms can result. Several species will self-sow themselves. Plant out in an enriched, well-drained soil in full sun. (Seed from some commercial sources and from all seed exchanges.)

Andropogon (Gramineae). Little Bluestem. A grass that can be increased by seed or division. Plant out in a light, well-drained soil in full sun. (Seed only occasionally occurs in seed exchanges, but plants are also available commercially.)

Anemone (Ranunculaceae). Anemones, Windflowers. This is a large and varied genus. The wood anemone group (*AA. nemorosa, blanda* etc.) has achenes of hard, buttercup-like seed as do the rivularis group (*AA. rivularis, narcissiflora* etc.); the de Caen group (*AA. pavonina, coronaria* etc.) has seed that is surrounded by a downy fur; the Japanese anemone group (*AA.* × *hybrida, hupehensis* etc.) have a similar woolly seed-head. All these should be sown fresh for the best results. Those with furry seed can be sown with the fur attached, but if it is difficult to separate the seed for an even sowing then the wool can be rubbed off. The rhizomatous roots of the wood anemone group are easy to divide, which is important as there are many named forms that will not come true from seed. They should be divided just before the foliage dies down, as this makes the small roots easier to find. The late-summer-flowering Japanese anemones can similarly be divided, but it is often better to take root cuttings in early winter, particularly as division is difficult to achieve without breaking the roots, which means that the resulting division usually ends up as a crude root cutting. Japanese anemones resent disturbance and it is often best to dig down beside the plant in late autumn

79

and remove a piece for a root cutting, or even make a division with a piece of root including a few fibrous roots and a few leaves, and pot up individually. Many of this group are named forms and therefore are best grown vegetatively. The *AA. pavonina* and *rivularis* groups come readily enough from seed and this is the best way of getting a quantity of plants, although the former can also have its tuberous roots divided, almost like bulbs. To tell when the seed of all groups is ripe, gently rub the seed between thumb and finger and it should come easily away from the seed-head. Seed of those forms with naked achenes (*A. nemorosa* for example) can be deceptive as the seed is generally still green when it is ripe. Plant out the wood anemone and the rivularis groups in a leafy moisture-retentive soil, preferably in light shade. The pavonina group likes full sun in a well-drained soil. The Japanese anemones will grow in any good garden soil, preferably in full sun, although they will take some shade. (Seed available mainly from the seed exchanges.)

Anemonopsis (Ranunculaceae). A monospecific genus represented by *A. macrophylla*, which can be reproduced by either seed or division. The seed should be sown fresh. Division can be either spring or summer. Plant out in a rich, lime-free, moisture-retentive soil that is in partial shade. (Seed is offered by HPS and other seed exchanges.)

Angelica (Umbelliferae). This herb comes very readily from seed, too readily sometimes as it will self-sow. Sow fresh or in spring. Plant out in ordinary garden soil that does not get too dry, in either sun or light shade. (Seed generally available from commercial and exchange sources.)

Anigozanthos (Haemodoraceae). Kangaroo Paw. Tender plants for warmer districts. The tuberous roots can be divided in spring or it can be grown from seed, which is becoming more available. Plant out in a very well-drained soil in full sun. (Seed available from some commercial sources and some exchanges. Plants are commercially available.)

Anthemis (Compositae). The easiest way to increase stocks is to take basal cuttings in spring. Cuttings can also be taken in summer. Many benefit by taking cuttings annually so that the plants can be renewed. *A. cupaniana* is most amenable as non-flowering (and even flowering) pieces can be broken off and stuck in the ground at any time of the year. Some plants can be divided. They will also come from seed, which is best sown fresh. Some, such as *A. sancti-johannis* will self-sow, but they must be moved young if they are to be transplanted. Many can be short-lived, so it is best to propagate regularly. Plant out in a sunny position in a well-drained but not too dry soil. (Seed available from some commercial sources and seed exchanges.)

Anthericum (Anthericaceae/Liliaceae). Bulbous, clump forming plants, easily divided in autumn. They will also come from seed, preferably sown fresh, or in spring. They may need pre-chilling if not naturally subjected to frosts. They will often self-sow. Generally an easy plant to propagate. Plant out in any good soil in full sun. (Seed available from both commercial and exchange sources.)

Antirrhinum (Scrophulariaceae). Snapdragons. A genus of plants much hybridized to produce strains of plants treated as annuals but, in fact, most are perennial. They can all be grown from seed sown in the spring, or autumn for early flowering. They will self-sow and the resulting plants tend to be more hardy than hand-raised ones. Some of the species, *A. molle* for example, will come quite easily from cuttings. I have not tried it on the hybrids, but there may be the possibility of perpetuating especially good forms in this way. Plant out in a fertile, well-drained soil in full sun. (Seed is available from most commercial sources, especially hybrid strains. True annuals and other species are best found in seed exchange lists.)

Apium (Umbelliferae). Water Celery. These water plants are easily increased by division in late spring. The divisions can be planted in baskets or directly back into the bed of the pond, making certain that they are well anchored, using lead strips if necessary to hold them down. They can also be grown from seed sown in pans kept submerged below water. Prick out seedlings into pots that are also kept below water, with the seedling just above the surface. Increase the depth of water as the seedling grows. Plant out in late spring. They are so easy to increase from division that seed is unimportant unless you have no plants to divide. (Seed not easy to obtain, but plants are available.)

Aponogeton (Aponogetonaceae). Water Hawthorn. Propagation is by seed sown in the spring. The pans of seed should be permanently stood in water or, better still, totally submerged. Seed is best sown fresh, but can be sown in spring, although it should not be allowed to dry out during storage. Prick out into pots or trays. Keep submerged so that the top of the seedling is above water. Continue to add water as the seedling grows. It can also be increased by simple division. Plant directly back into the bed of the pond or in a basket if these are used. Plant out in spring in deep water. (Seed is not easy to find but occasionally appears in seed exchanges. Plants are commercially available.)

Aquilegia (Ranunculaceae). Columbine. As with all Ranunculaceae, the seed benefits from being sown fresh, but can also be sown in spring, although germination can then be erratic. Pre-chilling in a refrigerator may help seed sown in spring. They tend to be promiscuous and cannot be guaranteed to come true, unless isolated from other species. Some of the strains, such as the double 'Norah Barlow' or 'Adelaide Addison' will come reasonably true from seed as long as they are isolated and any other forms are rogued out. Columbines will readily self-sow but rarely cause a nuisance as excess plants are easily removed. Mature plants can also be divided with care and may be the only sure way to keep plants true in borders where there are several forms present. Plant out in autumn for self-sown plants, or either spring or autumn from divisions. Plant out in a free-draining, moisture-retentive soil, in either sun or partial shade. (Seed available from commercial or seed exchanges.)

Arabis (Cruciferae). Increase is easily achieved from cuttings taken in the spring. If cuttings are taken later in the year, then the plant should be sheared over to produce new growth for suitable cutting material. Rooted cuttings can also be taken. They can also be propagated from seed, but as cuttings are so easy it is hardly worth it unless cutting material is not available. (Seed generally available.)

Aralia (Araliaceae). The herbaceous plants of this genus can be increased by either seed or division in spring, or root cuttings taken in late autumn. Plant out in a rich soil in sun or part shade. (Seed difficult to find although it does occur in some seed exchanges from time to time.)

Arctotis (Compositae). African Daisy. Only hardy in the warmer areas. They come very readily from cuttings taken in the autumn or can be sown as seed in the spring. Plant out in enriched, well-drained soil in full sun. (Seed available from most sources.)

Argemone (Papaveraceae). A small genus consisting mainly of annuals, although there are some perennials. All best propagated from seed sown in spring, under a gentle heat if you are in a hurry. They dislike disturbance so should be planted out while still young with a good root-ball of soil, or sown directly where they are to flower. Several have a tendency to self-sow but are not a nuisance. Both the seed and stems are poisonous. Plant out in a well-drained soil in full sun. (Seed available commercially and from seed exchanges.)

Argyranthemum (Compositae). Most are tender except in warmer districts. Since most are either named hybrids or cultivars, cuttings taken in autumn and overwintered is the first choice of propagation method. Cut back shoots in late summer to promote good growth for cutting material. Later-flowering plants can also be achieved from cuttings taken in early spring from greenhouse-forced plants, and rooted under heat. Seed can also be used, but is not always easy to come by. Sow fresh, if available, and overwinter any seedlings under glass. (Not commonly available but some species may be found still lurking under the name of *Chrysanthemum*.)

Arisaema (Araceae). These can be increased either from seed or from division of the tubers. Sow the seed fresh, first removing the flesh from the fruit to expose the one to four seeds per berry. If the berries have dried out, soak in warm water to soften them before removing the flesh. Sow thinly as they should not be pricked out for two years. Be careful with watering, as arisaema seedlings can rot off if overwatered and die if underwatered. Some species need at least two different clones to produce seed. They will take three to four years to reach flowering size. Mature tubers produce offsets that can be divided off in autumn, when the plant is dormant, to provide new plants. Plant out in a humus-rich soil that will not dry out, usually in light shade, although some will take sun if there is enough moisture in the soil. (Seed available from specialist commercial sources and from seed exchanges, especially alpine ones.)

Arisarum (Araceae). Mouse Plant. A small genus of two woodland species most easily increased by lifting and dividing the tubers in spring. They can also be grown from seed sown either fresh in the autumn or in the spring. Plant out in a woodland-type soil in light shade. (Seed available from specialist commercial firms and from seed exchanges.)

Aristea (Iridaceae). Tender plants that mainly need greenhouse conditions, but might be grown outside in warmer areas. Can be easily propagated from seed. Plant out in full sun in a well-drained soil as soon as the plant is large enough to transplant, as they resent being disturbed once developed. Some sources claim they can be divided but this is tricky because of the problem of disturbance. (Seed available from specialist commercial sources, HPS and other seed exchanges.)

Aristochia (Aristolochiaceae). The main species grown, *A. clematitis* is rather invasive and therefore easily lends itself to division. Other less rampant species can be increased from cuttings or from seed, neither of which is difficult. Plant out in full sun in a well-drained soil. (Seed available from specialist commercial sources and seed exchanges.)

Armeria (Plumbaginaceae). Thrift, Sea Pink. These come easily from either seed or cuttings. The larger forms can also be divided, with divisions easily taking root. All three methods can take place in spring. Named forms must be propagated vegetatively. Plant out in full sun in a well-drained soil. (Seed generally available from commercial sources and exchanges.)

Armoracia (Cruciferae). Horse-radish. Occasionally grown as an ornamental, especially the variegated form. It can be easily propagated by division of its invasive rootstock or, as anyone who has tried to get rid of this plant will know, by root cuttings. Seed can be used for the non-variegated form. Plant out in any garden soil in full sun or partial shade. (Seed mainly available from suppliers of herbal and vegetable seed.)

Arnebia (Boraginaceae). Prophet Flower. Only one species is *A. pulchra (echioides)* is normally grown. This can be increased by root cuttings taken in early winter, seed sown in spring or from heel cuttings taken in late summer or autumn. Plant out in a rich, well-drained soil in a sunny position. (Seed difficult to come by, but occasionally crops up in seed exchanges.)

Arnica (Compositae). A rhizomatous plant that can easily be divided. It will also come readily from seed, particularly if sown fresh. Plant out in a sunny position in a humus rich, but free-draining soil, which must be lime-free. (Seed available from specialist commercial sources and seed exchanges).

Artemisia (Compositae). Most of this genus are gently spreading and can easily be increased by division in autumn or spring. Many will also come from cuttings of non-flowering shoots in either spring or autumn. Some have preference for one or the other, for example *A. absinthium* is easiest from cuttings in autumn, while *A. a.* 'Lambrook Silver' is best from cuttings in spring. Other than named forms will come from seed, but this is a bit unnecessary with such easy vegetative means available. Plant out in a well-drained soil in full sun. (Seed available from commercial sources and seed exchanges.)

Arthropodium (Anthericaceae/Liliaceae). Tender plants that can be grown in warmer areas. These can be increased either by division of the fibrous roots or from seed. Plant out in a well-drained soil in a warm sunny position. (Seed occasionally available from one of the seed exchanges.)

Arum (Araceae). These curious plants will come from seed, often self-sowing themselves around the garden. Seed should be sown fresh in the autumn. If stored until the spring, it should not be allowed to dry out and should be kept in a domestic refrigerator. The seed will probably germinate in the first spring, but leaves will not appear until much later so do not throw away what appears to be an empty pot. *A. italicum* 'Pictum' has marbled leaves and will come true from seed although the marbling may not be seen for a year or so. The tubers usually clump up, producing offsets, and can easily be divided with the use of a knife if necessary. Plant out in a cool, moist woodland position in light shade. *A. creticum* needs a well-drained site in full sun. (Seed available from some commercial sources and seed exchanges.)

Aruncus (Rosaceae). Goat's Beard. They can be grown from seed sown in the spring. They are dioecious so both male and female plants are necessary if seed is required. Alternatively, as they are clump forming, they can be divided in autumn or in spring, if you are strong enough to cope with the woody rootstock. Plant out in a rich, moist soil in sun or partial shade. (Seed available from specialist commercial sources or HPS and other seed exchanges.)

Arundo (Gramineae). Giant Reed. This stoloniferous genus is usually increased by division in spring. It can also be sown from seed, also in spring, or by taking stem cuttings in summer and placing them in a compost kept constantly moist. New shoots will be formed at a node. Plant out in a moist, rich soil in full sun or partial shade. (Seed difficult to find but occasionally crops up in an exchange list. Plants commercially available.)

Asarina (Scrophulariaceae). This small genus, akin to *Antirrhinum*, comes readily from seed. It self-sows, but is difficult to transplant so it is best to grow new in pots and then plant out, rather than move self-sown seedlings unless they are dug up with a large root-ball. Plant out in shade in well-drained, lime-free soil. (Seed available from HPS and other seed exchanges.)

Asarum (Aristolochiaceae). Colonizing ground-cover plants that can easily be propagated by division or splitting off some of the spreading rooted shoots. They can also be grown from seed, preferably sown fresh in the autumn although sowing can be delayed until spring. (Seed available from all seed exchanges and some specialist commercial sources.)

Asclepias (Asclepiadaceae). Milkweed. There is plenty of choice with regards to the propagation of this genus. In the first place they can be sown from fresh seed (although seed is not frequently set in Britain) or, if necessary, from older seed in spring. A period of pre-chilling may be advantageous. Once acquired they can be increased from root cuttings taken in early winter, basal cuttings taken in spring, or careful division in spring. They object to being transplanted so all propagation should take place in pots and not open ground. Plant out in moisture-retentive, but well-drained soil. *A. incarnata* is a bog plant and can be easily divided. Plant out in a wet position. (Seed available from specialist commercial suppliers and from HPS and other seed exchanges.)

Asparagus (Liliaceae). Often grown as a foliage plant as well as a vegetable. Grown from seed sown in the spring. Soak seed in warm water for two or three hours and then sow directly into open ground, transplanting the young plants to final position in the following spring. The flowers are inconspicuous but the bright orange berries are very obvious and can be easily collected. It often self-sows, sometimes distributed by birds. The resulting plants can be transplanted in spring. Plant out in enriched but free-draining garden soil in full sun. (Seed available from commercial sources, often vegetable seed merchants, and all seed exchanges.)

Asperula (Rubiaceae). Woodruffs. These creeping plants can easily be increased by dividing their creeping rootstock in spring. They can also be grown from seed sown in the spring. Plant out in any soil in light shade, but does best in woodland conditions. Alpine species need a very well-drained soil in a sunny position. (Seed available from specialist commercial sources and all seed exchanges.)

Asphodeline (Asphodelaceae/Liliaceae). A satisfied plant will produce masses of seed that can be used for propagation, sowing it in the spring. They are likely to take up to three years to reach flowering size. The plants form a clump, which can be easily divided although it is preferable not to disturb established plants. Plant out into a well-drained soil in a sunny position. (Seed available from some specialist commercial sources and from HPS and other seed exchanges.)

Asphodelus (Asphodelaceae/Liliaceae). A small genus closely related to *Asphodeline* and increased in the same way from seed and by division. (Seed available from some specialist commercial sources and from HPS and other exchanges.)

Aspidistra (Convallariaceae/Liliaceae). This genus is only suitable for warmer districts. They are easily propagated by division in spring. Old plants, particularly if kept in pots, can have their roots hopelessly entangled so exercise patience when dividing. If not kept in pots the plants tend to have a more spreading habit and can be increased by removing rooted suckers. Their flowers (pollinated by slugs) and subsequent seed pods appear at ground level. Plant out in a well-drained soil in shade. (There does not seem to be any obvious source of seed, but plants are commercially available.)

Asplenium (Aspleniaceae). Spleenworts, Hart's Tongues (previously *Phyllitis*). These ferns are reproduced from spore or by dividing clumps of some species into separate crowns in spring. Bulbiferous species, *AA. bulbiferum* and *scolopendrium* for example, can be increased by separating off the bulbils and planting. Plant out in well-drained soil with added humus and mortar rubble. Does best on north sides of walls. (Spores may be available from pteridological spore exchanges and plants are commercially available.)

Astelia (Asteliaceae/Liliaceae). Grow from seed sown in the spring or from division of the tufted rhizome-forming plants. They are dioecious so plants of both sexes will need to produce seed. Plant in an enriched soil in full sun or partial shade. (Seed not easy to come by but does occur in some of the seed exchanges. Plants available commercially.)

Aster (Compositae). Asters, Michaelmas Daisies. The easiest way of reproducing all this group is by division of their clumps in spring. It is always best to take material from the edge of the clump and discard the woody centre portion. The divisions need only be one stem with roots on it. It is also possible to take basal cuttings in spring especially of the non-running forms, such as *A. × frikartii* or *A. amellus*, which are less easy to divide. Asters are one of the few genera that will tolerate the crude method of division using back-to-back forks or the even cruder use of a spade to chop the clump up into smaller portions, but it is still best to make proper divisions using the hands and fingers, discarding dead and broken material. To maintain the vitality of the planting, it is essential to propagate regularly, every two or three years at the most. The majority of asters grown in the garden are of named forms, so vegetative propagation is the best method, but it is quite possible to grow the species from seed and where faithful reproduction is not required. Seed should preferably be sown fresh in the autumn, although they can be sown in spring when they may benefit from a period of pre-chilling in a domestic refrigerator. Plant out in autumn or spring in good fertile soil in full sun. (Seed available from commercial sources and seed exchanges.)

Astilbe (Saxifragaceae). Most astilbe grown in the garden are of named varieties and so it is best to propagate them by vegetative means. As they are clump-forming, division can easily be achieved in either spring or autumn. Regular division benefits the continuing vitality of the plant, particularly in moister positions where they can clump up very quickly. The species can be grown from seed sown in the spring, although they may not flower until their second or even third year. Plant out in a rich moist soil in either full sun or part shade. (Seed available from commercial sources and seed exchanges.)

Astilboides (Saxifragaceae). A one-species genus represented by *A. tabularis*, which has recently arrived as a refugee from *Rodgersia*. The main method of increase is by division of its spreading rootstock in spring. It can also be grown from seed sown in spring. Plant out in a moisture-retentive soil in light shade or full sun if soil is not allowed to dry out. (Seed not available commercially but occasionally occurs in seed exchange lists, often under the name *Rodgersia tabularis*.)

Astragalus (Leguminosae). A very large genus that is becoming increasingly popular, especially in areas with milder climates. Most species are best increased from spring-sown seed, which may be slow to germinate. Sow in pots and plant in final positions as soon as possible as they resent being disturbed. Plant out in well-drained soil and in full sun. (Seed available from some specialist commercial sources and seed exchanges.)

Astrantia (Umbelliferae). Masterwort. The slowly spreading rhizomatous roots make this an easy plant to divide in spring or autumn. This is particularly important for the named cultivars which need to be kept true. It will also come readily from seed if sown fresh in the autumn or, if necessary, in the spring. They will generally self-sow giving a ready supply of young plants. Plant out in good garden soil in either sun or shade. (Seed available from specialist commercial sources and HPS and other seed exchanges.)

Athyrium (Athyriaceae). Lady Fern. Can be increased either from spore or from division. Plant out in a moist, humus-rich soil in shade. (Spores available from pteridological spore exchanges. Plants commercially available.)

Athamanta (Umbelliferae). These can be increased by either sowing seed or making divisions, both in the spring. Plant out in any good garden soil in full sun. (Seed not easy to find although it does turn up in some exchange lists from time to time. Plants commercially available.)

Aubrieta (Cruciferae). Easily propagated from cuttings. After flowering, closely shear over the plant and use the new growth that forms as cutting material. Seed of the species can be sown in the spring. There are now named strains that can be sown at the same time of year. These may benefit from sowing under glass in gentle heat. Plant out in a well-drained soil, preferably on a bank or wall, in full sun. (Seed available commercially and from seed exchanges.)

Aurinia (Cruciferae). See ***Alyssum***

Azolla (Azollaceae). Fairy Moss. A floating pond weed that is extremely easy to increase by simply breaking off pieces and refloating them on the water. (Plants commercially available.)

Baileya (Compositae). A small genus of relatively tender plants suitable only for warmer areas. Increased from seed sown fresh or in spring. Plant out in well-drained soil in a sunny position. (Seed not generally available but can occasionally be found in American exchange lists. Plants difficult to find in the UK but wider spread in the US.)

Baldellia (Alismataceae). A water plant that can be increased from freshly sown seed or by division. The pans of seed should be permanently stood in water or, better still, submerged until seedlings appear. Prick out the seedlings into pots or trays, again submerging them leaving the seedling just above water. Add more water as the seedling grows. Plant out in the spring in to shallow water direct into the bed of the pond or in baskets. Divisions can be returned straight back to the water as long as they are anchored to the bottom or placed in baskets. (Seed not easy to obtain, but plants available commercially.)

Ballotta (Labiatae). Cuttings can be taken at any time of the year but come more readily if taken in spring. To help prevent the cuttings from rotting, scrape off the 'wool' at the base. It can, of course, also be grown from seed sown in the spring. Plant out into a well-drained soil in a sunny position. (Seed does not appear to be available commercially but can be obtained from the HPS and other seed exchanges.)

Balsamita. See *Chrysanthemum*

Balsamorhiza (Compositae). Balsamroot. Increase from seed either sown fresh or in spring. Some species have tap roots, which means they should be planted in their final positions as soon as possible. Plant out into a well-drained soil in full sun. (Both seed and plants are difficult to find in the UK, but are available both from seed exchanges and as plants from commercial sources in the US.)

Baptisia (Leguminosae). Best grown from seed sown in spring. As with many of the legumes, it helps to soak the seed overnight in warm water before sowing. It is likely to take at least three years before the plant gives of its best. They can also be divided in spring, but since they are deep-rooted plants they resent disturbance and losses can be expected using this method. Plant out in a deep, humus-rich soil in full sun or partial shade. (Seed available from some commercial sources as well as HPS and other seed exchanges.)

Barbarea (Cruciferae). American Land Cress, Winter Cress. All species will come readily from seed sown in the spring. The variegated and double forms of *B. vulgaris* commonly found in gardens are best increased vegetatively by taking basal cuttings in spring. Surprisingly, a certain percentage of seedlings of the former will also be variegated. Plant out in moisture-retentive soil in full sun or partial shade. (Species used as salad vegetables are available from most seed merchants. Others, including *B. vulgaris* 'Variegata', are listed by specialist commercial firms and seed exchanges.)

Begonia (Begoniaceae). Some begonias are hardy in warmer districts, in particular *B. grandis*. Most can be increased from cuttings and from seed. The seed is very fine (about 50,000 to the gram!) and should be mixed with silver sand to make it easier to spread it evenly over a soil-less compost. Keep in a heated propagator at 18–21°C (65–75°F) ensuring that the compost stays moist. *B. grandis* can easily be increased from the bulbils that it readily produces. Plant out in good garden soil in a sheltered sunny spot. (Seed of the hardier forms is not easy to come by, but plants are commercially available.)

Belamcanda (Iridaceae). Blackberry Lily, Leopard Flower. A small genus of only two species of which *B. chinensis* is the most widely grown. Sow the shiny black seed in the autumn or spring. Germination can be helped by pre-chilling. They can also be easily divided in spring. Plant out in the following spring in a well-drained soil in a sunny or partially shaded position. (Seed available from seed exchanges and specialist commercial sources.)

Bellis (Compositae). Daisy. As most gardeners know to their cost, this is a very easy plant to propagate – place one plant in a lawn and you will soon have as many plants as you will ever need. There are, however, several named forms that need to be increased by division in either autumn or spring. Seedlings from these need to be rogued out as they are unlikely to come true. Some strains are sold by commercial sources as seed, but these also will deteriorate if left to self-sow. (Strains available from all commercial sources and named forms readily available as plants from nurseries.)

Bergenia (Saxifragaceae). All will come from seed sown in autumn or spring, although they will take two or three years to flower. Those sown in spring can be helped by a period of pre-chilling in a refrigerator. The named varieties need to be propagated vegetatively. This can easily be achieved in late autumn or winter by taking a section, about 2.5 cm (1 in) long, of the thick rhizomatous stem (ensuring that each has an 'eye' in the axils where an old leaf used to be – these are obvious when the stem is examined) and placing vertically just below the surface of the compost in a pot or tray, much in the manner of a root cutting. Many plants can be achieved in this way. A less productive, but less cumbersome method, is simple division in autumn or spring after flowering. These accommodating plants can be planted out in any garden soil in either sun or shade, although they will be at their best in a humus-rich soil and in partial shade. (Seed available from seed exchanges and specialist commercial sources.)

Berkheya (Compositae). A large genus of which *B. macrocephala* is the main herbaceous species in general cultivation. Propagation is from seed sown in autumn or spring, or division in spring although this is not always easy. Plant out in good garden soil in a warm sunny position. (Seed difficult to obtain, although it has occurred in seed exchanges. Plants for sale are likewise difficult to locate.)

Beschorneria (Agavaceae). A small genus of Mexican plants of which at least one, *B. yuccoides* is hardy in warmer areas. The simplest way of increase is by division of the basal rosettes in spring. They can also be grown from seed sown fresh or in spring, if necessary. Preferably sow in a temperature of about 21°C (70°F) and do not cover seed as light is beneficial to germination. Plant out in the following spring in very well-drained soil in a warm, sunny place. (Seed available from HPS and other seed exchanges, but rarely seen commercially. Plants available from specialist nurseries.)

Besseya (Scrophulariaceae). A small genus of American plants allied to *Synthyris*. The main method of increase is from seed sown in spring. Plant out in a woodland-type soil in light shade, although some species prefer a sunny well-drained position. (Seed difficult to obtain, although it does occasionally occur in seed exchanges.)

Bidens (Compositae). A moderate-sized genus of annuals and perennials. They can all be grown from seed sown in the autumn or spring. The perennials can also be increased vegetatively by dividing or taking cuttings in spring. Plant out in any good soil in full sun. (Seed of annual and half-hardy perennials are available commercially, while some of the species are occasionally seen in the seed exchanges.)

Betonica. See *Stachys*

Biscutella (Cruciferae). Like most crucifers this genus comes easily from seed sown in the spring. It can be sown directly into the open ground if required. Plant out into a well-drained soil in a sunny position. (Seed not generally available commercially but can be found in seed exchanges.)

Blandfordia (Liliaceae). Christmas Bells. A small, tender genus that can only be grown in milder regions. The main method of propagation is by sowing seed under glass either in autumn or spring. Slow to germinate. Refrain from watering seedlings when they have gone dormant. They can also be increased by division. Plant out in moisture-retentive, free-draining, acid soil in a warm position in full sun (or partial shade in hotter areas). (Seed available from some specialist commercial sources and some seed exchanges.)

Blechnum (Blechnaceae). Hard Fern. A large genus of ferns that can be propagated from fresh spores. They can also be increased by division in the spring, particularly those with a spreading and invasive habit such as *BB. chilense* or *penna-marina*. Plant out in spring in moisture-retentive soil (although they will take quite dry conditions) in partial shade or sun. (Spores available from pteridological societies' exchanges. Plants readily available from commercial sources.)

Bletilla (Orchidaceae). A small genus of which *B. striata* is commonly seen in cultivation. The only practical way of propagating is by division of the clumps of pseudo-bulbs in spring or after flowering. Plant out in a moisture-retentive but free-draining soil in full sun or partial shade. (Seed not generally available as it is extremely difficult to germinate, as with most orchids, although it is occasionally seen in exchanges. Plants commercially available.)

Bocconia. See *Macleaya*

Boltonia (Compositae). The main method of propagating these is by division of the spreading clumps into either smaller clumps or into individual slips in autumn or spring. Divide regularly to maintain vitality of the clumps. They can also be grown from seed sown fresh or in spring (particularly the annual members of the genus). Plant out in any good garden soil, preferably in sun, although they will take some shade. (Seed available from seed exchanges and some specialist seed merchants.)

Bomarea (Alstroemeriaceae/Liliaceae). A South American genus of twining plants that will survive in warmer areas. Increase by division of the roots in spring. They can also be propagated from seed sown fresh under glass at 19–21°C (65–70°F) for three weeks before chilling in a refrigerator for a further three weeks, and finally returning to the warmer temperature. Plant out in a warm sheltered position in a well-drained soil. (Seed not generally available but does occasionally occur in seed exchanges, particularly the American ones. Plants commercially available.)

Bongardia (Podophyllaceae/Berberidaceae). A monospecific genus consisting of *B. chrysogonum*. A tuberous plant that needs to be propagated from seed sown fresh or in spring. Plant out in a well-drained soil. (Seed available from alpine garden seed exchanges.)

Borago (Boraginaceae). Borage. *B. officinalis* is strictly an annual but it generously self-sows itself giving it a permanent place in the garden. *B. laxiflora* is a perennial very easily raised from seed and, again, usually providing sufficient seedlings by its tendency to self-sow. Plant out in any garden soil (even poor) in sun or shade. (Seed generally available from commercial sources and seed exchanges.)

Bothriochloa (Gramineae). Although perennials, these are often treated as annuals and sown as seed each spring directly into their final positions in a well-drained soil in a sunny position. They can also be treated as perennials by dividing the spreading rootstock in spring. (Neither seed nor plants are easy to come by, except from enthusiasts.)

Bouteloua (Gramineae). Mosquito Grass, Signal Arm Grass. These can be most easily propagated by division in spring or increased by sowing seed, also in spring. Plant out resulting plants in spring in well-drained soil in a sunny position. (Seed difficult to obtain but occasionally occurs in seed exchanges. Plants are commercially available.)

Boykinia (Saxifragaceae). (See also *Telesonix*.) Increase by dividing the clumps or sowing seed in spring. Plant out in a well-drained, humus-rich soil, preferably in partial shade. (Seed available from exchanges, especially the alpine garden exchanges. Occasionally available from commercial sources.)

Briza (Gramineae). Quaking Grass, Trembling Grass. Mainly annuals, but all can be grown from seed. Perennials can be divided in the spring. Plant out in a fertile soil in full sun. (Seed of the perennial species not generally available, but can occasionally be found in seed exchanges. Plants are commercially available.)

Brodiaea (Alliaceae/Liliaceae). (See also *Triteleia*.) Similar to alliums and can be propagated in the same fashion, i.e. from dividing the numerous bulbous offsets in autumn (it is best to do this at least every three or four years otherwise they become congested) or by sowing seed in autumn or spring. Plant out in a well-drained soil in full sun. (Seed available from seed exchanges and occasionally from specialist commercial sources.)

Brunnera (Boraginaceae). An easy-going genus for the propagator as it can be readily increased by either division or seed, the former in autumn or spring, the latter in spring. It is also one of that small band of genera that can be propagated from root cuttings, which should be taken when the plant is dormant in late autumn or early winter. Use either of the two vegetative means for reproducing named forms. Plant out in a moisture-retentive soil in partial shade, although it will take full sun if the soil is not too dry. (Seed available from HPS and other seed exchanges but generally not seen in commercial catalogues.)

Bulbine (Asphodelaceae/Liliaceae). The main method of increase is by seed sown in spring under glass. They can also be propagated by division of the bulb-like clumps in spring. Although other methods are more than satisfactory, *B. caulescens* can also be increased by taking cuttings in spring. Plant out in late spring into a well-drained soil in a warm, sunny position. (Not easy seed to find, but occasionally offered in alpine garden exchanges. Plants commercially available.)

Bulbinella (Asphodelaceae/Liliaceae). These can be increased by division of the clumps of fleshy roots in late spring or in autumn if they are lifted for over-wintering. Can also be increased by seed sown fresh or in spring, but do not cover deeply as light is beneficial to germination. *B. rossii* tends to be dioecious and therefore needs both male and female plants to be present in order to set seed. Plant out in spring into a moisture-retentive soil (preferably not alkaline) in partial shade or full sun. (Seed available from HPS and other exchanges as well as some specialist commercial sources.)

Bupthalmum (Compositae). A small genus of which two species, *B. salicifolium* and *B. speciosum*, are generally grown. The easiest way of increase is by division for which the spreading plants (*B. speciosum* is particularly rampant) provide plenty of material. Seed is equally easy and, again, the plants helping by providing self-sown seedlings. Plant out in moisture-retentive soil in part shade or full sun. (Seed available from specialist commercial sources and from seed exchanges.)

Bupleurum (Umbelliferae). The easiest method of propagation is from seed sown fresh or in spring. The main decorative species, *B. falcatum*, is a vigorous self-sower providing ample seedlings but it is tap rooted so, if used, should be moved to its final positions as early as possible. Some of the other species can be divided. Plant out in any garden soil, preferably in full sun. (Seed available from HPS and other exchanges, as well as some specialist commercial suppliers.)

Butomus (Butomaceae). Monotypic genus. *B. umbellatus* can be propagated by division in spring. Can also be reproduced from bulbils collected in late summer. Place bulbils in a pot of potting compost containing extra leafmould. Keep compost wet by standing pot in a tray of water until the plants are large enough to plant out. No real need to grow from seed, but it is possible by sowing in a soil-less compost, which is kept moist by standing in a tray of water as with the bulbils. Plant out on the margins of water either in the damp surrounding soil or in shallow water. (Seed not commercially available, but can be found in the HPS seed exchange. Plants widely obtainable.)

Caccinia (Boraginaceae). A small genus easily propagated from seed sown in spring, or by dividing in autumn or spring. Dividing is not always successful as the plants dislike being disturbed. It can also be increased by taking root cuttings during early winter. Plant out in a well-drained soil in a sunny position. (Seed not easy to come by but occasionally occurs in HPS seed exchange. Plants also difficult to find.)

Calamintha (Labiatae). A good plant to propagate as you get such a pleasing scent from it as you divide it in spring, or by taking cuttings during early summer. It can, of course, also be grown from seed, which should be sown in spring. Plant out in a well-drained soil in full sun. (Seed not often available from commercial sources, but occurs in most seed exchange lists. Plants commercially available.)

Calamagrostis (Gramineae). As with most grasses, these can be either divided in spring or sown from seed in autumn or spring. Plant out in any good garden soil in sun. (Seed not easy to find except occasionally in seed exchanges. Plants commercially available.)

Calanthe (Orchidaceae). As with most orchids, the only viable way of reproducing is by division of the bulbous rootstock just after the flower has faded. Plant out in a sheltered position in a humus-rich, woodland soil in partial shade. (Plants commercially available.)

Calla (Araceae). Bog Arum. Monospecific genus. *C. palustris* can be propagated by division in autumn or spring. When replanting divisions ensure that they are anchored down if they are planted in shallow water. It can also be easily increased by taking stem cuttings, each section of which should contain a latent bud. Pot into a soil-less compost, which is kept permanently wet by standing in a shallow tray of water. Although easy to increase by vegetative means, it can also be grown from seed, which should be sown fresh in late summer in compost that is kept moist. Plant out on the margins of water, either in damp ground or in shallow water. (Seed not easy to find, but does occur occasionally in seed exchanges. Plants commercially available.)

Callirhoe (Malvaceae). Poppy Mallow. A small genus of both annuals and perennials. The latter can either be grown from seed sown in the spring either in pans or directly in the soil where they are to grow. They can also be increased by division in spring or from cuttings taken at the same time of year. Plant out in a free-draining soil in full sun. (Seed not readily available commercially, but does occur in HPS and other seed exchanges.)

Caltha (Ranunculaceae). Kingcups, Marsh Marigolds. Divide after flowering in early spring. *C. leptosepala* is slow to re-establish itself after dividing. *C. polypetala* can be easily propagated by layering the radiating shoots. If replanting divisions in shallow water make certain that they are anchored down. They can also be increased from seed, which should be sown fresh if possible. If not, sow in spring. Ensure the compost stays moist. The double form, *C.p.* 'Plena', should be increased vegetatively. A percentage of the white forms will come from seed. Plant out in a moisture-retentive soil in sun or partial shade. Can be treated as marginals and planted in boggy ground or shallow water. (Seed available from specialist commercial sources or from HPS and other seed exchanges.)

Camassia (Hyacinthaceae/Liliaceae). Bulbous plants that happily increase themselves, but require a helping hand with the occasional splitting up of the clumps in the autumn. Starting from scratch can be easily achieved by sowing seed, preferably fresh. Seedlings can take up to four years to reach flowering size. Plant out in a moisture-retentive soil in full sun. (Seed available from the seed exchanges and some specialist seed merchants.)

Campanula (Campanulaceae). Bellflowers. A big genus with a large number of species in cultivation. The main methods of propagation are seed and division. All apart from named forms can be raised from seed, which can be sown in autumn or early spring so that it catches some of the frosts. (Pre-chilling in a refrigerator for three weeks is a good alternative.) Do not cover as light is beneficial for germination. Some, *C. thrysoides* being the prime example, are monocarpic and die after flowering and setting seed (may be a year or more after germination). These should be sown every year to ensure a continuance of the plants. *C. pyramidalis*, although a perennial, should be raised from seed every year and treated as a biennial in order to ensure the best plants. Campanulas generally set plenty of seed but some gardeners have difficulty in finding it as the seed capsule is disguised in the back of the calyx; look closely and you will soon discover its secret. Some, such as *C. persicifolia*, provide plenty of self-sown seedlings. All clump-forming species and cultivars can be increased by division, which is best undertaken in spring. Use the younger growths round the edges of the clump, discarding the woodier centres. They can be planted out or potted up as individual slips or in larger clumps. All benefit from regular division every three or four years. Some are stoloniferous rather than clump forming (*CC. rapunculoides* and *takesimana* being particularly invasive examples) and rapidly spread outwards. These can also be easily divided by taking one stem plus its associated roots. An alternative vegetative method is by taking basal cuttings from the young spring growth. Plant out in moisture-retentive, but free-draining soil in full sun. (A limited number of forms are stocked by commercial seed merchants, but the various seed exchanges cover an astonishing number of varieties between them.)

Canna (Cannaceae). The normal method of increasing existing plants is by making divisions of the rhizomes in late winter. A section bearing a bud is cut off and laid in compost in the manner of a root cutting. Water sparingly and keep at around 15°C (60°F). They can also be raised from seed sown in spring. The seed case is hard and needs the same treatment as sweet peas, i.e. soaking in warm water, filing, or shaking vigorously with sharp sand, to allow penetration of moisture. Plant out in spring after the last frosts in a rich soil in full sun. (Available from specialist seed merchants and most seed exchanges.)

Cardamine (Cruciferae). This genus now includes most of the species that were previously in *Dentaria* and these, in common with the older members, can be easily increased by division of the wandering roots at any time when the weather allows, although some growers prefer to divide before growth starts in the spring. As anyone who has bitter-cress (*C. hirsuta*) as a weed in the garden (and who hasn't?) will know, cardamines can also be readily increased from seed either when fresh or in spring. *C. bulbifera* can be increased by 'sowing' the bulbils that form in the axils of the leaves. Plant out in a humus-rich soil in partial shade or full sun. (Seed available from wild-flower seed merchants and seed exchanges.)

Cardiocrinum (Liliaceae). These lilies are monocarpic and hence die after flowering and producing seed. Fortunately they produce offsets before dying. These are the best means of increase as they only take a few years to reach flowering size, whereas seed can take up to eight years of patient waiting. Seed is produced in copious amounts and should be sown fresh if possible. Leave the seedlings in the same pot for two years before potting on, providing them with a liquid potash feed as well as water. If possible sow some every year to get a collection of different ages and a continuance of plants. Plant out in a very rich soil with plenty of humus in partial shade. (Seed available from some specialist seed merchants, and HPS and other seed exchanges.)

Carduncellus (Compositae). A small genus of thistles, some distinguished by their beautiful rosettes of leaves. They can be easily propagated by seed, preferably sown fresh. Plant out as soon as possible as they resent root disturbance. Plant in a well-drained soil in full sun. (Seed available from some specialist commercial sources and from seed exchanges.)

Carex (Cyperaceae). Sedge. An enormous genus of plants that can easily be propagated either by simple division or by sowing seed. Both operations can be carried out in spring, the latter benefitting from a little gentle heat. Plant out in any moisture-retentive soil in the shade or in full sun if there is sufficient moisture. Some can be planted in shallow water; make sure these are anchored down. (Surprisingly with such a large genus there is not a great deal of seed available. Some species are offered by specialist seed merchants, including those specializing in wild flowers, and others are offered in seed exchanges.)

Carlina (Compositae). Thistles. Despite gardeners' natural aversion towards thistles, there are some that make interesting, if not good, garden plants. They all come readily from seed that should preferably be sown fresh, but can also wait until spring. Plant out as soon as possible, preferably in spring, as they develop tap roots and therefore resent disturbance. The tap roots are another source of increase as most species can be propagated from root cuttings taken in early winter. A well-drained soil and a sunny position is best. (Seed available from specialist seed merchants and seed exchanges.)

Catananche (Compositae). Blue Cupidone, Cupid's Dart. This small genus can be propagated either by sowing seed in spring or by taking root cuttings in early winter. Plant out in a well-drained soil in a sunny position. (Seed available from most seed merchants as well as seed exchanges.)

Catharanthus (Apocynaceae). Madagascar Periwinkle, Rose Periwinkle. A small genus hardy only in the warmest areas, treat as annual elsewhere. It can be increased from seed or by taking cuttings. The seed needs to be germinated in darkness and under heat (21°C, 70°F) in spring. Plant out in a moisture-retentive soil in full sun. (Seed available from some commercial sources and some seed exchanges.)

Caulophyllum (Berberidaceae). Blue Cohosh, Papooseroot. A small genus of two species grown mainly for their decorative berries, which also provide one way of increase. Sow fresh or in spring. Do not harvest the seed too early. The seed case splits exposing the seed before it is ripe. Although naked, the seed continues to swell until it is ripe – indicated by the change to a blue colour. The plants are rhizomatous and can be divided in spring. Plant out in a woodland soil in light shade. (Seed not easy to come by although both species appear in seed exchanges from time to time. Plants of *C. thalictroides* also commercially available.)

Cautleya (Zingiberaceae). A genus for warmer areas, although some are surprisingly hardy. Propagation is by careful division of the thick rootstock or by sowing seed in spring. The hard seeds should be scarified and soaked in warm water before sowing. Plant out in a well-drained but moisture-retentive soil in a warm protected position in full or part sun. (Seed available from some commercial sources and from seed exchanges.)

Cedronella (Labiatae). Most species have been moved to **Agastache** but C. *triphylla* (*C. canariensis*), Balm of Gilead, remains. Can be easily increased from seed sown in the spring or from cuttings taken in the autumn and overwintered. Plant out in a well-drained soil in full sun. (Seed difficult to find, but may be available from commercial sources specializing in herbs. Also occasionally occurs in seed exchange lists. Plants commercially available.)

Celmisia (Compositae). This genus can be increased from seed, preferably sown fresh, but also in spring if stored properly in chilled conditions. It is also possible to propagate it vegetatively, either by division or by taking cuttings in spring. Plant out in a well-drained but moisture-retentive soil in a protected position in sun. (Seed available from some specialist commercial sources and from seed exchanges.)

Centaurea (Compositae). Knapweeds, Hardheads. A very large genus of which the majority in cultivation can be easily increased by simple division in the autumn or spring, either by dividing into single slips and potting up or directly planting out, or by dividing into small clumps. Clumps should be divided regularly to keep plants vigorous. Most (except named varieties) will come from seed sown in the spring. Many, particularly C. *montana* are happy to self sow. Another characteristic of this plant and quite a number of others, including CC. *dealbata* and *hypoleuca*, is that they can be increased from root cuttings taken in early winter. C. *cinerea* (*C. gymnocarpa*) can be propagated from stem cuttings taken in autumn and kept in a propagator that is partly ventilated. Can be grown from seed but the silver qualities that are one of the main reasons for growing the plant will in all probability be lost. Plant out in well-drained but moisture-retentive soil in sun. (Seed available from specialist commercial sources and HPS and other seed exchanges.)

Centranthus (Valerianaceae). Red Valerian. This is most easily grown from seed sown either fresh or in the spring. They can be sown directly into the open ground. It self-sows so readily that there is little need for the gardener to sow it again once it is established, although it is important to move seedlings when they are young. Another method of increase is to take basal cuttings. Plant out in a well-drained soil (it naturally seems to prefer old walls or banks) in sun. (Seed available from commercial and seed exchanges.)

Cephalaria (Dipsacaceae). Propagation is usually by division or from seed, both in the spring. They can be sown directly into the open ground if required. Some forms seem to be sterile and produce no seed. Although these two methods should be adequate, they can also be increased from root cuttings taken in early winter. Plant out in any good garden soil. (Seed is available from specialist commercial sources and the HPS and other seed exchanges.)

Cerastium (Caryphyllaceae). Snow-in-Summer. Most gardeners feel that this increases readily enough by itself without a helping hand. All three main methods lend themselves to propagating this genus, C. *tomentosum* in particular. Seed can be sown in spring. Cuttings can be taken in summer (shearing over first to get some good new growth) or the creeping growth can easily be divided at virtually any time, spring or autumn being best. Plant out in any good garden soil in full sun. (Seed available from some commercial sources and all seed exchanges.)

Ceratophyllum (Ceratophyllaceae). Hornworts. Hardy submerged water plants easily increased by taking cuttings in spring. The cutting compost should be kept moist by standing the pot in a tray of water. They can also be divided. Make certain when planted out that they are anchored down until they have rooted into the pond. They will tolerate deep water and shade. (Plants available commercially.)

Ceratostigma (Plumbaginaceae). This genus are really shrubs but can be called honorary herbaceous plants, particularly *P. plumbaginoides*, which is herbaceous in habit. This species' creeping habit means that it can easily be divided, as can *C. willmottianum*. These, along with the other species, can also be increased from soft cuttings taken in early summer or half-ripe cuttings in summer. They can also be grown from seed sown in the spring. Some, *C. willmottianum* for example, will self-sow. Plant out in well-drained soil in a sunny position. (Seed available from specialist commercial sources and from seed exchanges.)

Cestrum (Solanaceae). Shrubby plants easily propagated from half-ripe cuttings taken in summer. (*C. parqui* can also be from soft cuttings.) They will also come from seed sown in spring. Plant out in spring in well-drained soil in a sunny position. (Seed available from some specialist commercial sources and all seed exchanges.)

Chaerophyllum (Umbelliferae). These are most easily increased from seed sown in the spring. They can also be propagated by careful division in the spring. Plant out in any good soil in full sun or part shade. (Seed available from HPS and occasionally other exchanges. Plants available commercially.)

Chamaelirion (Liliaceae). Blazing Star, Rattlesnake, Wand Lily. Closely related to *Veratrum*, this monospecific genus is represented by *C. luteum*, which can be either grown from seed sown fresh, or by having its tuberous rootstock divided in spring. Plant out in a rich woodland soil in partial shade. (Seed not easy to find, but occasionally available from seed exchanges. Plants commercially available, although difficult to find.)

Chara (Characeae). Stoneworts. Hardy submerged water plants easily increased by division by simply anchoring the pieces that have been split off into the mud. (Plants are commercially available.)

Chasmanthe (Iridaceae). The simplest method of increase for this genus is by the division of the offsets, produced by the corms, during autumn when the plant goes dormant. They can also be easily grown from seed, which should be sown fresh. Plant out resulting seedlings in the following summer or the spring after that in a well-drained soil in a sunny position. (Seed available from some specialist commercial sources and seed exchanges.)

Cheilanthes (Adiantaceae). Lip Ferns. As with all ferns, these are easily propagated from spores collected in the autumn. Plant out in a very well-drained, open position. (Spore possibly available from pteridological society spore exchanges. Plants commercially available.)

1 *Anemone blanda* 'White Splendour'
Divide the roots just before the foliage dies down.

2 *Aquilegia vulgaris* 'Adelaide Addison'
Surprisingly, this cultivar comes true from seed, preferably freshly sown.

3 *Asclepias tuberosa*
This accommodating plant can be increased by virtually any method.

4 *Aster tongolense*
Division is probably the easiest method of increase but sowing seed is equally effective.

5 *Caltha palustris* 'Plena'
Division after flowering is the best way of propagating this double form.

6 *Camassia leichtlinii alba*
The bulbs of this plant multiply quite
quickly and can be easily divided.

7 *Cardamine heptaphylla*
The running nature of this cardamine
makes it easy to divide.

8 *Corydalis flexuosa*
This rare corydalis is embarrassingly easy
to increase from either division or seed.

9 *Dactylorhiza grandis*
Division is the only realistic way to
increase this orchid.

10 *Dianthus deltoides*
This small pink can easily be propagated
by cuttings, or if colour is not important,
from seed.

11 *Erythronium* 'Pagoda'
Being a cultivar the only method of
increase is by division of the bulbs.

12 *Geranium* × *riversleaianum* 'Russell Prichard'
Careful division is the normal method of propagating this
geranium.

13 *Hesperis matronalis*
This plant usually provides self-sown
seedlings, ready for use.

14 *Hieracium aurantiacum*
This plant can increase all too readily by
itself, but can be propagated by division
or from seed.

15 *Hosta undulata albo-marginata*
Division is the only method of increase for hosta cultivars.

17 *Ixia uranus*
These bulbs naturally increase forming a large clump and can be easily split up.

16 *Iris pallida*
Most of the larger irises are best increased by division.

18 *Lilium pyrenaicum*
A variety of methods are available for growing lilies, either seed or scales can be used for this species.

20 *Meconopsis cambrica*
The Welsh poppy comes all too readily from seed, often self-sowing prodigiously.

19 *Lupinus*
Lupins should be propagated regularly from seed or basal cuttings to provide vigorous young plants.

21 *Paeonia officinalis* 'Rosea Plena'
Cultivar peonies must be propagated by vegetative methods, either division or root cuttings.

22 *Papaver orientale* 'Goliath'
Root cuttings are really the only method to increase the named forms of oriental poppies.

23 *Paris polyphylla*
This rare plant can be increased by
careful division in autumn.

24 *Potentilla* 'Gibson's Scarlet'
Division in autumn is the normal
method of propagating potentilla
cultivars.

25 *Pulmonaria saccharata*
Division after flowering gives the best
results for propagating the lungworts.

26 *Pulsatilla vulgaris*
Semi-double form
A surprisingly large percentage of
semi-double plants are produced from
freshly-sown seed.

27 *Pulsatilla vulgaris*
By far the easiest method of production
is from seed, but it must be freshly sown.

29 *Salvia involucrata* 'Bethellii'
Being a cultivar vegetative methods such
as division or cuttings must be used to
increase it.

28 *Roscoea cautleoides*
The roscoeas are clump-forming plants and can easily
be divided.

30 *Sanguinaria canadensis* 'Plena'
This beautiful plant can easily be propagated by dividing its spreading rhizomes.

31 *Scoliopus bigelovii*
Division is the easiest method of increase, but seed can be used if it can be acquired.

32 *Senecio tanguticus*
Being rather invasive this plant can very easily be divided.

33 *Shortia uniflora*
Careful division is the best method of increase, seed being rather difficult to germinate.

34 *Veronica spicata* 'Alba'
Simple division of the spreading clump is the easiest method of increase for many veronicas.

Cheiranthus (Cruciferae). (See also *Erysimum*). Named varieties and good forms can be kept going by taking cuttings of non-flowering shoots (taken with a heel) in mid-summer. Softwood cuttings can also be taken in spring and kept under mist or in a closed frame. Species and mixtures can equally be increased by seed sown in spring. The so-called biennials sold by seed merchants are in fact short-lived perennials and will last more than one season, although they tend to be better in their first. These can be sown in rows in the open and then transplanted to their flowering positions in late summer or autumn. Any particularly good colour form of these can be perpetuated by regularly taking cuttings as above. Plant out in any good, well-drained soil in a sunny position. (Seed available from all commercial seed sources and exchanges.)

Chelidonium (Papaveraceae). Greater Celandine, Swallow Wort. A monotypic genus of which the solitary *C. majus* is sometimes grown as a cottage garden plant. It comes very easily from seed and can often be increased from self-sown seedlings, which should be transplanted when young. The double form *C.m.* 'Flore Pleno' will also come true in a high percentage of cases. The form *C.m.* 'Laciniatum Flore Pleno' can be increased (as can the others) by division in early spring. Plant out in any soil and either in sun or part shade. (Seed available from some specialist commercial sources and seed exchanges.)

Chelone (Scrophulariaceae). Turtlehead. The easiest way of propagation is by simple division of the clumps formed by the spreading roots. It can also be grown from seed sown in the spring. Ensure that the compost is very free-draining. A period of pre-chilling may be advantageous and some growers find that light also increases germination rate. Basal cuttings taken in the spring are another vegetative method that can be useful. Plant out in any moisture-retentive soil in sun or part shade. (Seed available from some commercial sources and from HPS and other seed exchanges.)

Chenopodium (Chenopodiaceae). Both the annuals and the perennials can be raised from seed sown in the spring. The perennials can also be increased by division in spring. Plant out in any soil in full sun. (Seed can be obtained from commercial sources (some listed under vegetables or herbs) and seed exchange lists.)

Chionochloa (Gramineae). Tussock Grass. This genus can be grown from seed, which should be sown fresh. The clumps can also be divided in spring, just as they are coming into growth. Plant out in the spring in well-drained, moisture-retentive soil. (Seed difficult to find but might be available through New Zealand exchange lists. Some species available commercially as plants.)

Chionographis (Liliaceae). A small genus of Japanese woodland plants, which are rhizomatous and can easily be propagated by dividing the dormant crowns in autumn. It can also be grown from seed sown in autumn or spring. Plant out in a woodland-type soil in light shade. (Seed not commercially available but occasionally appears in seed exchanges. Plants difficult to find commercially.)

Chlorophytum (Anthericaceae/Liliaceae). St Bernard's Lily. Plants mainly for the warmer regions, these can be most easily increased by division in spring. They can also be grown from seed sown in spring. Some plants produce small plantlets on the thin flowering stems and these can be potted up and grown on in a similar fashion to strawberry runners. Plant out in a well-drained soil in a protected, sunny position. (Seed difficult to find although they occasionally occur in seed exchange lists. Some plants commercially available.)

Chlidanthus (Amaryllidaceae/Liliaceae). There is little problem in increasing this genus as the bulbs readily reproduce themselves and can be easily divided. They can also be grown from freshly sown seed but can take several years to flower. In warmer areas plant out in well-drained soil in a sheltered sunny position. It will need protection in other areas. (Seed not easy to find, but plants of C. *fragrans* commercially available.)

Chrysanthemum (Compositae). This genus has recently been split up amongst a number of new and existing genera but the old familiar name has been retained in this book as the changes have not yet found widespread acceptance. Genera involved include *Argyranthemum, Balsamita, Chrysanthemopsis, Dendranthema, Leucanthemella, Leucanthemopsis, Nipponanthemum,* and *Tanacetum.* Those that have spreading roots, such as C. *uluginosum* (now *Leucanthemella serotina*) or C. *maximum* (*Leucanthemum maximum*), can easily be divided in spring. Those, such as the florists' chrysanthemums (*Dendranthema*), that grow from a single stem can be increased from basal cuttings taken in the spring (or taken in mid-winter from plants forced into early growth by lifting them and taking them into frost-free conditions or even into a little warmth). All can be increased from seed, preferably sown fresh, although named varieties will not come true (except for specially-bred commercial strains).

Chrysanthemopsis (Compositae). See **Chrysanthemum**

Chrysogonum (Compositae). Goldenstar. This monotypic genus, represented by C. *virginianum,* is treated as an annual in most places and grown from seed, but it is a perennial and can overwinter in warmer districts. As a perennial it can also be divided. Plant out in well-drained soil in a protected, sunny position. (Seed difficult to find but available from some seed exchanges. Plants commercially available.)

Chrysopsis (Compositae). Golden Aster. The easiest way of propagation is by division in spring. They can also be grown from seed, preferably sown fresh. Plant out in any well-drained soil in a sunny position. (Seed not easy to come by but can occasionally be found in seed exchange lists. Some plants commerically available, although difficult to find.)

Cichorum (Compositae). Chicory. The easiest method of propagation is probably from seed either sown in pots or direct into the soil. In either case move to their flowering positions while the plant is still young. Can also be increased vegetatively by root cuttings taken in early winter or by very careful division, in spring, of the thick, forked rootstock, ensuring that each piece has a shoot or bud on it. Plant out in a well-drained soil in full sun. (Seed available commercially and from most seed exchanges.)

Cimifuga (Ranunculaceae). Bugbane. This genus can easily be propagated by division in the spring or autumn. It can also be grown from seed, preferably sown fresh or, if necessary, in spring. Plant out in a rich, moisture-retentive soil in partial shade or, if the soil is moist enough, in sun. (Seed available from specialist commercial sources as well as HPS and other seed exchanges.)

Cirsium (Compositae). Thistles. On the whole this genus should be avoided as they reproduce themselves only too readily without any help. However, there are some garden-worthy plants that can easily be propagated. The simplest method is by division of the creeping rootstock in spring or autumn. Alternatively, they can be grown from seed, preferably sown when fresh, but also in spring. Plant out in any good garden soil, preferably in sun for best results. (Seed available from specialist commercial sources and seed exchanges.)

Claytonia (Portulacaceae). Spring Beauty. This genus can be easily propagated from seed. Indeed, it self-sows itself quite happily and can be a source of supply of young plants that costs the gardener little effort. They can also be increased by division in the spring. Plant out in a moist woodland-type soil in partial shade, although they will also take sun if the soil is moist enough. (Seed not easy to come by from commercial sources, but available from seed exchanges. Plants commercially available.)

Clematis (Ranunculaceae). Although the majority of this genus are shrubby climbers, there are a number of herbaceous perennials, which can be propagated in a number of ways. Most of these herbaceous clematis form clumps that can be carefully divided in spring to provide more plants. Basal cuttings taken in spring are another vegetative method of increase. Cuttings are prone to rot and a weekly spray of a fungicide may be necessary. Layering provides yet another method of this type of propagation, but with the herbaceous types the layer must succeed by the autumn. Alternatively, all but named forms can be increased by seed, although the quality of the plants may vary and some, such as the purple form of *C. recta*, cannot be guaranteed to come true. Seed should preferably be sown fresh and pre-chilled in a refrigerator if sown in spring. Plant out in a rich soil in a site that provides a cool root run, although the top should be in the sun. (Seed available from specialist commercial sources and HPS and other seed exchanges.)

Clinopodium (Labiatae). Propagate by division in spring or from seed sown at the same time of year. Plant out in any good garden soil in sun. (Seed not easy to come by but occasionally occurs in seed exchanges.)

Clintonia (Convallariaceae/Liliaceae). This genus can be propagated by the division of their creeping rhizomes or, in some cases, the dense clumps of crowns. Division can be hazardous as *Clintonia* seem to resent disturbance. An alternative method is by sowing seed either fresh or in the spring, ensuring that the compost is always kept moist. Fresh seed might be difficult to find as *Clintonia* do not seem to set seed well in cultivation. Plant out in a moist woodland soil in part shade. (Seed not easy to find but is available from some specialist commercial sources and seed exchanges.)

Clivia (Amarylaceae/Liliaceae). Kaffir Lily. Only hardy in the warmest of regions. The best method of increase is by careful division of the mass of fleshy roots in spring. If offsets are produced these can be split off from the parent plant and potted up. They can also be raised from freshly sown seed, but will take four to five years to reach flowering size. Plant in a rich, well-drained soil in spring and keep well watered until autumn. (Seed available from specialist commercial sources and occasionally from seed exchanges.)

Cobaea (Polemoniaceae). A small genus of climbing plants generally considered as annuals, although they are perennial and can be overwintered in warmer areas. They are grown from seed sown in the early spring. Seed may not ripen in a cold, damp autumn, but seed pods, on their stems, may be stood in water until they are ready. Plant out in a rich but well-drained soil in a sheltered, sunny position. (Seed available from most commercial sources and seed exchanges.)

Cochlearia (Cruciferae). All species of this genus are too small to be considered in this book, the only eligible one, *C. armoricia*, having been moved to **Armoracia** as *A. rusticana*.

Codonopsis (Campanulaceae). The normal way of propagating these plants is to grow them from seed either sown fresh or in spring. They can also be grown from basal cuttings taken in the spring. With a great deal of care it is also possible to divide them in spring, but the tubers resent disturbance so success may be limited. Plant out in a moisture-retentive but free-draining soil in either sun or part shade. (Seed available from some specialist commercial sources and from HPS and other seed exchanges.)

Colchicum (Colchicaceae/Liliaceae). Autumn Crocus. It is generally the large-flowered species that can be grown outside. These can most easily be increased by division of the corms from around the parent plant. This can be done when the leaves show above ground in spring so that you can see where they are. Alternatively, it can be carried out at or immediately after flowering. The latter is preferred by many gardeners. They can also be grown from seed, which should preferably be sown fresh. Plant out in any good garden soil in partial shade or full sun. (Seed available from specialist seed merchants and from seed exchange lists, especially the AGS.)

Commelina (Commelinaceae). This is quite an easy genus to propagate in that those with a running tuberous rootstock can readily be divided in spring or in autumn if they are lifted for winter storage. Some species root at the nodes and these can be transplanted or potted up as with strawberry runners. Basal cuttings can also be taken in spring. They can also be grown from seed sown in the spring. Do not cover seed too deeply. Plant out in any free-draining soil in full sun. (Seed available from some specialist seed merchants and from seed exchanges.)

Convallaria (Convallariaceae/Liliaceae). Lily-of-the-Valley. *C. majus*, and its various forms, is the species most commonly grown in gardens. The normal method of increase is by division of its wandering roots, virtually at any time of year but preferably after flowering or in very early spring before growth begins. Sometimes they can be difficult to establish, but once settled they increase rapidly. One way of increasing the chances of getting it established is to dig up a large clump and plant it in one piece instead of dividing it up into individual rhizomes. If plants are unavailable, grow from seed, preferably sown fresh. They will grow in most soils, including chalk, but planting out in a leafmould or peaty woodland soil gives the best chance of getting established. (Seed very difficult to find but does occasionally occur in seed exchange lists.)

Convolvulus (Convolvulaceae). A genus that is a mixture of terrible weeds and superb garden plants. Most of the latter tend, unfortunately, to be slightly tender and can only be grown in warmer areas. Elsewhere they need propagating each year. Two of the best, *CC. sabatius* and *cneorum*, along with most of the others, can be easily increased by taking cuttings in spring. They tend to continue flowering even as cuttings so all flower buds should be removed as soon as they are seen. The more rampant forms, such as *C. althaeoides*, can be readily increased by division. All species can, of course, be grown from seed, which can benefit from being soaked overnight in warm water. Plant out in any soil, preferably well-drained, in a sunny position. (Seed available from some specialist commercial sources and most seed exchanges.)

Coreopsis (Compositae). Division in spring is the easiest method of propagation and, indeed, is a necessity for the various named forms (except seed merchants' strains). Clumps can get congested and benefit from division every three years or so. An alternative vegetative method is to take basal cuttings. Species can be grown from seed, which should preferably be sown fresh. Plant out in any good garden soil in a sunny position. (Seed available from commercial sources and all seed exchanges.)

Coriaria (Coriaceae). These herbaceous and shrubby plants can be vegetatively increased from cuttings taken in early summer or by divisions of suckering rootstock. The more shrubby types can also be layered. They will also come from seed sown in the spring (the fruit is poisonous). Plant out in any good garden soil in a sheltered, sunny position. (Seed unavailable commercially, but can be found in the HPS and, occasionally, other seed exchanges.)

Cortaderia (Gramineae). Pampas Grass. The usual way to increase this popular grass is by division in spring. The roots of many plants, particularly older ones are very tangled and a great deal of force may be necessary to separate them (use a sharp knife or even a spade). A less strenuous method is to grow the plants from seed, which should be sown in the spring. Plant out in a well-drained soil in full sun. (Seed available from some commercial sources and from seed exchanges.)

Cortusa (Primulaceae). This small genus of primula-like plants is treated in the same way as its relation. Plants can be divided in spring or can be increased by sowing seed, preferably fresh. Plant out in a rich moisture-retentive soil in part shade. (Seed available from some commercial sources and from the seed exchanges, particularly those devoted to alpines.)

Corydalis (Papavaraceae). A large genus of which most species are more suited to the alpine garden. It is the non-bulbous varieties that are mostly grown in the open borders or in walls, such as *CC. lutea, cheilanthifolia, ochroleuca*, or *sempervirens*. These are grown from seed, which must be sown as fresh as possible. If the bulbous varieties are grown, *C. solida* or *C. caucasica* for example, these can be increased either by seed or by dividing the naturally-increasing tubers in the summer after the foliage has died down. Plant in a well-drained soil in a sheltered position in full sun or part shade. (Seed available from some commercial sources and from seed exchanges, particularly those devoted to alpine plants.)

Cosmos (Compositae). This genus is mainly treated as an annual to be sown from seed but some, such as *C. atrosanguineus*, are perennials. These are mainly increased vegetatively, in the same way as one deals with *Dahlia*, by taking basal cuttings as early in the spring as possible or by very careful division of the fleshy tubers, also in the spring, making certain that each piece has an eye. Seed is another possible method of increase but in colder regions *C. atrosanguineus* is very shy in setting seed. Plant out in a moisture-retentive but well-drained soil in full sun. (The annual seed is readily available, but it is more difficult to find seed of the perennial species although it can occur in American seed exchanges.)

Cotula (Compositae). Normally these are considered as alpine plants but some, *C. coronopifolia* in particular, are suitable for planting in the front of borders. This spreading genus can be increased either by sowing seed, preferably fresh, or by division in the spring. They generally prefer a well-drained position, but the example mentioned above likes a moister soil in full sun. (Seed not normally available commercially but can be found in most seed exchanges, particularly the alpine ones.)

Crambe (Cruciferae). Seakale. The usual method for increasing these is by taking root cuttings in early winter. An alternative vegetative method is by careful division of the thick roots in spring. Seed can also be sown in spring. It can be sown in open ground where it is to grow. Plant out in a deep well-drained soil in full sun. (Seed available commercially and from the HPS and other seed exchanges.)

Craspedia (Compositae). A large genus of plants for warmer areas. They can be increased from seed, preferably sown fresh. Alternatively, clumps can be divided or basal cuttings taken in spring. Plant out in a well-drained soil in full sun. (Seed available from some commercial sources and occasionally from seed exchanges.)

Crassula (Crassulaceae). A very large genus of succulent plants suitable for warmer areas. They can be increased vegetatively from either stem or leaf cuttings at any time of the year, although spring generally produces the best results. They can also be grown from seed sown in the spring. Plant out in a well-drained soil in a warm sheltered position. (Seed available from some specialist commercial sources and from seed exchanges, especially those connected to cacti and succulent societies.)

Crepis (Compositae). Hawksbeards. A large genus of which CC. *aurea* and *incana* are the two normally grown. Plants can be increased by either sowing seed fresh or in spring. *C. incana* can be shy of setting seed so be certain to sow seed and not just the empty pappus. Some plants can be increased vegetatively by careful division in spring or by taking root cuttings in early winter. Stem cuttings from new growth can also be taken in spring. Plant in a rich but free-draining soil in full sun. (Seed available from some commercial sources as well as HPS and other seed exchanges.)

Crinum (Amaryllidaceae). This genus develops enormous bulbs from which young offsets are produced. These can be divided off from the parent in spring. Do not allow bulbs to dry out before replanting (also avoid buying bulbs that have dried out too much). The plants resent disturbance and require a long time to settle down again, so should be disturbed as little as possible. A good alternative therefore is to grow from seed, although it takes a number of years for the bulb to reach flowering size. Seed should be sown as soon as it ripens. The plant is viviparous, meaning that seed will often germinate while still on the plant. This can be carefully potted up. Plant out in a well-drained but a rich, moisture-retentive soil in a sunny position. (Seed available from some specialist commercial sources and seed exchanges.)

Crithmum (Umbelliferae). Samphire. This can be sown from seed, preferably as soon as it is ripe. Alternatively, it can be divided. Plant out in a well-drained position in full sun. (Seed not generally available commercially, although it can be found in some catalogues specializing in unusual vegetables. Occasionally available from seed exchanges. Plants commercially available.)

Crocosmia (Iridaceae). Montbretia. This accommodating genus does the propagating for you by producing many offsets that form large clumps. New corms form on the end of stolons, often some distance from the parent plant. These can be easily divided. They can also be easily grown from seed and will self-sow. Sown seed cannot be used to reproduce named forms. Plant out in full sun in any good garden soil that is well-drained. (Seed available commercially and from all seed exchanges.)

Crocus (Iridaceae). A genus with a large number of species and cultivated forms. The former can be readily grown from seed sown either fresh or in the autumn. Both can be easily propagated vegetatively by simply dividing the new corms that grow next to their partners. Plant out in any good garden soil in full sun. (Seed available commercially and from all seed exchanges, especially the alpine ones.)

Crucianella (Rubiaceae). (See also **Phuopsis**.) Some herbaceous plants remain in this genus. These can be increased either by division or from seed, both in spring. Plant out in any good garden soil in sun or partial shade. (Seed not easily available from any sources.)

Cunila (Labiatae). Dittany. These herbs can be easily grown from seed sown in spring or by division at the same time of year. Plant out in any good moisture-retentive garden soil in full sun. (Seed generally available from all sources.)

Curtonus (Iridaceae). Similar to *Crocosmia* and can be propagated in the same way, namely by the division of the corms in spring and by sowing seed either fresh or in the spring. Plant out in a well-drained soil in full sun. (Seed not very widely available, but plants can be commercially obtained.)

Cyclamen (Primulaceae). These can be propagated from seed, which must be sown as freshly as possible. Seed that has dried out should be soaked for a few hours in tepid water to which one drop of washing-up liquid has been added. Germination from dried seed is likely to be erratic. Tubers that have two or more distinct areas of roots and leaf production can be increased vegetatively. Slice through the corms between these areas, treat the cut surfaces with fungicide and pot up. This method can be used for *CC. hederifolum, purpurascens* and *rohlfsianum*. Those that sometimes produce extensions to their tubers, such as *C. coum*, can have them cut off and again treated with a fungicide and potted up. These are extreme measures and for all practical purposes seed is the best way. Plant out in any well-drained garden soil in part shade or sun. (Seed available commercially and from all seed exchanges, particularly the Cyclamen Society's and those for alpine plants.)

Cymbalaria (Scrophulariaceae). Ivy-leaved Toadflax. The best way of increasing these tiny plants is from seed sown in the spring. Seed can be sown direct into its favourite sites – old walls or rocky banks – by placing a few seeds on the palm of the hand and blowing them into a crack with the aid of a drinking straw. If they can be detached from their position, they can also be divided. Plant in ordinary garden soil. (Seed available from some commercial sources and seed exchanges.)

Cynara (Compositae). Cardoon, Globe Artichoke. The main method of propagation is by division of the offsets in early spring. Root cuttings, taken in the early winter, provide another vegetative means of increase. They can also be raised from seed sown fresh or in spring, although this method cannot be recommended if the globe artichokes are intended for eating. Viable seed is not frequently set, but viability is retained for several years for that that does. It can be sown directly where it is to grow. Plant out in a rich but well-drained position in full sun. (Seed available from a few specialist commercial sources and from seed exchanges.)

Cynoglossum (Boraginaceae). Hound's Tongue. Propagate from seed sown fresh or in spring. This can be sown where the plants are to flower. The main vegetative means of increase is by root cuttings taken in the early winter. It is also possible to increase it by careful division in spring. Plant out in any garden soil in a sunny position. (Seed available from specialist seed merchants and from HPS and other exchanges.)

Cypella (Iridaceae). These bulbous plants for warmer areas can be easily increased from freshly-sown seed, which is produced in large amounts. They will seed themselves around saving the gardener the trouble. They can also be increased by dividing the offsets produced around the parent bulb. Plant out in a well-drained soil in a sunny, sheltered position. (Seed available from seed exchanges. Bulbs commercially available.)

Cyperus (Cyperaceae). The easiest method of increase is by division in spring. Seed can also be sown in spring. Plant out in a moisture-retentive soil in a warm, sunny position. (Seed available from some commercial sources and occasionally from seed exchanges.)

Cypripedium (Orchidaceae). Lady's Slipper Orchids. A very difficult orchid to propagate. The only means is vegetative, namely division. New methods are being experimented with and there is hope that these plants will become more widely available. Plant out in a rich, peaty soil in a cool shady position. (Plants occasionally available from commercial sources.)

Cyrtomium. See **Phanerophlebia**

Cystopteris (Aspleniaceae). Bladder Ferns. As with other ferns this can be propagated from spore collected in autumn. They can also be divided in spring. Plant out in a well-drained, shady position such as dry-stone walls. (Spore possibly available from pteridological society spore exchanges. Plants commercially available.)

Daboecia (Ericaceae). Heath. These shrubby plants can be increased from cuttings taken in summer or autumn. Take cuttings of non-flowering shoots with a heel of old wood. They can also be layered by covering the plants with compost with only the tops of the stems showing. Keep the compost moist. Remove and pot up the stems when they have produced roots. Plants can be divided. Seed should be sown in spring on a soil-less potting compost that contains no lime. Plant out in a well-drained, lime-free soil in full sun. (Seed can be found from some specialist seed merchants and from seed exchanges.)

Dactylis (Gramineae). A monotypic genus of a grass easily propagated by division in spring or from seed sown at the same time of year. Plant out in any good garden soil in sun or part shade. (Seed not easily obtainable. Plants commercially available.)

Dactylorhiza (Orchidaceae). This is one of the easier orchids to propagate. Although quite difficult to increase from seed, it is relatively easy to divide the tubers in late summer or autumn. Self-sown seedlings appear from time to time, sometimes at some distance from the parent plant. Shaking seed, which must be fresh, around the parent plants encourages self-sowing as the necessary mycorrhizal fungus is present in this area. Plant out in a humus-rich soil in either sun or part shade. (Seed available from seed exchanges, but its viability is doubtful. Plants commercially available.)

Dahlia (Compositae). Several methods can be used to propagate these tuberous plants. The tubers themselves can be divided in spring. Take basal cuttings as early as possible in spring, forcing the tubers into premature growth in warmth if necessary. Seed can also be sown, preferably fresh or in the spring. Apart from commercial strains, named forms will not come true from seed. Plant out in a well-drained, fertile soil in full sun. (Seed available from seed merchants and seed exchanges.)

Damasonium (Alismataceae). Starfruit. A marginal water plant mainly grown from seed, either sown fresh or in spring. Sow seed in a soil-less compost, keeping it moist by standing it in a tray of water. Pot on seedlings, again keeping them moist by a similar method. Large clumps can also be divided. Plant in the mud or shallow water round a pond. Make certain that any planted-out material is well anchored if it is in water. (Seed not easy to find but plants are commercially available.)

Darlingtonia (Sarraceniaceae). Carniverous plants for warmer areas that can be increased by division in the spring. They can also be grown from seed sown on sphagnum moss, which is kept moist. Plant out in a moist peat and sphagnum moss bed in sun. (Seed available from some specialist commercial suppliers and from specialist society seed exchanges.)

Darmera (Saxifragaceae). Umbrella Plant. Formerly known as *Peltiphyllum*, this monotypic genus can easily be increased by the division of the creeping rhizome during the spring, planting it directly back into the ground. Can be sown from seed either sown fresh or in spring. Keep seed moist. Plant out in a boggy or, at least, a moisture-retentive soil, in either part shade or sun. (Seed available from specialist commercial sources as well as HPS and other seed exchange lists.)

Datisca (Datiscaceae). A genus of two species for warmer areas that can be propagated from seed sown in spring. The plants are dioecious and so both male and female are needed to produce seed. The mature plants can also be divided in spring. Plant out in good garden soil in a sunny position. (Both seed and plants difficult to find.)

Datura (Solanaceae). Thorn Apple. A small genus of annuals and shrubby perennials that are increasingly finding their way into borders, particularly in warmer areas. They can easily be sown from seed, placing each seed into individual pots in spring under glass and with gentle heat. Some of the annuals will self-sow. The fruits are poisonous. Cuttings of the perennial forms can be taken in spring, overwintering the young plants under glass. Plant out in a well-drained soil in full sun. (Seed available both commercially and from the seed exchanges.)

Davallia (Davalliaceae). Haresfoot Fern. These are generally creeping, rhizomatous ferns that can easily be divided in spring. All, including those without rhizomes, can be increased from spore sown in spring. Plant out in a woodland-type soil in part shade. (Spores possibly available from pteridological societies.)

Decodon (Lythraceae). Water Willow. A marginal water plant best grown from stem cuttings taken in the summer. Stems root very easily and can often be detached with roots already formed where they are touching the mud. Needless to say, the plant can also be divided. Keep cuttings and divisions moist by standing them in a tray of water. Sow fresh or in spring in a soil-less compost, keeping it moist as for cuttings. Plant in the mud or shallow water round a pond. Make certain that any planted out material is well anchored if it is in water. (Seed not easy to find but plants commercially available.)

Deinanthe (Hydrangeaceae). A small genus easily propagated by dividing the spreading rhizomes. They can also be increased by growing from seed. Plant out in a rich, moisture-retentive soil in partial shade. (Seed not available commercially but can be found in the seed exchange lists. Plants commercially available.)

Delphinium (Ranuculaceae). Sow seed fresh in late summer or autumn or, if stored properly in air-tight containers in the salad compartment of a refrigerator, in spring. Germination rates can be erratic with dark blue cultivars taking longer to germinate than their lighter counterparts. Germination can be speeded up by using a temperature of between 15–20°C (60–68°F) but too high a temperature will cause dormancy. They can also be sown in open ground in May or June, but slugs and snails can be a problem unless controlled. Delphinium seed is poisonous. Basal cuttings can be taken as they appear in spring. Many of the older cultivars are now getting weak and do not produce very strong plants. If the cut section of the cutting shows a black ring then the plant is becoming too weak to reproduce satisfactorily by this method. It may be possible to continue propagation by dividing the plant for a few more years but it is weakening all the time. It is possible to shear off all stems in summer to produce new growth for taking cuttings, but the shoots are very difficult to strike and the take-up rate is well below that of spring cuttings. Eye cuttings can be taken during the summer. These are the dormant buds waiting to provide the following year's flowering stems. Cut off the eye as close to the crown as possible and place it in a pot or tray with the top of the shoot just appearing above the compost (use a cutting compost). Divide in spring by cutting the crown with a sharp knife into segments with strong shoots, or dormant buds, and healthy roots. Rotting can occur on the cut portions of the crown and losses can be high. Seed and basal cuttings are the easiest methods of increase. Plant out in a humus-rich soil in full sun. (Seed available from most commercial sources and all seed exchanges, especially that of the Delphinium Society. Alpine exchanges are good for seed of species.)

Dendranthema (Compositae). See **Chrysanthemum**

Dennstaedtia (Dennstaedtiaceae). Invasive ferns easily increased by division in spring. As with all ferns, they can also be propagated from spore sown in the autumn. Plant out in a cool, humus-rich soil in part shade. (Spore may possibly be available from pteridological society exchanges.)

Dentaria (Cruciferae). Most of what were known as *Dentaria*, such as *DD. digitata* and *polyphylla*, have been moved out into the genus *Cardamine*. Of those that remain, *D. californica* is one that crops up from time to time. This woodlander can easily be propagated by division in spring or seed sown at the same time of year. The seedlings are curious in that the seed leaves appear on two different stems, each thrown up from the developing rhizome below ground. The unwary can think that these two (or sometimes more) leaves come from different seedlings and try to separate them when pricking out, thus destroying the young plant. Plant out in woodland soil in part shade. (Seed not easy to find but crops up occasionally in seed exchange lists. Plants also difficult to find.)

Deschampsia (Gramineae). Hair-grasses. These can be easily propagated in spring by either dividing up the clumps or by sowing seed. Plant out in any good garden soil (*D. caespitosa* prefers it moist) in part shade or sun. (Seed not generally available but plants can be bought without too much difficulty.)

Dianella (Phormiaceae/Liliaceae). Flax Lilies. Plants for warmer areas easily propagated by division in spring or seed sown at the same time of year. The black seed should be separated from the blue fruit before sowing. Plant out in a well-drained, lime-free position in full sun. (Seed not available commercially but does occur occasionally in HPS and other seed exchanges.)

Dianthus (Caryophyllaceae). Carnations, Pinks. This large genus comes very readily from seed sown either fresh or in the following spring. Sow thinly. Apart from commercially-named strains, named varieties and colour forms will not come true from seed. Many dianthus will self-sow, especially *D. deltoides* and other species. Be certain to rogue out any that do not come true or are not worth keeping otherwise the quality of the stock will deteriorate. Vegetative propagation is also very straightforward. All can be increased from nodal cuttings taken during the summer from non-flowering shoots. Some, especially the mule pinks such as the legendary *D.* 'Napoleon III', are so floriferous that they are liable to flower themselves to death. All shoots tend to be flower shoots so it is necessary to designate one plant for cuttings and keep the flower shoots cut back so that the new growth can be used for cuttings. Pipings are a traditional way of increasing pinks. This is just a form of cutting where the top of a shoot is held firmly between finger and thumb and pulled so that a part of the stem is pulled out of the 'socket' at one of the nodes. This is then treated as a cutting. Many can be layered by bending and pinning down a long shoot either into the ground or into a buried pot of compost. The stem should be partially split through at the point below ground. Keep the soil or compost at the layer moist. *Dianthus* are not generally long-lived plants so should be reproduced regularly. Plant out in a well-drained position in full sun in the autumn. (Seed available from commercial sources and all seed exchanges; seed of species best obtained from the alpine plant exchanges.)

Diascia (Scrophulariaceae). A surprisingly large genus of about 150 species of tender and near tender plants that have become increasingly popular border plants. They are very easily increased from cuttings taken at any time of the year, although September or October is the optimum time. This is also a good time to take cuttings for overwintering in a greenhouse or frame to ward against losses during the winter. Diascias have hollow stems, so the cuttings should be nodal. Some species, such as *D. anastrepta*, root where their stems touch the ground and can be increased by detaching and planting rooted portions. They can be grown from seed but vegetative propagation is so easy that it hardly seems worthwhile. They are reluctant to set seed due to self-incompatability, but this can be overcome by the presence of more than one clone in the bed. Instinct says that these plants should be grown in well-drained soil, but they grow in damp areas in the wild and consequently should have a moisture-retentive soil in cultivation in a sunny position. (Seed not easy to find but a few species are available from HPS and alpine seed exchanges.)

Dicentra (Papaveraceae). Bleeding Hearts. All species come readily from seed, especially if sown fresh in the autumn. Seed sown in spring should be pre-chilled in a refrigerator for best results. The rhizomatous species *DD. eximia* and *formosa* can be easily divided in spring. *D. spectabilis* can be increased by digging up in winter and carefully dividing by cutting up the crown with a sharp knife, each section having a bud and roots. The divisions can be replanted or potted up to grow on. It can also be propagated by basal cuttings taken in spring. Root cuttings can be made in winter, bedding them out in a sandy soil or in a tray of cutting compost. *D.s.* 'Alba' can be propagated as above or from seed as it comes true; the white seedlings having yellowish-green leaves and stems. *D. macrantha* is increased by seed or by careful division as with *D. spectabilis*. All should be planted out in a leafy soil in light shade. (Seed available from seed exchanges and commercial sources.)

Dichelostemma (Alliaceae/Liliaceae). Bulbs can be divided after the foliage has died down. They can also be grown from seed sown either fresh or in spring. Plant out in a well-drained soil in a warm, sunny spot. (Seed not easy to find but occasionally occurs in seed exchange lists.)

Dicksonia (Dicksoniaceae). Tree Fern. These are plants for milder regions and can only be reproduced from spore sown in the autumn. Plant out in a cool, humus-rich soil in part shade. (Spore may be available from pteridological societies.)

Dictamnus (Rutaceae). Burning Bush, Dittany. Sowing seed is the normal method of increase. It should be sown as fresh as possible. If sown in spring, germination is likely to be at least a year, although this can be improved by pre-chilling. Plants grown from seed will not flower for at least three years. Seed capsules explode violently so should be enclosed in a bag if the seed is to be collected. The plants can also be carefully divided in spring, but are slow to settle down as *Dictamnus* resents disturbance. Plant out in any good garden soil in full sun. (Seed available from the specialist commercial sources and from all seed exchanges.)

Dierama (Iridaceae). Angel's Fishing Rod, Wand Flower. These grass-like plants can be increased from seed sown in spring. They resent disturbance and it is best, if space is available, to sow the seed singly in individual pots. They can also be propagated by very careful division in the spring. Take care as the roots are very brittle. Do not plant out until at least the spring after germination. Plant out in a well-drained soil (even those planted near water, where they look at their best, need this) in full sun. (Seed available from commercial sources and all seed exchanges.)

Dietes (Iridaceae). Iris-like plants for warmer regions that spread forming large clumps easily divided in spring. Clumps will need splitting from time to time to prevent congestion. They can also be grown from a spring sowing of seed. Plant out in a well-drained soil in full sun. (Seed and plants are not easy to come by but may be found in specialist societies.)

Digitalis (Scrophulariaceae). Foxgloves. The easiest method of propagation is from seed, which can be sown in autumn or spring. Most will come from seed scattered on the open soil and many will self-sow, often abundantly. If only the white form of *D. purpurea* is required, all purple ones should be regularly rogued out and after a few years the population will be predominantly white. The white seedlings can be recognized by their green leaf-stems as opposed to the purple-streaked ones of the usual purple-flowered form. Light is beneficial to germination. The beautiful crosses between *DD. purpurea* and *lutea* are sterile and need to be propagated vegetatively. This can be done by division in spring or by stem cuttings taken from the flowering stem in early summer. Sections of the stem, each containing a leaf, are placed in a pot or tray of compost with the leaf just touching the surface. The young plants develop from the nodes. The other *D. purpurea* cross, *D. × mertonensis*, comes true from seed. The clump-forming perennial species can be divided in spring. Plant out in a well-drained soil in part shade or full sun. (Seed available from commercial sources and seed exchanges.)

Dimorphotheca (Compositae). See *Osteospermum*

Diphylleia (Podophyllaceae/Berberidaceae). Umbrella Leaf. A small genus of two or three species. They are rhizomatous plants that can be reproduced by the division of the rhizomes in spring or from seed (berries) sown fresh or in spring. The latter method is slow to produce mature plants. Needs a moist shady position when planted out. (Seed available from alpine seed exchanges.)

Diplarrhena (Iridaceae). Butterfly Flag. This small genus for warmer regions can be increased by division of the creeping rhizomes of the evergreen tussocks in spring. They can also be grown from seed sown either fresh or in the spring. Plant out in a well-drained, sunny position. (Seed available from specialist commercial sources and seed exchange lists.)

Dipsacus (Dipsacaceae). Teasels. Monocarpic plants easily increased from seed sown in the spring directly into the ground. They tend to self-sow generously so there are normally plenty of seedlings available. If they need to be moved do so while they are young. Plant in a well-drained soil in sun or light shade. (Seed available from seed merchants, particularly those specializing in wild flowers, and seed exchanges.)

Disporum (Convallariaceae/Liliaceae). Fairybells. This increasingly popular genus can most easily be propagated by the division of creeping rootstock in spring, making certain that each piece has a 'nose'. They can also be sown from seed, preferably fresh, or in spring after pre-chilling. Some, in particular *D. smithii*, self-sow producing enough seedlings for most uses. Plant out in a cool, peaty woodland soil in part shade. (Seed available from specialist commercial sources and seed exchanges.)

Dodecatheon (Primulaceae). Shooting Stars. Propagation can be either division in spring (they divide like their near-relatives the primulas) or from seed sown fresh. Another easy method is by taking root cuttings in early winter. They are mainly woodlanders and need planting out in a moisture retentive soil in part shade or sun if the soil is not too dry. (Seed available from specialist commercial sources and seed exchanges. Seed from both sources do not always come true to type.)

Doronicum (Compositae). Leopard's Bane. These accommodating plants are very easily split up by dividing them after flowering or in autumn. They can also be grown from seed either sown fresh or in spring. Plant out in any good garden soil, preferably moisture retentive, in sun or part shade. (Seed obtainable from commercial sources or seed exchange lists.)

Doryncium (Leguminosae). A genus of perennials and shrubs. Like many of this family, the seed benefits from being scarified or chipped before soaking in warm water overnight. Sow in spring. They can also be increased from cuttings taken in summer. Plant out in a well-drained, warm position in full sun. (Seed available from specialist commercial sources and seed exchanges.)

Dracocephalum (Labiatae). These can be easily increased by splitting the clumps formed by this creeping plant in spring. They can also be propagated by taking basal cuttings from the new growth in spring. Seed can be sown, also in spring. Plant out in any good, well-drained garden soil in full sun. (Seed available from specialist commercial sources and seed exchanges.)

Dracunculus (Araceae). Dragon Plant. The rhizomatous roots of this genus can easily be divided when the plant is dormant. Cut the rhizome into sections, ensuring that each contains a dormant bud. They need regular dividing every few years. It can also be grown from seed (extracted from the red berries) sown fresh or in spring. Plant out in a humus-rich, woodland soil in sun or part shade. (Seed available from specialist commercial sources and some seed exchanges.)

Dryas (Rosaceae). A genus of shrubby ground-coverers that can be increased by taking semi-ripe cuttings (with a heel) in late summer. They can also be propagated by dividing off some of the rooted stems in spring. Seed can be sown, preferably fresh, but also in spring. Plant out in a well-drained soil in a sunny position. (Seed available from specialist commercial sources and all seed exchanges.)

Dryopteris (Aspleniaceae). Ferns that can be propagated in the usual way of either sowing spore in autumn or by dividing the slow-spreading clumps in spring. Plant out in a humus-rich, moisture-retentive soil in part shade or sun. (Spore available from pteridological societies. Plants are commercially available.)

Ecballium (Curcurbitaceae). Squirting Cucumber. A monotypic genus represented by *E. elaterinum*. Although often treated as a half-hardy annual, this plant is in fact perennial in warm areas. Sow in spring under glass in gentle heat as one would culinary cucumbers. It self-sows and will provide sufficient seedlings once established. Plant out in a free-draining soil in a sunny position. (Seed available from commercial sources and occasionally from seed exchanges.)

Eccremocarpus (Bignoniaceae). A small genus of climbing plants of which *E. scaber* is the most commonly grown. Although often treated as an annual, this is a perennial plant and can be grown as such in warmer areas. It can be grown very easily from seed, which is produced in copious amounts, sown in spring. Do not cover the seed as it germinates better in light and do not use temperatures above 18°C (65°F) as this is likely to bring about dormancy. It is likely to self-sow. Plant out in a well-drained soil in a warm position where it can climb. (Seed available from commercial sources and seed exchanges.)

Echeveria (Crassulaceae). Hens-and-Chickens. A large genus of succulent plants for warmer areas that can be increased from seed sown in the spring or from leaf cuttings. One of the easiest methods is to divide off the offsets that are produced, often in large numbers. Plant out in a very well-drained soil in a warm position in full sun. (Seed available from specialist seed merchants and occasionally seed exchanges, especially those connected with cacti and succulent societies.)

Echinacea (Compositae). There is no problem in increasing this genus. Take basal cuttings from the young shoots or divide the spreading clumps in spring. They can also be grown from seed sown fresh or in spring. Seed cannot be used with named forms (except for commercial strains) if you wish to keep them true. Plant out in a rich, free-draining but moisture-retentive soil in full sun. (Seed available from commercial sources and various seed exchanges.)

Echinops (Compositae). Globe Thistle. The usual method of increase is a vegetative one. They can either be divided in spring, or cuttings taken from their thick roots in early winter. They will also grow from seed, which can either be sown fresh or in spring. If seed heads are left on many will self-sow. Plant out in any well-drained soil in full sun. (Seed available from commercial sources and all seed exchange lists.)

Echiodes (Boraginaceae). See *Arnebia*

Echium (Boraginaceae). Bugloss. Most of these tend to be either biennial or monocarpic and these can all be increased by seed sown either fresh or in spring. The perennial species, which are not likely to be hardy in colder districts, can be increased in a like manner. The shrubbier perennials can also be increased from cuttings taken in spring. Even layering can be tried on some of these last species. Plant out in a well-drained soil in full sun. (Seed available from specialist commercial sources and seed exchange lists.)

Eichhornia (Pontederiaceae). Water Hawthorn. An attractive, somewhat tender, floating water plant that can be grown in warmer areas or overwintered elsewhere. Propagation can be achieved by cutting off the young plants produced on runners and potting these up in mud or compost that is kept permanently moist by being placed in a bowl of water (plants can be overwintered in this manner). Alternatively, return directly to the water. Propagation is normally confined to producing plants to overwinter or for use in other water features, as they spread quite happily by themselves and, indeed, have to be restrained. Plant out in water in spring. (Plants commercially available.)

Eleocharis (Cyperaceae). Hair Grass. A submerged pond weed whose carpets can easily be divided. Anchor the divisions to the bottom of the pond. (Plants commercially available.)

Elodea (Hydrocharitaceae). Canadian Pondweed. Once considered an aquatic pest, the less-vigorous are now valued as submerged oxygenators. It can easily be divided, but divisions are best anchored to the bottom of the pool. (Plants commercially available.)

Elsholtzia (Labiatae). These are normally increased by vegetative means. They can be divided in spring or cuttings taken in summer. They can also be increased from seed sown in spring. Plant out in any good garden soil in full sun. (Seed available from specialist commercial sources and seed exchange lists.)

Elymus (Gramineae). A very invasive grass whose spreading rhizomes can be easily divided in spring. Should you want another method of increase, it can be grown from seed sown fresh or in spring. Plant out in any well-drained soil in full sun. (Like all grasses seed, it is not easy to obtain but does occur in the HPS seed exchange list.)

Eminium (Araceae). These can be propagated by division of the tubers, which produce offsets, in autumn. They can also be increased by sowing seed either fresh or in spring. Plant out in a well-drained, light soil in full sun. (Seed not easy to find but plants are commercially available.)

Endymion (Hyacinthaceae/Liliaceae). See **Hyacinthoides**

Eomecon (Papaveraceae). Dawn Poppy, Snow Poppy. These colonizing plants can easily be divided in spring. They can also be propagated by taking root-cuttings in early winter or by sowing seed either fresh or in spring. Plant out in a moist, woodland-type soil in part shade. (Seed not generally commercially available, but does occasionally occur in exchange lists. Plants commercially available.)

Epilobium (Onagraceae). Willow Herbs. As gardeners know to their cost, willow herbs come very easily from seed. However, they do need a certain amount of light to germinate, so the seeds should not be covered too deeply; some diffused light should be allowed to penetrate down to them. Not only are they invasive by seed but also by running and consequently can be increased by dividing in spring. Take cuttings of *E. glabellum* in early autumn. Plant out in any well-drained soil in full sun. (Seed offered by specialist seed merchants and most seed exchanges.)

Epimedium (Berberidaceae). These spreading plants can easily be divided in either autumn or spring. They can also be grown from seed, preferably be sown fresh. Delay in sowing will lead to delay in germination. Plant out in a humus-rich, woodland-type soil in part shade or sun. (Seed available from specialist commercial sources and seed exchange lists.)

Epipactis (Orchidaceae). As with most orchids, growing from seed is not a practical proposition. Increase is achieved by dividing the slowly increasing rootstock, ensuring that each piece has a 'nose' on it. Plant out in a peaty, woodland type soil in part shade. (Plants commercially available.)

Equisetum (Equisetaceae). Horsetails. Not plants that one would normally allow anywhere near a garden, but there are a few well-enough behaved to be introduced if you are brave enough. The creeping rhizomatous roots can easily be divided in autumn or spring. Their reproductive methods are similar to ferns and thus they can be increased from spore sown when it is ripe. Plant out in any soil in sun or light shade. (Spore not generally available, but plants are commercially available.)

Eragrostis (Graminae). Love Grass. These grasses can be increased either by division in spring as is usual with grasses or by sowing seed in autumn or spring. Plant out in a well-drained soil in full sun. (Seed and plants difficult to find.)

Eranthis (Ranunculaceae). Winter Aconites. The easiest way to propagate these plants is to divide the tuberous rhizomes, but do not allow them to dry out in the process. (Never buy packets of dried rhizomes from garden centres.) They can also be sown from seed but it should be sown fresh. Aconites provide plenty of self-sown seedlings that are usually growing close to the parent plant. These can easily be pricked out and grown on. Plant in a humus-rich soil in part shade. (Seed available from specialist seed merchants and from all society seed exchanges.)

Eremostachys (Labiatae). These can be propagated by sowing seed in spring or taking cuttings in summer. Plant out in a well-drained soil in full sun. (Both seed and plants are difficult to find but the former do occasionally crop up on seed exchange lists.)

Eremurus (Asphodelaceae/Liliaceae). Foxtail Lilies. The easiest method of propagation is, after the foliage has died down, to lift the crowns in late summer or autumn and divide them. Lift very carefully to avoid damage to the roots. Separate crowns under water or leave for a couple of days for them to shrink a little, which helps with the separation. The clumps must be periodically divided to maintain vitality. They can also be grown from seed sown in the spring but it can take up to six years for plants to reach flowering size. Darkness is required for germination. Plant out in a well-drained soil in full sun. (Seed available from specialist commercial sources and seed exchanges.)

Erianthus (Graminae). This genus of grasses can be divided in spring or grown from seed sown either in autumn or spring. Plant out in well-drained soils in full sun. (Both seed and plants are not very easy to find.)

Erica (Ericaceae). Heather. These shrubby plants are usually increased by taking semi-ripe cuttings during the summer or autumn. Take non-flowering shoots that have a heel of old wood on them. Another method of propagation is a form of layering. The plant is covered with peaty potting compost, which is worked well down between the branches with just the tips of the stems showing. This should be kept moist. In time roots grow on the buried portions of the shoots, which can then be removed from the parent plant and individually potted up. An ericaceous, lime-free compost should be used for sowing seed. It is unlikely that seed will come true, but new forms might be grown. Plant out in a well-drained, lime-free soil in sun. (Seed available from specialist commercial sources and seed exchange lists.)

Erigeron (Compositae). Fleabanes. Like most of the daisies, these can be increased by dividing or taking basal cuttings in spring. If necessary, they can also be grown from seed, preferably sown fresh but also in the spring. Some, such as *E. karvinskianus*, will self-sow providing a lot of seedlings best transplanted (if required) before they get too large. *E. philadelphicus* can be layered. Plant out in a good, well-drained garden soil in full sun. (Seed available from specialist commercial sources and seed exchange lists.)

Erinus (Scrophulariaceae). Fairy Foxgloves. There is generally no problem in germinating seed sown in spring, indeed it self-sows itself, which is a useful source of plants. Seed can be sown directly where it is to flower. If sowing in crevices in a wall (a favourite habitat) put a few seeds on the palm of your hand and blow them into the crevice using a drinking straw. The plants are said to divide in spring but they are so easy from seed it hardly seems worth the bother unless if you want to keep some particularly good form going. Plant out in a well-drained soil in sun. (Seed available from commercial sources as well as seed exchanges.)

Eriogonum (Polygonaceae). Wild Buckwheat. Most of this large genus are propagated by seed sown in spring. A few, such as *E. umbellatum*, can be increased by cuttings taken in spring. Others can be carefully divided but on the whole they do not like to be disturbed. Plant out in a very well-drained soil in a warm position in full sun. (Seed available from specialist seed merchants and seed exchanges.)

Eriophyllum (Compositae). A spreading daisy easily increased by dividing in spring. It can also be increased by seed sown fresh or in spring, sowing directly into the open ground if desired. Plant out in a good, well-drained garden soil in full sun. (Seed available from specialist seed merchants and seed exchanges.)

Erodium (Geraniaceae). Storksbills. Most come readily from seed, but the setting of seed is unreliable in many species. There is also a high risk of hybridization. Of the larger ones *EE. absinthiodes, alpinum, chrysanthum* and *guicciardii* are dioecious and need both male and female plants to set seed. Many of the round-leaved species are poor producers of seed, with the noted exceptions of *EE. pelargoniflorum* (*pelargonifolium*) and *trifolium*, which will often self-sow. Much apparent seed is non-viable. They can also be propagated from basal cuttings including part of the rhizome of those that have them. These are best taken in the summer. Those that are clump-forming can be divided in spring. Plant out in a well-drained soil in full sun. (Seed available from specialist seed merchants and all seed exchanges, especially alpine ones.)

Eryngium (Umbelliferae). Sea Hollies. Probably the easiest means of increase of this genus is by sowing seeds, either fresh or in spring. *E. giganteum* is monocarpic and can only be increased by seed. It self-sows itself quite prodigiously so there should be no shortage of plants. However, they have deep roots and if they need moving, do so early in their life. *Eryngium* can also be increased vegetatively by taking root cuttings in the early winter or careful division. Plant out in a deep well-drained soil in full sun. (Seed available from commercial sources and all seed exchange lists.)

Erysimum (Cruciferae). Wallflowers. These and the closely related *Cheiranthus* can be increased from cuttings of non-flowering shoots taken in summer. Most are short-lived perennials and it is a sensible precaution to take cuttings every year. They may also be grown from seed sown in the spring but named forms are unlikely to come true. Plant out in a good, well-drained garden soil in full sun. (Seed available from commercial sources and seed exchange lists.)

Erythrina (Leguminosae). Coral Tree. A large genus of plants only hardy in warmer districts. They can be increased from seed sown in the spring. They can be vegetatively propagated by taking heeled cuttings in spring. The herbaceous species, which are not hardy, can also be divided. Plant out in a warm spot in a well-drained soil in full sun. (Seed available from specialist commercial sources and occasionally from seed exchanges. Plants are commercially obtainable.)

Erythronium (Liliaceae). Dog-tooth Violets. Bulbous plants that are not too difficult to propagate. Clump forming species and cultivars such as *EE. tuolumnense* and 'White Beauty' can be easily lifted and divided in the early autumn. Other species can raised from seed although this can be a long process, taking from three to five years. Seed should be sown when fresh or as soon as possible in a gritty compost that contains a little extra peat or leafmould. They need a frost to break germination and should be kept in a shady position. Keeping the seedlings in growth for as long as possible by paying constant attention to moisture levels, speeds up the growth rate and helps to ensure early flowering. The quickest way to get the seedlings established is to plant out the potful as a whole, after the first year, into their final flowering position in a semi-shaded area in a humus-rich soil. Alternatively, the individual bulbs can be potted on after their second year. (Seed available from specialist commercial sources and seed exchanges.)

Eschscholzia (Papaveraceae). Californian Poppy. Although normally treated as an annual this is a short-lived perennial and behaves as such in warmer areas. The usual method of propagation is by sowing seed in spring. They resent disturbance so sow directly where they are to flower. They will self-sow but most colour strains of *E. californicum* will revert to the typical orange colour. Plant out in a well-drained soil in a sunny position. (Seed available from most commercial sources and seed exchanges.)

Eucomis (Hyacinthaceae/Liliaceae). Pineapple Flower. These can be increased from seed sown under cover in spring. Plants will take three to four years to reach flowering size. They can also be divided when in their dormant state during autumn or early winter. Plant out in a warm spot in well-drained soil rich in humus. (Seed available from specialist commercial sources and seed exchanges.)

Eupatorium (Compositae). Bone Set, Hemp Agrimony. A very large genus of clump-forming plants easily increased by division in autumn or in spring. It is also possible to grow them from seed sown fresh or in spring. Plant out in a moisture-retentive soil in sun or part shade. (Seed available from commercial sources, and the HPS and other seed exchanges.)

Euphorbia (Euphorbiaceae). Spurge. An enormous genus of around 2,000 species of which the hardy perennials form a part. They can nearly all be grown easily from seed, preferably sown soon after it has been harvested. The seed capsules ripen and suddenly explode scattering seed, so keep an eye on it if you need to collect it. Some of the harder-cased seed may need soaking overnight in warm water to aid germination. If sown in spring a period of pre-chilling may also help. Many will self-sow around the garden, some such as *E. lathyrus* becoming a nuisance in this respect. Those that have a running rootstock, such as *EE. griffithii* or *sikkimensis*, can easily be divided in spring or autumn. Others that form tighter clumps, such as *EE. polychroma* and *palustris*, can be similarly divided, but the woodier, central portions should be discarded. Many forms, such as *E. palustris*, can be increased by taking soft tip cuttings. Many, particularly the woodier forms, do better if these are from young shoots, which can be promoted by cutting the plant back. Some, such as *E. griffithii*, come well from lateral cuttings, although in this case division is a better alternative. When cut, euphorbias exude a sticky latex. This must be sealed at once, either by dipping it in sand or powdered charcoal, or by holding the cut end over a lighted match. This latex can cause irritation of the skin and should, under all circumstances, be kept away from eyes. Cuttings can be taken in autumn. Many species, such as *EE. characias wulfenii* or *nicaeensis* seem to resent too close an atmosphere and more air should be allowed to circulate around the cuttings. Most prefer a well-drained soil in full sun, but others such as *E. robbiae*, will tolerate quite deep shade, while others, *E. sikkimensis* for example, prefer a dampish soil and do well in light shade. (Seed available from all the seed exchanges and specialized commercial sources).

Euryops (Compositae). Shrubby perennials that can be increased by taking cuttings in summer or by layering. Seed should be sown fresh or in spring. Plant out in a well-drained soil in a sunny position. (Seed available from specialist seed merchants and occasionally from seed exchange lists.)

Eustoma (Gentianaceae). Propagate from seed in a free-draining compost. Do not overwater. Sow seed fresh in late summer. Germinate between 20–27°C (68–92°F) with best temperature about 24°C (82°F). Prick out and grow on in long-toms and avoid wildly fluctuating temperatures. Again avoid overwatering. An easier method of propagation is by taking root cuttings in early winter. Protect all plants in their first winter. Plant out in a warm, sheltered spot in full sun in a well-drained soil. (Seed available from specialist commercial sources and seed exchanges, particularly American ones.)

Evolvulus (Convolvulaceae). Subshrubs for warmer areas that can be increased either from cuttings taken in summer or from seed sown in spring. Plant out in a well-drained soil in full sun. (Seed not easy to find, but plants commercially available.)

Fallopia (Polygonaceae). A genus of vigorous refugees from *Polygonum* and *Reynoutria*. The spreaders such as *FF. japonica* or *sachalinensis* can easily be divided, either in spring or autumn. The climbers, such as *FF. aubertii* or *baldschuanicum*, can be increased from semi-ripe cuttings taken in summer. They can all be grown from seed, except the cultivars of *FF. japonicum* and *baldschuanicum*, which seem shy of setting much seed in cultivation. Plant out in any garden soil in sun or light shade. (Seed not available commercially but occasionally crops up in exchanges, often still under the name *Polygonum*. Plants widely available.)

Felicia (Compositae). Propagate from cuttings taken in August or September. Shear over part of the plant two or three weeks before required to remove flowering heads, and feed to encourage new growth for cutting material. In warmer areas where the genus is truly perennial, older plants can be carefully divided in the same way as chrysanthemum stools. Can also be grown from seed sown fresh or in spring. Plant out in a well-drained soil in a warm, sunny position. (Seed available from commercial sources and seed exchanges.)

Ferraria (Iridaceae). This genus of bulbous plants can be increased by the division of the offsets when they are dormant. They can also be grown from seed sown in the spring. Plant out in a well-drained soil in a warm, sunny position. (Seed not commercially available, but does occur in the seed exchanges.)

Ferula (Umbelliferae). Fennel. The main method of propagation is by seed, which should preferably be sown fresh but can also be sown in spring. Seedlings should be pricked out into long-toms or planted out before the long roots are too developed. They can also be sown directly where they are to flower. Division has also been advocated as a method but *Ferula* resent being disturbed because of their deep root system. Plant out in a deep, well-drained soil in full sun. (Seed available from commercial sources and seed exchanges.)

Festuca (Graminae). Fescue. As with most grasses, the best method of increase is by division or seed sown in spring. Plant out in a well-drained, light soil in sun. (Seed available from specialist commercial sources as well as HPS and other seed exchanges.)

Filipendula (Rosaceae). Meadowsweets. The main method of propagation is by division in spring or autumn. They can also be grown from seed fresh or in spring. Plant out in a moist soil in part shade or full sun if the soil can be kept moist. *F. vulgaris* needs a well-drained soil and full sun. (Seed available from specialist commercial sources and HPS and other seed exchanges.)

Foeniculum (Umbelliferae). Fennel. The problem with this plant is not how to propagate it, but how to stop it propagating itself. It produces large quantities of seed that self-sows everywhere. Seed should preferably be sown fresh but can be sown in spring. Seedlings should be pricked out into long-toms or planted out before the tap roots are too developed. They can also be sown directly where they are to flower. Division in spring has also been advocated as a method but plants resent being disturbed because of their deep root system. Plant out in a deep, well-drained soil in full sun. (Seed available from commercial sources and seed exchanges.)

Fontinalis (Fontinalaceae). Willow Moss. A hardy, submerged aquatic plant whose clumps can be easily divided in spring. Plant out, preferably, in running water, anchoring it to the bottom. (Plants commercially available.)

Fragaria (Rosaceae). Strawberries. Most produce runners which either root themselves or can be pegged down to produce roots. These can then be severed from the parent plant and transplanted. The larger plants can also be divided. Vegetative means are important for the various named and colour forms. Species, such as *F. vesca* (*alpina*), can also be grown from seed. Plant out in a rich soil in full sun although some forms will take a degree of shade. (Seed available from specialist commercial sources and seed exchanges.)

Francoa (Saxifragaceae). Bridal Wreath. This can be vegetatively propagated by dividing plants or by taking basal cuttings from young shoots, both in spring. It can also be grown very easily from seed sown in spring. Plant out in well-drained but humus-rich soil in full sun. (Seed available from specialist commercial sources and seed exchanges.)

Fritillaria (Liliaceae). Fritillaries. These can easily be grown from seed, preferably sown fresh, but also in spring. Keep seedlings in growth for as much of the year as possible, watering and lightly feeding until the leaves die down. Keep shaded at this stage. Pot on whole pots of seedlings, without dividing, into larger pots. Divide up after their second year and either put into pots or direct into their flowering position. Germination to flowering can take three to five years, *F. imperialis*, one of the commonest garden varieties, can take up to seven years. They can also be increased vegetatively by dividing the offset bulbs that are slowly produced. *F. imperialis* can be increased in this way but resents disturbance and can take a season or more to settle down again. Some fritillaries produce 'rice' (tiny white grains) that can be sown in pots or in the open to grow on into full size bulbs. Some of the larger bulbs, such as *F. imperialis*, lend themselves to scaling (*see* p. 69). Plant out in a well-drained soil in full sun, although some prefer a light shade. *F. camtschatcencis* prefers a moisture retentive soil. (Seed available from commercial sources and all seed exchanges.)

Fuchsia (Onagraceae). Although technically shrubs, these can be considered honorary herbaceous plants as they are usually cut back in the winter, if not by frosts, then by the gardener. The normal method of increase is by taking cuttings in early summer. In spite of their being shrubs, many can be lifted and divided, preferably in late spring. As so many of the cultivated plants are cultivars or hybrids there is little point in growing from seed unless you are looking for new varieties or are growing species. Seed should be sown in spring under glass at a minimum temperature of 18°C (65°F). The best time for planting out is in late May in a fertile, moisture-retentive soil in sun. (Seed available from specialist commercial sources and from seed exchanges.)

Gaillardia (Compositae). Blanket Flower. A small, North American genus of annual and perennial plants. These can be grown from seed sown in the spring in pans, possibly under glass in gentle heat, or directly into open ground when the soil has warmed up a bit in late spring. They can also be propagated vegetatively either by careful division in spring or by taking root cuttings in early winter. A third method is to take stem cuttings in late summer or early autumn. Plant out in spring in any good garden soil in a sunny position. (Seed available both from commercial sources and seed exchange lists.)

Galanthus (Amaryllidaceae). Snowdrops. Bulbous plants that can be divided immediately after flowering while leaves are still green. They can, in fact, be divided at any time as long as the bulbs are not allowed to dry out. Avoid buying dried out bulbs. Bulbs that are slow to increase can be twin-scaled (*see* p. 69). Species will also grow from seed sown as soon as it is ripe. Plant out in a woodland-type soil in full sun or part shade. (Seed available from specialist commercial sources or seed exchanges.)

Galax (Diapensiaceae). This monotypic genus can be increased by division in autumn or spring, or from seed sown as soon as it is ripe. Plant out in an acid, woodland-type soil in part or full shade. (Seed not commercially available but obtainable from seed exchanges.)

Galeobdolon (Labiatae). See *Lamium*

Galega (Leguminosae). Goat's Rue. There are quite a number of named forms of the two species that make up this genus so vegetative propagation is important. This can be carried out by either dividing the plants in spring or autumn, or by taking basal cuttings of the new shoots in early spring. They can also be grown from seed sown in spring either directly in the soil or in pots. Plant out in any good garden soil in full sun. (Seed commercially available and from seed exchange lists.)

Galium (Rubiaceae). Bedstraws. This genus, which contains many weeds, has a few plants suitable for the wild garden that can be readily increased from seed sown in spring. They can also be easily divided at the same time of year. Plant out in any garden soil in sun or part shade. (Seed available mainly from wild-flower seed specialists. Plants commercially available.)

Galtonia (Hyancinthaceae/Liliaceae). Summer Hyacinth. These bulbous plants are very easily grown from seed sown either fresh or in spring. They will self-sow providing a source of seedlings. Mature clumps can be divided, but are slow to increase and unhappy about being disturbed, and can take a while to settle down again. Plant out in a well-drained, but moisture-retentive soil. (Seed available from specialist commercial sources and seed exchanges.)

Gaura (Onagraceae). Short-lived perennials best raised from seed. They can be sown in early spring under glass at about 16°C (61°F) so that they will flower in the same year or sown directly in the border in mid-spring. They can also be increased from summer cuttings. Plant out in a well-drained soil in full sun. (Seed available from commercial sources and seed exchanges.)

Gazania (Compositae). Tender perennials for warmer areas (overwinter elsewhere) that can be propagated from cuttings taken in mid to late summer. They can also be grown from seed sown in early spring. Plant out in late spring in any good garden soil in full sun. (Seed available commercially and from seed exchanges.)

Gelasine (Iridaceae). The corms of this bulbous plant can be divided in their dormant period after flowering. They can also be grown from seed sown fresh or in spring. Plant out in a warm, sunny spot in a well-drained soil. (Seed not commercially available but does occur in seed exchange lists, especially the alpine ones.)

Gentiana (Gentianaceae). Gentians. A large genus best propagated from seed sown when ripe or, if necessary, in early spring when a pre-chilling in a domestic refrigerator may help germination. The seed need light to germinate so do not cover. Mix the fine seed with sand if this makes it easier to sow. Clump-forming species, such as *G. sino-ornata* or *G. acaulis*, can be divided in spring. Cuttings can be taken from many, such as *G. verna* or *G. sino-ornata*, at the same time of year. Some gentians, *G. farreri* or *G. veitchiorum* for example, root easily at their nodes and can be layered. Plant out in a moisture-retentive soil in sun or part shade. (Seed available from commercial sources and all seed exchanges, especially the alpine ones.)

Geranium (Geraniaceae). Cranesbill, Hardy Geraniums. A large genus with many forms in cultivation. The best way of propagation for all except named forms, which are unlikely to come true, is from seed. This can be sown in spring, although better germination may come from seed sown in autumn. The seed capsules are explosive so the seed should be collected just as the capsule is turning brown or by covering the seed head with a bag. *G. bohemicum* is reported (P. Yeo) as germinating best after a fire: a fire lit on the site of a plant will produce seedlings in its wake. Many geraniums self-sow but beware of inferior forms if these are grown on. Most of the perennial geraniums can be divided in spring. Stem cuttings can be taken in spring for some species, such as *GG. cinereum, incanum,* and *sanguineum.* Root cuttings can be taken in autumn for species such as *GG. cinereum* and *sanguineum. G. procurrens* has a tendency to produce its own layers, which can be readily used as a source or new plants. Its hybrid 'Anne Folkard' unfortunately does not do this and is quite difficult to propagate; cuttings taken in spring are occasionally successful, but it is mainly increased by very careful division. Plant out in a good garden soil, preferably in a sunny position although some will tolerate part shade. (Seed available from commercial sources and all seed exchanges, particularly the HPS.)

Gerbera (Compositae). Plants for warmer regions that can be readily increased from seed sown in the spring under glass (21–24°C (70–75°F) with gentle heat. Seed should be sown with the sharp end downwards and they should not be completely covered. Plants do not give of their best until their second or third year. Heeled side shoots can be taken as cuttings in summer. These are tap-rooted plants and resent disturbance so plant out as soon as possible. Plant in a warm, sheltered spot in full sun in a well-drained soil. (Seed available from commercial sources and from seed exchanges.)

Geum (Rosaceae). The easiest way of propagating these is by dividing established plants in spring, although this will mean forgoing most of that season's flowers. Plants should be regularly divided to prevent them becoming congested. They can also be grown from seed sown fresh or in spring, but this method cannot be used for named forms. Germination may be slow or erratic but can be improved by using gentle heat. Plant out in a good fertile soil in sun or part shade. (Seed commercially available and from all seed exchanges.)

Gillenia (Rosaceae). A small genus of two species that can be propagated by seed sown preferably fresh or in spring, when it will benefit from pre-chilling in a refrigerator. Germination can be slow. They can also be divided but will be unhappy about it and may prove difficult. An alternative vegetative means is by taking cuttings in spring but the 'take' rate is usually low. Plant out in a good, moisture-retentive garden soil in sun or partial shade. (Seed available from specialist seed merchants or seed exchanges.)

Gladiolus (Iridaceae). There are two distinct groups of *Gladiolus*: the species and the modern hybrids. The former can be propagated by division in their dormant period or by sowing seed either fresh or in spring. Some, such as *G. byzantinus*, self-sow providing seedlings for transplantation. The modern hybrids can only be increased by division when lifting in the autumn. Plant in a well-drained soil in sun. (Seed available from specialist commercial sources and seed exchanges.)

Glaucidium (Paeoniaceae). The single species of this monotypic genus can be increased by careful division of the clumps in spring. It can also be grown from seed sown as soon as it is ripe. The resulting plants take several years to reach flowering size. Plant out in a rich woodland-type soil in part shade. (Seed not available commercially although most seed exchanges carry it. Plants commercially available.)

Glaucium (Papaveraceae). Horned Poppies. These produce masses of seed that germinates readily if sown in spring. The plants deeply resent disturbance so either plant out while the plants are still small or sow directly in their flowering position and then thin to the required number of plants. Plant out in a well-drained, light soil. (Seed available from specialist seed merchants and seed exchange lists.)

Globularia (Globulariaceae). Globe Daisy. The method of increase for most species is by growing them from seed sown in early spring. Germination can be increased by a three weeks' pre-chilling if the seed is unlikely to receive it naturally. A number of the herbaceous species can be divided in the spring. The more shrubby species can be propagated by taking cuttings, also in spring. Plant out in a well-drained soil in full sun. (Seed available from some specialist commercial sources and seed exchanges.)

Glyceria (Gramineae). Reed Meadow Grass, Reed Sweet Grass. The creeping colonies can easily be split up in spring to produce new plants. The species, but not the variegated forms, can also be increased by seed sown in spring. Plant out in moist soil (even shallow water) in a sunny position. (Seed not commonly found, but plants commercially available.)

Glycyrrhiza (Leguminosae). Liquorice. The normal method of increase is by division of the roots in spring, making certain that every piece has a viable bud. Seed can be sown in spring. Plant out in a moisture-retentive soil in full sun. (Seed not commercially available and only occurs occasionally in seed exchange lists. Plants obtainable commercially.)

Goodyera (Orchidaceae). One of the easiest of the orchids to grow. Seed still presents a problem, but the creeping rhizomes can easily be divided in spring, just as growth recommences, or in autumn. Plant out in a woodland-type soil in part shade. (Plants commercially available.)

Grindellia (Compositae). These can be sown from seed in autumn or spring. They can be divided in spring or basal cuttings taken at the same time of year. Plant out in a well-drained soil in a sunny position. (Seed not available commercially but does occasionally occur in HPS and other seed exchanges.)

Gunnera (Gunneraceae). Chilian Rhubarb, Prickly Rhubarb. These giant (and tiny, cf. *G. prorepens*) plants can best be increased by division. Unless you wish to hire a mechanical digger, the easiest way is to split a small piece with roots from the side of a mature plant, or deliberately keep plants small by constant division. The former can be achieved by cutting off a chunk of rooted rhizome with a bud attached in late spring. Sow seed as soon as it is ripe, when germination is quite free. Plant out in spring after frosts have passed in a rich, humus-laden, moist soil in sun or partial shade. (Seed can be obtained from specialist commercial sources and seed exchanges.)

Gymnospermium (Podophyllaceae/Berbideraceae). Tuberous rooted plants that need to be propagated from seed sown fresh or in spring. Plant out in a well-drained sunny situation. (Seed available from alpine seed exchanges. Plants commercially available.)

Gynura (Compositae). Plants for warmer regions generally increased by taking cuttings in the spring or early summer. They can also be grown from seed sown fresh or in spring. Plant out in a well-drained soil in sun. (Seed difficult to find but does occasionally occur in seed exchange lists. Plants commercially available.)

Gypsophila (Caryophyllaceae). Baby's Breath, Chalk Plant. The easiest way to increase this genus is by sowing seed in spring, either in pots or directly into the soil. The named cultivars of *G. paniculata* need to be increased vegetatively by taking cuttings of young side shoots (with a heel) in the spring or early summer. They are not too happy about being kept in a closed atmosphere so keep this as short as possible. Cuttings of named forms such as 'Bristol Fairy' and 'Flamingo' are often reluctant to take and better results may be had by grafting them onto stock of *G. paniculata*. Some of the perennial forms can be increased by taking root cuttings in early winter. Although the main herbaceous species are deep rooted and dislike disturbance the lower, mat forming species can be divided in spring. Plant out in a deep, well-drained soil in a sunny position. (Seed available commercially and from all seed exchanges.)

Hacquetia (Umbelliferae) Monotypic genus. *H. epipactis* can best be increased from seed sown fresh. Do not cover pricked-out seedlings too closely in the frame as they are prone to damping off; just stand in a shady, draught-free spot. Self-sown seedlings frequently appear and are a good source of new plants, but they must be transplanted while still young. It is possible to divide, with extreme care, after flowering but the deep roots dislike disturbance and it is often impossible to re-establish. Plant out in a free-draining, woodland-type soil in part shade. (Seed not available commercially but commonly available from all the seed exchanges. Plants commercially available.)

Hakonechloa (Gramineae). These are rhizomatous species that can easily be divided, as with all grasses, in spring. Since most of the taxa grown are of coloured forms, seed cannot be used, but any of the species can be grown from seed if it can be found. Plant out in any moisture-retentive soil in part shade. (Plants commercially available.)

Haplocarpha (Compositae). Needing winter protection in all but the warmest areas, these plants can be increased by taking cuttings from young growth in the spring. If seed can be found, this should be sown either fresh or in spring. Plant out in a well-drained soil in a warm position in full sun. (Seed very difficult to find, but plants commercially available.)

Haplopappus (Compositae). Most of this genus are for warmer areas although some, such as *HH. coronopifolius* and *spinulosus*, are reasonably hardy. Propagation can be from cuttings taken in spring, or by division for those that are clump-forming. Some, such as *H. coronopifolius*, produce roots along stems that are in contact with the ground and these can be used as rooted cuttings. They can also be grown from seed sown fresh or in spring. Plant out in any free-draining garden soil in full sun. (Seed does not seem to be commercially available but can be found in seed exchanges.)

Hedychium (Zingiberaceae). Although considered tender, many will tolerate temperatures down to −10°C (14°F) and can be used for permanent plantings. Easily propagated by the division of their rhizomes in spring. Sections of the rhizome 15 cm (6 in) long, each containing roots and adventitious buds, are placed in pots or trays. Avoid disturbing in autumn. Can also be grown from seed sown in spring. Seed benefits from being soaked in warm water before sowing. Plant out in a rich, moisture-retentive soil in full sun. Note that plants are late into growth, about late May. (Seed occasionally available from American Rock Garden seed exchange and commercial sources.)

Hedysarum (Leguminosae). Most can be grown readily from seed sown in spring, either in pots or directly into the soil. Semi-ripe cuttings can be taken in late summer. Some such as *H. microcalyx* can be divided in spring. Plant out in a well-drained soil in sunny position. (Seed available from some specialist seed merchants and seed exchanges.)

Helenium (Compositae). Sneezeweed. These soon form large clumps easily divided in autumn or spring to provide new plants, either replanting individual slips or small clumps. Old clumps should be divided every three or four years to prevent them getting too congested. Division will produce as many plants as required, but it is also possible to propagate by taking basal cuttings in spring. Since the majority of taxa in gardens are named forms there is little point in growing them from seed although it is possible to do so, sowing either when the seed is fresh in autumn or in spring. Plant out in any good, humus-rich garden soil in full sun. (Seed available from commercial sources as well as seed exchanges.)

Helianthella (Compositae). A clump-forming genus easily propagated by division in autumn or spring. Basal cuttings can be taken from young shoots in spring. Seed can be sown in either autumn or spring. Plant out in a moisture-retentive soil in full sun. (Both plants and seeds are hard to find.)

Helianthemum (Cistaceae). Rock Rose, Sun Rose. These shrubby plants play an important part in the border. They can be propagated by sowing seed fresh in autumn or, if necessary, in spring. For named forms it is best to take semi-ripe cuttings in summer and autumn. Plant out in a well-drained soil in a sunny situation. (Seed available from specialist commercial sources and seed exchanges.)

Helianthus (Compositae). Sunflowers. The main method of propagation is by division of the clump-forming plants in autumn or spring. They should be divided every three to four years to prevent congestion. Basal cuttings can be taken in spring. The species can be grown from seed, either sown fresh or in spring. Plant out in a rich, moisture-retentive soil in full sun. (Seed available from some specialist commercial sources and seed exchanges. Seed of annual species more generally available.)

Helichrysum (Compositae). Strawflowers. A large genus that all have one thing in common − a dislike of wet conditions. This means that although cuttings can be taken from many of them they must not be kept under close conditions, otherwise they will rot. Similarly divisions, which can be taken in spring, should not be cossetted too closely if put into pots rather than the open ground. Many can also be sown from seed, either fresh or in spring. Plant out in a well-drained soil in a sunny position. (Seed available from commercial sources and seed exchanges.)

Helictotrichon (Gramineae). Grasses best propagated by division in spring. They can also be grown from seed in spring if it can be found. Plant out in a well-drained soil in full sun. (Seed difficult to find but plants widely available.)

Heliopsis (Compositae). Ox-eye. Clump-forming perennials easily divided in autumn or spring. They ought to be divided every three or four years to prevent the clumps from becoming too congested and consequently dying out from the centre. They can also be propagated from basal cuttings of young shoots taken in spring. All but named varieties can be grown from seed, sown either fresh or in spring. Plant out in a moisture-retentive soil in full sun. (Seed available from commercial sources and seed exchanges.)

Heliotropum (Boraginaceae). A large genus of annuals and perennial subshrubs of which a number are in cultivation, in particular plants derived from *HH. arborescens* (*peruvianum*) and *corymbosum*. These are tender perennials that can normally be grown from seed, usually under gentle heat, but older varieties such as 'Chatsworth', 'Gatton Park', 'Lord Roberts' and 'P. K. Lowther' need to be taken from cuttings in autumn. Plant out in early summer in a well-drained soil. (Seed of perennials not generally available, but plants can be found commercially.)

Helleborus (Ranunculacae). Hellebore. Sow seed fresh in summer or autumn, when best germination will be achieved, or, if necessary, in spring. Divide mature plants in spring while the plants are still in bloom or immediately they finish flowering. Named forms must, of course, be increased by division. Split the clumps into small pieces each with individual shoots with roots attached, to be potted up or replanted in the open soil. Plant out in a rich, moisture-retentive soil in partial shade or full sun if soil is moist enough. (Seed available commercially and from seed exchanges.)

Helonias (Liliaceae). Swamp Pink. A single species genus represented by *H. bullata*. It produces offsets that can be divided from the parent plant in spring. It can also be grown from seed sown fresh or in spring. Plant out in a woodland-type soil in light shade. (Seed not available commercially but occasionally occurs in seed exchange lists. Plants not commercially available.)

Heloniopsis (Melanthiaceae/Liliaceae). A small genus of rhizomatous plants from Japan, all of which are readily increased by division in autumn. They can also be grown from seed sown fresh or in spring. Plant out in a cool, moisture-retentive soil in part shade. (Seed difficult to find but plants commercially available.)

Hemerocallis (Hemerocallidaceae/Liliaceae). Day lilies. The standard way of increase for all day lilies and, in particular, named forms is by division of mature clumps in spring or autumn. Congested clumps may need dividing as a way of revitalizing them. Seed can be sown of species, or any forms on which you want to gamble, in early spring, pre-chilling in a refrigerator for six weeks if they are unlikely to receive it naturally. Plant out in any good garden soil in autumn or spring in sun or partial shade, although they flower better in the former. (Seed available from the more specialist seed merchants and from seed exchanges.)

Hepatica (Ranunculaceae). Increase by division soon after flowering. Also from freshly-sown seed. The seed appears very early in the year so do not miss it. It should be harvested as soon as it can be rubbed from the pod, at which stage it is still green. Double-flowered plants can only be propagated from division; single from either division or seed, although to maintain colour forms division will be necessary. Young plants can take a while to settle down and begin to flower. Plant out in a woodland-type soil in part shade. (Seed available from specialist seed merchants and all the seed exchanges.)

Heracleum (Umbelliferae). A medium-sized genus of which many are weeds. The monocarpic *H. mantegazzianum*, giant hogweed, is the species normally grown. This is grown from seed sown fresh or in spring. It self-sows freely and the seedlings can be an easy source of plants. Move or plant out as soon as possible. Plant out in a deep moist soil in part shade or sun. Be careful as many people are allergic to the sap, which can cause nasty skin complaints. If you have to touch it use gloves and do not allow it to come into contact with any exposed skin or eyes. (Seed available from seed merchants and seed exchanges.)

Hermodactylus (Iridaceae). This iris relative has creeping tubers that can be lifted and divided in autumn. It can also be grown from seed sown either fresh or in spring. Plant out in very well-drained soil in a warm sunny spot. (Seed not commonly available but can be obtained from some seed exchanges.)

Hesperantha (Iridaceae). Plants similar to *Ixia* that can be grown in the open in warmer areas. The offsets provide a ready means of increase in autumn, or they can be grown from seed sown when fresh or in spring. Seed takes three to four years to flower and should be left undisturbed in the pot for at least one year after germination. Plant out in a well-drained soil in a warm, sunny position. (Seed difficult to find but some plants commercially available.)

Hesperis (Cruciferae). Sweet Rocket. A small genus of biennial herbs easily grown from seed either *in situ* or in pots. The main plants of interest to herbaceous gardeners are the old double forms of *H. matrionalis*. Being double, these cannot be grown from seeds and, being biennial, they need to be regularly propagated vegetatively to ensure their continuance. If big enough they can be divided in spring, or they can be increased from cuttings after the plant has flowered. Stem cuttings can be taken from the old flowering stem or it can be cut back inducing secondary growth, which again can be used as cuttings. Commercially they are increased by micropropagation methods. (Seed available from seed exchanges and commercial sources.)

Heuchera (Saxifragaceae). The usual method of propagating heucheras is by division either in autumn or spring, many gardeners preferring the former. Plant divisions deeply or work in some old potting compost round the new crowns so that the rhizomes are buried. The species can be increased by seed. *H. micrantha* 'Palace Purple', although given a cultivar name, has from its first raising been grown from seed. Make a careful selection of the seedlings to ensure that the colour remains true. Other named forms are not so obliging and should be propagated by vegetative means. Plant out in a humus-rich soil in part shade or full sun if the soil is not too dry. (Seed available from specialist seed companies and all seed exchanges.)

× **Heucherella** (Saxifragaceae). These bigeneric hybrids can only be propagated by vegetative means. This means that the only viable method is by division either in autumn or spring. The parent plants of this cross are *Heuchera* and *Tiarella* and there is plenty of opportunity for the adventurous to try new hybrids from seed. Plant out in a rich, well-drained but moisture-retentive soil in part shade or sun if the soil is not too dry. (Plants available commercially.)

Hibiscus (Malvaceae). Mallow. This genus contains annuals, perennials and shrubs. All can be grown from seed sown in the spring; the annuals directly in the soil where they are to flower. Chip and soak the seed for 24 hours before sowing. The perennials can also be divided. The shrubby ones (some of which are used in herbaceous borders) can be increased from cuttings taken in autumn or by layering in late summer. Some shrubs can also be grafted but that is stepping outside the limits of this book. Plant out in any good garden soil in a warm, sunny position. (Seed available from specialist commercial sources and from seed exchanges.)

Hieraceum (Compositae). Hawkweeds. Some of these can indeed be considered weeds as their vernacular name suggests; they self-sow themselves to give more than enough plants for most uses. In a more controlled situation seed can be sown either when ripe or in spring. Those that spread by stolons forming clumps or mats, such as *HH. aurantiacum* or *villosum*, can be easily divided in spring. Plant out in any well-drained garden soil in sun. (Available from commercial suppliers as well as seed exchanges.)

Hippocrepis (Leguminosae). Horse-shoe Vetch. These edge-of-border plants can be increased either by seed sown in spring or by division in autumn or spring. Plant out in a well-drained soil in full sun. (Seed not easy to find but may be listed by wild-flower seed specialists. Plants commercially available.)

Holcus (Gramineae). *H. mollis* 'Albovariegatus' is the only form of this genus likely to be found in cultivation. Being variegated the only method of increase is by division in the spring. Plant out in a well-drained soil in sun or partial shade. (Plants widely available.)

Homeria (Iridaceae). Plants similar to *Ixia* that can be grown in the open in warmer areas. The offsets provide a ready means of increase in autumn or they can be grown from seed sown when fresh or in spring. Seed takes three to four years to flower and should be left undisturbed in the pot for at least one year after germination. Plant out in a well-drained soil in a warm, sunny position. (Seed difficult to find but some plants commercially available.)

Homogyne (Compositae). A small genus of perennial herbs that can be divided in spring, or grown from seed sown fresh or in spring. Plant out in a moist soil in part shade or sun. (Seed available from specialist commercial sources or from seed exchanges, especially those specializing in alpine plants.)

Hordeum (Gramineae). Both annuals and perennials are grown from seed sown in spring. Plant out in any garden soil in sun. (Annual seed can be obtained from commercial sources. A wider range can be found in seed exchange lists. Plants commercially available.)

Hormium (Labiatae). A monotypic genus of which the only member, *H. pyrenaicum*, presents no difficulty in being propagated either by division in spring or from seed sown at the same time of year. Plant out in a free-draining soil in full sun. (Seed not commercially available but can be found in seed exchange lists.)

Hosta (Funkiaceae/Liliaceae). Plantain Lilies. A genus of about 40 species and innumerable cultivars and hybrids. They can be increased by seed sown fresh or in spring, but there is no guarantee as to what plant will result except in the case of isolated species, which are likely to come true. Do not allow compost to dry out. Seedlings take several years to reach flowering size. The normal method of increase is by division in spring or autumn (or even summer if they are being potted up or weather conditions are suitable for open ground). Roots can be terribly entangled and to get the best divisions use a bucket of water to help release the various pieces, using a knife to cut through sections. Most gardeners will not have the time nor the temperament to spend hours untangling the more congested clumps and a clean cut with a spade or large knife will produce chunks of hosta that can be replanted. However, this is one plant where patience and care in dividing it will bring rewards in the number of new plants. It is possible to dig out a section from a large clump without removing the latter from the soil. Each section can then be divided or replanted whole. Another, more sophisticated, method that has been employed in recent years for those hostas that are reluctant to bulk up. This involves sticking a sharp kitchen knife through a bud just above where it joins the rootstock and cutting downwards through the latter. A second cut can be made at right angles. The operation can be achieved without removing the plants from the soil. The soil is scraped back and the incisions made, dusted with fungicide and the soil pushed back. Calluses will form over the cuts and a new plant will be initiated on each section. This operation can be undertaken in spring when the leaf buds have started to elongate. Plant out in a rich, moisture-retentive soil in part shade or sun if the soil is not too dry. (Seed available from commercial sources and seed exchanges.)

Hottonia (Primulaceae). Water Violets. Submerged aquatic plants easily increased by taking cuttings in summer. These should be tied together in bunches and bound with a lead strip to hold them in the growing medium, which should be submerged in water. When planted out they should be likewise firmly anchored down. (Plants commercially available.)

Houttuynia (Saururaceae). A monotypic genus whose only member, *H. cordata*, is very invasive, creeping underground, and can be easily divided in spring to produce new plants. Plant out in a woodland-type soil in part shade or full sun if soil is not too dry. (Seed not available, but plants easy enough to find commercially.)

Humulus (Urticaceae). Hops. The easiest method of increase is by dividing the crowns in early spring. They can also be grown from seed but since they are dioeceous both male and female are required to produce seed. It is the female form that bears the attractive 'hops' and since it takes several years from seed to flowering, and hence to be able to determine its sex, it is best to use divisions if you want to be certain that you have a female form. Seed can be sown in pots or *in situ*. The golden form *H. lupulus aureus* needs to be propagated vegetatively. (Seed sometimes available from specialist commercial sources and, very occasionally, from seed exchanges. Plants commercially widely available.)

Hyacinthus (Hyacinthaceae). Hyacinths. Most hyacinths seen in gardens are cultivars and need to be increased vegetatively by dividing the offsets that are reasonably freely produced. To produce a larger number the base of the bulbs should be scored (*see* p. 69). Species can be increased from seed if it can be found. Plant out in any good, well-drained garden soil in sun or light shade. (Seed most commonly found in the alpine seed exchange lists. Bulbs very readily available.)

Hyacinthoides (Hyacinthaceae). Bluebells. These are only too easy to propagate and many gardeners have rued the day that they were introduced into certain borders. Bluebells are really only suitable for the wild garden. The bulbs readily increase and can easily be divided when the plant is dormant in summer or autumn. They will also come readily from seed and many self-sown seedlings can usually be found. Plant out in a woodland-type soil preferably in part shade, although they will take full sun. (Seed available from commercial sources, especially those specializing in wild flowers, and from seed exchanges.)

Hydrangea (Hydrangeaceae). A genus of shrubs allowed in as honorary herbaceous plants as they are frequently used in borders. These are increased from cuttings, either as soft tip cuttings in summer or as harder cuttings later in the season. The species can of course be grown from seed but it is normally only undertaken with newly introduced seed. It should be sown in the spring. Plant out in any good garden soil in light shade or full sun if the soil is moist enough. (Seed available from at least one commercial source and occasionally from seed exchanges. Best material comes from seed-collecting expeditions.)

Hydrastis (Ranunculaceae). A small genus of two species of which *H. candensis* is occasionally seen in gardens. It can be increased by the division of its tuberous rootstock in spring. It can also be raised from freshly sown seed, removing the flesh from around the seed before sowing. Plant out in a woodland-type soil in light shade. (Seed not commercially available but occasionally occurs in seed exchanges. Plants can be found commercially.)

Hylomecon (Papaveraceae). A monotypic genus solely represented by *H. japonicum*. This is a delightful spreading plant easy to divide in the spring. It can also be sown from seed in spring. Plant out in a woodland-type soil in part shade. (Seed available from specialist commercial sources as well as all seed exchanges.)

Hymenocallis (Amaryllidaceae/Liliaceae). These bulbous plants for warmer areas can be propagated vegetatively by removing offsets in the dormant period. They can also be grown from the large seed sown when fresh or in the spring. Plant out in a well-drained soil in a warm, sunny position. (Seed not easy to find but bulbs commercially available.)

Hyoscyamus (Solanaceae). Henbane. A small genus of biennials often grown in herbaceous borders. Grow from seed sown in spring. They will self-sow once established but seedlings thus raised must be moved to their final flowering positions while the plant is still young as they resent disturbance. Alternatively, sow where they are to flower. Germination can be erratic. The seed and the plant are poisonous. Plant out in well-drained soil in a sunny position. (Seed available from specialist commercial sources and from seed exchanges.)

Hypericum (Guttiferae). A genus of herbaceous and shrubby plants that are good border plants. Vegetative propagation can be from semi-ripe cuttings taken in summer or autumn. Those with a creeping habit, such as *H. calycinum*, can easily be divided in spring. Seed can be sown of any species in spring. Plant out in any good garden soil in full sun. (Seed available from specialist commercial sources and seed exchanges.)

Hypolepis (Dennstaedtiaceae). Invasive ferns easily divided in spring. They can also be grown from spore sown when collected. Plant out in a woodland-type soil in part shade or sun. (Spore possibly available from pteridological spore exchanges. Plants commercially available.)

Hyssopus (Labiatae). Hyssop. These can be increased vegetatively by dividing the plants in spring or taking cuttings at the same time of year, or indeed summer and autumn. They can also be increased from seed sown in autumn or spring. Plant out in any good garden soil in full sun. (Seed very readily available, both from commercial sources or from seed exchanges.)

Hystrix (Gramineae). This small genus of grasses can be increased either by division in spring or sowing seed at the same time of year. Plant out in good garden soil in full sun. (Seed hard to find and plants not much easier, although some are commercially available.)

Iberis (Cruciferae). Candytuft. These can be easily increased by taking cuttings in summer or by dividing the plants after flowering. They can also be readily grown from seed sown in the spring. Plant out in a free-draining soil in full sun. (Seed available from most commercial sources and all seed exchanges.)

Impatiens (Balsaminaceae). Balsams, Busy Lizzies. A large genus of over 1,000 species of which a handful are grown as annuals and perennials. All perennials come very readily from cuttings taken at any time. While germination of seed of some species is easy, it is often difficult in others. Seed should be sown in autumn and overwintered in the open to experience cold periods. Pre-chill seed in a refrigerator if it is not exposed to frosts. Do not cover seed as light is needed for germination. It is also beneficial to keep humidity high until germination is complete. Some readily self-sow, particularly *I. glandulifera*, which can become invasive. Plant out in moist soil in a shady position, although sun will be tolerated if the ground is kept moist. (Seed available from HPS and alpine seed exchanges as well as commercial sources.)

Incarvillea (Bignoniaceae). Trumpet Flower. A large genus of plants of which a few are hardy. These are generally propagated from seed sown preferably as soon as ripe, or in the spring. It takes three to four years for the plants to reach flowering size. Some lend themselves to careful division but *Incarvillea* resent disturbance once established. Cuttings can be taken in spring from others, such as *I. olgae*. Plant out in a well-drained but fertile soil in full sun. (Seed available from specialist commercial sources and seed exchanges.)

Indigofera (Leguminosae). A large genus of shrubby plants, some of which are hardy and fit well into a border. These can be increased by taking soft-wood cuttings in late spring or early summer. They can also be grown from seed sown in spring under glass in gentle heat (10°C, 50°F). Soak the seed for 24 hours before sowing. Overwinter under glass and plant out in the spring of their second year. Plant out in a fertile, well-drained soil in full sun. (Seed can be obtained from specialist commercial sources and seed exchanges.)

Inula (Compositae). The most usual method of increase is by division in either autumn or spring. They can also be grown from seed sown either fresh or in spring. Seed can be sown in pots or directly into the soil. In either case light seems to be beneficial to germination, so do not cover too deeply. Plant out in a moisture-retentive soil in full sun although they will also take part shade. (Seed available from specialist commercial growers and seed exchanges.)

Ipheion (Alliaceae/Liliacae). These bulbous plants spread to form quite large colonies that can easily be divided in autumn or, after flowering, in late spring. They can also be grown from seed sown in spring, except named forms, which need to be divided. Plant out in a moisture-retentive soil in part shade although they will grow in reasonably dry conditions in sun. (Seed available from specialist commercial sources and all seed exchanges.)

Iris (Iridaceae). A very large genus of thick rhizomatous, thinner creeping and bulbous species. The first, which mainly comprise the germanic bearded irises, can be divided after flowering or in autumn or spring. Sections of rhizome can be cut away from the parent plant, each piece having a fan of leaves and roots. Plant so that the roots are buried but the rhizome remains above ground. Reduce the leaves to a short fan. The old pieces of rhizome should be discarded. They can also be grown from seed but, except in the case of species, are unlikely to come true to their parents. Seed should be sown fresh, although it will remain viable for at least 15 years as long as it is stored properly. Older seed is erratic in germination. Germination can be improved by soaking the seed in water for several days, changing it every day, and then pre-chilling for four weeks. The creeping varieties, which include those that like moist soil and even grow in water, as well as those like *I. unguicularis* that need very well-drained sites, have smaller rhizomes and these can be divided off in a similar manner and planted firmly in the ground, again after flowering. They can also be grown from seed sown in the spring. The bulbous varieties produce offsets that can be easily divided in their dormant period, never later than autumn. These can also be sown from seed in the spring. Plant out in a variety of soils from well-drained to pondside marginal planting according to species. Most prefer full sun. (Seed available from all commercial sources as well as all seed exchanges including iris societies.)

Isatis (Cruciferae). Woad. A genus of annual, biennial and perennial herbs that can very easily be increased by seed sown in spring. They will happily self-sow if allowed to and this will produce sufficient seedlings for most purposes. Indeed, the annuals can be considered perennial in that they copiously self-sow and continue year after year. Seed can be either sown in pots or directly into the soil. Some plants can be increased by division in autumn. Plant out in any garden soil in full sun. (Seed available from specialist commercial sources and seed exchanges.)

Isoetes (Isoetaceae). Quillwort. Submerged aquatic plants that can only be increased by division, which is undertaken in late spring. Anchor the divisions down into the growing medium or they will fail to take. (Plants commercially available.)

Isopyrum (Ranunculaceae). A small genus of woodland plants grown from seed sown as soon as it is ripe. They are creeping plants and can easily be divided. Plant out in a rich, woodland-type soil in part shade. (Seed available from specialist commercial sources and seed exchanges.)

Ixia (Iridaceae). Corn Lilies. A tender genus of bulbs that can only be grown in warmer areas. The naturally increasing clumps can be divided after flowering, autumn at the latest as they come into growth through the winter. They can also be grown from seed sown thinly in autumn, leaving the resulting seedlings at least one season before potting on or planting out. Plant out in a well-drained soil in a warm, sunny position. (Seed not commercially available, but can be found in seed exchanges. Plants commercially available.)

Ixiolirion (Ixioliriaceae/Liliaceae). A small genus of bulbous plants easily increased by lifting the clumps of naturally increasing bulbs and dividing them. They can also be grown from seed in spring. Plant out in a well-drained soil in full sun. (Seed not available commercially, but can be found in most seed exchanges. Plants commercially available.)

Jaborosa (Solanaceae). This invasive plant can easily be increased by division in spring. Should another vegetative method be needed, it is also possible to take cuttings of the young shoots in spring. Seed, if it can be found, can be sown, also in spring. Plant out in a well-drained soil in a warm, sunny position. (Seed not available commercially, but it does occur in seed exchanges. Plants sometimes commercially available.)

Jasione (Campanulaceae). These can be grown from seed sown fresh or in spring. Some species can also be divided in spring. Plant out in a well-drained soil in full sun. (Seed available from specialist commercial sources and seed exchanges.)

Jeffersonia (Berberidaceae). This small genus can be increased by careful division in spring or by sowing seed as soon as it is ripe. Plant out in a rich, woodland-type soil in part shade. (Seed available from specialist commercial sources and seed exchanges.)

Juncus (Juncaceae). Rushes. Pondside, marginal plants best increased by division in late spring. It is also possible to increase them by sowing seed in very moist compost as soon as it is ripe. Plant out in water at the edge of a pond or stream making certain that the plants are anchored down. (Seed not easily available although it does occur in some seed exchanges.)

Kentranthus (Valerianceae). See *Centranthus*

Kirengeshoma (Hydrangeaceae). The normal method of increase is by dividing the plants in spring. They can also be grown from seed sown in spring. Make certain the compost does not dry out. Plant out in a moisture-retentive soil in part shade. (Seed not commonly available from commercial sources but can be found in HPS and other seed exchange lists.)

Knautia (Dipsacaceae). These relatives of the scabious can be increased by division in spring or autumn. They can also be grown from seed preferably sown fresh, or in the spring. If necessary, they can be sown directly into the open ground. Plant out in a moisture-retentive soil in full sun. (Seed available from specialist commercial sources as well as HPS and other seed exchanges.)

Kniphofia (Asphodelaceae/Liliaceae). Torch Lilies, Red Hot Pokers. An easy genus to propagate as division is simple to achieve at any time of the year while the plant is in active growth, although spring is usually considered to be the best time. Evergreen forms can be divided in autumn, but this does not seem to be so suitable for deciduous varieties. The production of side shoots on slow-growing forms can be speeded up by sheering over the crown of the plant. Unless required for division, clumps can be left in the same position for many years. Removing all the soil and manipulating the plants in a bucket of water can facilitate division. Reduce the length of the old roots and sheer over the foliage a few inches above the base. Pot up or replace in the ground. Species will come true from seed if the parents are in fact true themselves, but named forms must be propagated vegetatively unless new forms are being sought. Seed should be sown fresh or in spring. Plants should be planted out in spring into a fertile, moisture-retentive, light soil in a sunny position. (Seed available from HPS and other seed exchanges and commercial sources, although in all cases the results are likely to be variable.)

Koeleria (Gramineae). These grasses can readily be increased by division in spring. They can also be grown from seed sown in spring either in pots or direct in the soil. Plant out in any garden soil in sun. (Seed not easy to find commercially but occasionally listed in seed exchanges. Plants commercially available.)

Lactuca (Compositae). Blue Lettuce. Both the annuals and perennials can be raised from seed sown in spring, either in pots or direct in the soil. The perennials can have invasive roots, especially *L. bourgaei*, and these can easily be divided in autumn or spring. Plant out in any garden soil in sun. (Seed not commercially available but can be found in HPS and other seed exchange lists.)

Lamiastrum (Labiatae). Yellow Archangel. *L. galeobdolon* wanders like a lost soul between *Lamiastrum*, *Lamium* and *Galeobdolon*. The plant itself has a very marked tendency to wander, even to the point of invasiveness. This, however, makes it easy to propagate as it can easily be divided, by removing the rooted runners, in either autumn, or spring. It will also come very readily from seed sown in spring. It self-sows with abandon so there are always plenty of seedlings to use. The silver variegated form normally comes true from seed as well as the species. Plant out in any garden soil in part shade or sun. (Seed not available commercially but occurs in seed exchanges. Plants widely available.)

Lamium (Labiatae). Deadnettles. There seems to be no problem in propagating these. The most common method is by division to which they lend themselves quite readily. They can also be grown from seed sown in spring. Plant out in any garden soil in either sun or part shade. (Seed not available from commercial sources, but can be found in seed exchange lists. Plants commercially available.)

Lapeirousia (Iridaceae). A medium-sized genus of bulbous plants of which *L. laxa* is commonly grown in warmer areas. The corms can easily be divided in the dormant period. They will also come readily from seed sown in spring. Light is beneficial to germination, so do not cover too deeply. They will self-sow themselves generously. Plant out in a well-drained soil in sun or even light shade. (Seed available from specialist commercial sources and seed exchanges.)

Lathyrus (Leguminosae). Peas. A large genus of annuals and perennials, some of which are climbing plants. Both perennials and annuals can also be grown from seed. The seed needs scarifying by chipping, rubbing with sandpaper, or vigorously shaking along with sharp sand in a jar, and then soaking overnight before sowing. Several of the perennial species, of which *L. latifolius* is a good example, can be increased vegetatively by taking cuttings from young shoots in spring. Clump-forming species, of which *L. vernus* is typical, can be divided in autumn, or spring after flowering. Plant out in a well-drained soil in sun, although some such as *L. grandiflorus* will take a modicum of shade. (Seed available from specialist commercial sources and from all seed exchanges.)

Lavandula (Labiatae). Lavender. A small genus of shrubby plants frequently found in perennial borders. Probably the easiest means of propagation is to take soft tip or semi-ripe stem cuttings during the summer or, indeed, at almost any time of the year. Lavender also comes very readily from seed sown in spring, although the resulting colours may be variable. Plant out in a well-drained soil in full sun. (Seed available from specialist commercial sources and occasionally from seed exchanges.)

Lavatera (Malvaceae). Tree Mallow. There are several methods of propagation available with this genus. The most common is to take cuttings in spring or autumn for the more tender forms, such as *L. maritima*, to ensure that they overwinter. Some multi-stemmed, clump-forming species can be divided in spring or autumn. They will all come from seed although some gardeners feel that non-seed setting plants are more free-flowering and would therefore advocate vegetative propagation for a plant of that type rather than a seed-producing one. Annuals, of course, must be raised from seed. Plant out in a well-drained soil in full sun. (Seed available from commercial sources and from seed exchanges.)

Leontice (Podophyllaceae/Berberidaceae). Tuberous plants that can only be propagated by removing offsets in early spring from seed sown fresh or in spring. Seed should only be covered sparingly. Planting out in a well-drained sunny situation. (Seed available from alpine seed exchange. Some plants commercially available.)

Leontopodium (Compositae). Edelweiss. All the species, including the dwarf forms, can be grown from seed sown in late winter or early spring. If unlikely to receive frosts, then a period of pre-chilling will be beneficial. They can also be divided in spring, but if potted up should not be enclosed in too close a frame or the damp atmosphere will rot the plants. Plant out in a well-drained sunny position. (Seed available from some commercial sources and seed exchanges.)

Lespedeza (Leguminosae). A medium-sized genus of shrubs and subshrubs that die back each winter like an herbaceous plant and can easily be divided in early spring. They can also be grown from seed sown in early spring. Plant out in a well-drained soil in full sun. (Seed occasionally available from some specialist commercial sources and seed exchanges. Plants commercially available.)

Leucanthemella (Compositae). See **Chrysanthemum**

Leucanthemopsis (Compositae). See ***Chrysanthemum***

Leucojum (Amaryllidaceae). Snowflakes. These bulbous plants naturally increase and the resulting clumps can be divided in late summer or early autumn. They can also be increased by seed sown as soon as it is ripe or in spring. Resulting seedlings should not be potted on until their second year. It can take up to four years to get flowering plants from seed. Plant out in a woodland soil in part shade. (Seed commercially available and from seed exchange lists.)

Lewisia (Portulaceae). A popular genus of North American plants for which the main method of propagation is from seed. This is ideally sown fresh in the autumn. If sown in spring or if it is unlikely to experience frosts then a period of pre-chilling is beneficial. Leave the deciduous species, such as *LL. pygmaea* or *rediviva*, in their pots until their second autumn before pricking out (the deciduous species are difficult to grow in the open garden). Those species that make offsets can be propagated vegetatively by cutting off the offsets and placing them in moist sand in a close atmosphere. Plant out in a well-drained soil in light shade. (Seed available from specialist commercial sources, including specialist nurseries, and seed exchanges, especially alpine ones.)

Liatris (Compositae). Kansas Gay Feather, Button Snakeroot. The easiest method of increase is by division carried out in autumn or spring. The solid, almost tuber-like plates from which the stems and roots emerge may need to be cut with a knife, which in any event will give a cleaner edge than making the division by snapping the plates. They will also grow from seed sown either fresh or in spring. Plant out in sun in any good garden soil that, although well-drained, is not too dry. (Seed available from many commercial sources and from HPS and other seed exchanges.)

Libertia (Iridaceae). These clump-forming plants can easily be divided in spring. Alternatively, they can be increased from seed sown in spring. Some, for example *L. formosa*, will quite happily self-sow, providing ample offspring for most purposes. Plant out in a well-drained, but moisture-retentive, soil in a sheltered spot in sun. (Seed available from some commercial sources and seed exchanges.)

Ligularia (Compositae). Most gardeners would increase these by division in autumn or spring. They can also be grown from seed sown in spring. Seed would not normally be used for cultivars, but *L. dentata* 'Desdemona' and 'Othello' will usually produce seedlings identical to the parents. Non-typical ones should be rogued out. Some, such as *L. veitchiana* and *L.d.* 'Desdemona' mentioned above, produce a large number of self-sown seedlings that can be used as a ready source of plants. Plant out in a humus-rich, moisture-retentive soil in part shade, or sun if soil is kept moist. (Seed available from specialist commercial sources and from HPS and other seed exchanges.)

Lilium (Liliaceae). Lilies. Lilies are not particularly difficult to propagate, but there are so many varying methods of vegetative increase and different aspects to seed germination that a whole book could be written on the subject. Indeed, anyone keen enough should search out monographs specifically on lilies. There are several different types of lily bulb and those that are of a stoloniferous or rhizomatous nature can be divided in autumn. The concentric type, which are rounded and produce no offsets in any form, cannot be increased division. All bulbs can increased by scaling, which involves snapping off the scales (easily recognized with a bulb in your hand) as close to the base as possible. Just a few scales from the edge of the bulb can be taken or the whole bulb can be used to provide a large number of new plants. Place the scales into pots or trays in a well-drained but humus-rich compost, and keep in a close frame. Alternatively, they can be placed in a polythene bag and mixed up with moist vermiculite. The bag is tightly closed and kept in an airing cupboard until bulblets are formed and roots are seen. It can then be removed and the scales potted up in a well-drained but humus-rich compost. Keep enclosed in a frame or propagator to start with and then gradually harden off. Scales can be taken at any time, but early spring and after flowering are the favoured times. Some lilies produce bulblets on the stems between the main bulb and the soil surface. These can be removed and potted up in a compost as directed above for scales. Another type of bulbs, namely bulbils, are produced by some lilies in the leaf axils. These can be picked and sown as seed either in pots or in the open ground. Sometimes, roots are already present before the bulbils would naturally drop to the ground. Seed is another obvious method of increase and has the advantage that it is the only method that does not transfer the dreaded virus diseases from parent plants to offspring. Its main disadvantage is that it can take several years to obtain flowering plants by this method. For those not interested in the mechanics of lily germination, the easiest way is to sow the seed when it is fresh and patiently wait until it germinates. For those who are, there are two types of germination: epigeal and hypogeal. In the former the seed leaf appears above ground after germination, usually with the seed coat still attached. In the latter the seed produces a small bulb and the seed leaf, plus seed case, remain below ground with the first leaf to emerge being the first true leaf. To add to the complications both epigeal and hypogeal germination can be immediate or delayed. There is a tendency for epigeal germination to be immediate and hypogeal germination to be delayed. There is no problem with immediate germination as these can be sown as normal, but with lilies that have delayed germination it is best to sow in a moist mixture of sharp and peat and keep enclosed in a polythene bag. Place in an airing cupboard or propagator at about 21°C (70°F) until the bulbils are seen to form. Germination is likely to stick at this point for several months or even years and to break the dormancy the bag should be put in a domestic refrigerator (not freezer) for six to eight weeks. Pot up the resulting plants. Alternatively, sow as normal when the seed is fresh and leave the pots outside during the winter, but it may take a couple of winters to break the dormancy. There is no way to tell which lilies have immediate epigeal germination and which delayed hypogeal without either previous experience or by consulting reference books on lilies. Most lilies like a well-drained soil and full sun but there are others that require more moisture and shade. Again, consult reference books for individual species. (Seed available from specialist commercial sources and seed exchange lists, especially the RHS Lily Group's list.)

Limonium (Plumbaginaceae). Sea Lavender, Statice. These can be propagated by division in spring. Some, in particular *L. latifolium*, lend themselves to increase by taking root cuttings in winter. Seed sown in spring can be used for annual and perennial species, but named forms need to be increased vegetatively. Plant out in a well-drained soil in full sun. (Seed available from commercial sources and all seed exchanges.)

Linaria (Scrophulariaceae). Toadflax. These are more-or-less self-propagating. Many are invasive and spread by underground runners, which can be divided or used as root cuttings at any time of the year as long as the soil is moist and it is neither too hot nor too cold. Those that are clump forming, such as *L. purpurea*, tend to self-sow, providing sufficient seedlings for most uses. Seed can also be sown in spring either in pots or where they are to grow. If difficulty is experienced a period of pre-chilling may help. The pink form 'Canon Went' will provide a large number of pink seedlings if not grown close to the typical purple form. The white form is very difficult and does not appear to come true from seed. It is possible that it may come from cuttings. Plant out in a light, well-drained soil in full sun. (Seed available from specialist seed merchants and seed exchanges.)

Lindelofia (Boraginaceae). A small genus of annual and perennial plants of which the latter can be divided in autumn or spring. An alternative vegetative method is to take root cuttings in the winter. They can also be grown from seed sown either fresh or in spring. Plant out in any good garden soil in sun. (Seed does not appear to be commercially available but can be found in HPS and other seed exchange lists.)

Linum (Linaceae). Flax. These can generally be grown from the copiously-produced seed sown in the spring. Some self-sow producing ample seedlings for most requirements. They can also be increased vegetatively (particularly the named forms such as *L. flavum* 'Gemmel's Hybrid') by taking cuttings either in spring or summer. Some can also be carefully divided in spring. Plant out in a well-drained soil in full sun. (Seed available from specialist commercial sources and seed exchanges.)

Liriope (Convallariaceae/Liliaceae). These clump-forming plants can easily be divided in spring, as can those that have a tendency to creep underground. With the exception of named forms they can also be grown from seed. Plant out in any good garden soil in part shade. (Seed available from some specialist seed merchants and seed exchanges.)

Lobelia (Campanulaceae). A large genus, many of which are perennials in spite of their use as annual bedding plants. Seed provides an easy method of propagation although division is no more difficult. Discard the central portion of the clump when dividing as this becomes woody and dies out. *L. cardinalis* comes true from seed but its hybrids with *L. fulgens*, including clones such as *L.* 'Queen Victoria', need to be propagated by division or stem cuttings. Short lengths of stem each bearing a leaf are placed in cutting compost with the leaf axil just resting on the surface. New plants appear from the axils. If the leaves are large, reduce the area by a third with a sharp knife. Cuttings should be taken in summer or after flowering and the rooted plants left to overwinter in their trays until the following spring before potting up. Plants potted up in autumn are liable to rot. Stem cuttings are not restricted to hybrids, they can be taken from any of the other herbaceous forms, although seed and division are easier. Trailing and cushion-forming annual varieties are best grown from seed, which is very fine and should be sown with silver sand to help make an even distribution. Perennials may benefit from a period of pre-chilling. These will often self-sow but not necessarily coming true. (Seed available from all seed exchanges and most commercial sources.)

Ludwigia (Onagraceae). False Loosestrife. A genus of mainly tender aquatic plants but at least one, *L. palustris*, is suitable for planting on the margins of ponds. It can be increased vegetatively, probably most easily by division at any time during the early summer. It can also be increased by seed sown in spring, keeping the compost wet by standing the pot in a tray of water. Plant out in shallow water at the edge of a pond or in a stream. (Seed not generally available but plants can be purchased from pond specialists.)

Lunaria (Cruciferae). Honesty. Of the two perennials *L. rediviva* is the one usually grown in gardens. This can be sown from seed in autumn or spring or increased by division in spring. The biennial *L. annua* can only be sown from seed, again in autumn or spring. If not cut down before its seed ripens, it will usually self-sow. Forms with either variegated leaves or variegated flowers generally come true from seed, particularly if reverted forms are rogued out. All may be sown directly into open ground. Plant out in any garden soil in sun or light shade. (Seed commercially available and can also be found in the HPS and other seed exchanges.)

Lupinus (Leguminosae). Lupins. These come readily from seed sown in spring, but to ensure an even germination the seed can be scarified or chipped and then soaked in warm water overnight prior to sowing. Sowings can be made in pots or direct in open ground. They can also be increased by taking basal cuttings in spring, which is an important method for propagating named hybrids. Constant vegetative propagation tends to weaken the plants and many of the old, named varieties have disappeared. Modern colour forms are developed as strains and these come reasonably true from seed. They can also be increased by careful division in spring, but if vegetative means is required it is best to take cuttings as the plants age relatively quickly. Lupins are not long lived and benefit from regular propagation every two or three years. In many cases they are best treated as biennials and grown afresh from seed each year (this of course also applies to the annual species). Many will self-sow in borders and supply sufficient replacement plants, although the colours of the commonly-grown hybrids are eventually likely to revert to a muddy purple. Plant out in a well-drained, humus-rich soil in full sun. Young plants should be placed in their final positions in autumn. (Species mainly obtained from seed exchanges, strains commonly available from seed merchants.)

Luzula (Juncaceae). Woodrush. A large genus with a few garden-worthy plants. They can be increased either by sowing seed in spring or by division at the same time of year. Some, such as *L. sylvatica*, produce offsets that can easily be broken off and either potted up or planted direct into the soil. Some plants, *L. nivea* for example, readily self-sow. Variegated and named forms need propagating vegetatively. Plant out in either sun or shade in most garden soils. (Seed of some species is available from commercial sources but seed exchanges are the main sources of supply.)

Lychnis (Caryophyllaceae). Catchflies. Seed, sown in spring, is by far the easiest method of growing most of these border plants. Some, *L. coronaria* in particular, will self-sow, often in profusion, providing plenty of replacement plants. Most colour forms, white (or off-white) in particular, will produce a fair percentage of true seedlings. Most (*L.* × *haageana* being an exception) can also be increased by division either in autumn or spring. Plants are not long lived and regular propagation should be practised to ensure replacement. Plant out in a well-drained, fertile soil in full sun. (Seed generally available from seed merchants and seed exchanges).

Lycopus (Labiatae). Bugleweed, Gypsywort, Water Horehound. A small genus usually grown as medicinal herbs. They are stoloniferous and therefore can easily be divided, either in autumn or spring. They will also come very easily from seed sown in spring. They will self-sow, often aggressively. Plant in moisture-retentive or damp soil in full sun or light shade. (Seed not generally available but may be found from distributors of wild flower or herb seed. Some plants commercially available.)

Lycoris (Amaryllidaceae). A small genus of bulbous plants for warmer areas. The quickest method of propagation is by lifting the plants after the foliage has died down and removing the offsets. They can also be raised from seed sown in autumn and kept under gentle heat (minimum 13°C, 55°F). Plant out in a well-drained soil in a warm sunny position. (Seed not generally available from commercial sources, but can occasionally be found in seed exchanges. Bulbs are available.)

Lysichiton (Araceae). Skunk Cabbage. A small genus of two species, both of which are in cultivation. The best method of increase is from seed sown as soon as it is harvested. Keep the compost wet, preferably by standing the pot in a shallow tray of water. Self-sown seedlings can be found in spring around the parent plant. These need potting up or transplanting before they are suffocated by the large leaves of the parent. The clumps can also be divided, although with some difficulty. This should be done in spring, before flowering. Plant out in a wet, boggy position, on the margins of ponds or ditches, for example. (Seed available from the more specialist commercial sources and seed exchanges.)

Lysimachia (Primulaceae). Loosestrifes. A very large genus (up to 200 species) of which only a few are commonly grown in cultivation. Most are either clump-forming or spreading (often invasive) which makes them ideal subjects for division either carried out in autumn or spring. *L. nummularia*, Creeping Jenny, can be increased by taking stem cuttings in spring or summer. They can also be grown from seed sown in spring, ensuring that the compost is kept moist. Plant out in a moisture-retentive soil either in full sun or light shade, although the former is preferred. (Seed available from seed merchants and HPS and other seed exchanges.)

Lythrum (Lythraceae). Purple Loosestrifes. These are best propagated by vegetative means, especially the named forms. As they are clump-forming they can be divided either in autumn or spring. A large stock can also be raised by taking basal cuttings from the young shoots in spring. They can also be grown from seed sown in spring. The seeds require a certain amount of light in order to germinate, so do not cover them too deeply, but just sufficient to allow diffused light to penetrate. Pre-chilling may also help. Plant out the young plants or divisions into a moisture-retentive soil in full sun or a light shade, although they will flower best in the sun. (Seed available from specialist commercial sources and HPS and other seed exchanges.)

Macleaya (Papaveraceae). Plume Poppy. A genus of two species, both of which are grown in gardens. They are both spreading plants (sometimes invasive) which makes them ideal candidates for division, particularly from the suckers produced, either in spring or autumn. The other vegetative method of propagation is by taking root cuttings in winter. This method can often be achieved without disturbing the plants, simply by digging up some of the spreading roots. Since vegetative propagation is so easy there is generally no need to use seed but this can be used as a means of increase with sowing taking place in spring. Plant out in any soil in full sun or light shade. (Seed available from specialist commercial sources and HPS and some other seed exchanges.)

Maianthemum (Convallariaceae/Liliaceae). May Lily, Twin-leaved Lily of the Valley. A single species (*M. biflora*) genus. The normal method of increase is by division of its creeping rootstock in autumn. It can also be grown from seed, removing it from the berries and sowing in autumn. Plant out new plants or divisions in the following autumn in a cool leaf-mould soil in a light shady position. (Seed occasionally available from specialist commercial sources and alpine seed exchanges.)

Malephora (Aizoaceae). Only suitable for warmer areas. Low, succulent plants easily propagated from cuttings taken during the growing season. They can also be grown from seed sown in spring. If sown under gentle heat, they may flower in their first year. Plant out in a well-drained soil in full sun. (Seed more generally available in USA than UK from commercial sources. Plants quite readily available in both countries.)

Malva (Malvaceae). Mallows. These can be increased either by seed or cuttings. The seed can be sown in either autumn or spring. Can be sown in open ground in late spring. Some, such as *M. moschata*, can produce plenty of self-sown seedlings, which provide a good source of new plants. Cuttings can be taken from side shoots in summer. These are short-lived plants and should be propagated regularly to maintain the stock. Plant out in a fertile soil in full sun. (Seed available from seed merchants and seed exchanges.)

Malvastrum (Malvaceae). Quite a large family of perennials and subshrubs of which not all are hardy. They are easily increased from cuttings taken in summer or from seed sown in autumn or spring. Some with running rootstocks, such as *M. coccineum*, can be divided. Plant out in a fertile soil in a warm, sunny position. (Seed available from some specialist commercial sources and HPS and other seed exchanges.)

Mandragora (Solanaceae). Mandrake. A small genus of which *M. officinarum* is grown as a medicinal herb or out of sheer curiosity. They can be propagated from seed cleaned from the many-seeded berries and sown fresh or in spring. It is also possible, with care, to divide the forked roots. The various parts can be poisonous so wash your hands after handling and under no circumstances eat any part. Plant out in a well-drained soil in full sun. (At least one specialist commercial seed merchant supplies seed and it can usually be found in HPS and other exchange lists.)

Marrubium (Labiatae). White Horehound. Quite a large genus although only a few are in cultivation. There is a choice of propagation methods, all of equal convenience. They can be increased from seed sown in spring. Vegetatively they can either be divided in spring or raised from basal cuttings taken in spring from the young shoots. Plant out in a well-drained soil in full sun. (Seed available from some specialist commercial sources as well as HPS and other seed exchanges.)

Marsilea (Marsileaceae). Pepperwort, Water Clover. Aquatic ferns that can be only be grown in warmer areas. Increase is mainly by division or by cuttings taken from the rhizomes, both undertaken in spring. May also be increased from spore sown when fresh. (Spore difficult to obtain, but may possibly be available from pteridological societies.)

Marshallia (Compositae). A small genus of which *M. grandiflora*, Barbara's Buttons, is the main species grown. They can be grown from seed sown in autumn or spring or from division carried out in spring. Plant out in a moist soil in either sun or a light shade. (Seed not easily available in the UK but more generally obtainable in the USA.)

Matricaria (Compositae). Although some species of this genus have been removed, a few garden-worthy plants remain, *M. recutita* (syn. *M. chamomilla*), being the main one. These can be increased by taking cuttings of side shoots in autumn or by division in autumn or spring. They also come readily from seed and several varieties, although perennial, are offered as half-hardy annuals. Plant out in any ordinary soil in full sun. (Seed available from most merchants and seed exchanges.)

Matteuccia (Aspidiaceae). Ostrich Fern. Spreading, even invasive, plants easily propagated by dividing off the young plants that are formed, often at a distance, from the parent. They can also be increased by sowing the fresh spore. Plant out in a moist, humus-rich soil in light shade. (Spore may be available from pteridological societies' exchanges.)

Matthiola (Cruciferae). Stocks. A genus of mainly annual or biennial species but it does contain some perennials, although they are often short-lived. All can be increased from seed sown fresh or in spring. Some of the perennials can be divided in spring, in particular the delightful *M. fruticulosa valesiaca*, which has a running habit. Plant out in a fertile, well-drained soil in a sunny position. (Seed of non-perennials generally available from seed merchants but the perennials mainly restricted to the seed exchanges.)

Meconopsis (Papaveraceae). Blue Poppies. There are about 45 species of *Meconopsis* and quite a number of hybrids and other forms, but apart from *M. betonicifolia* not many are grown except by devotees. Although often considered perennial many are monocarpic for example, *MM. horridula, napaulensis, regia* and *dhwojii*. Many others act as if they were biennial and die out after flowering for example, *M. punicea*. Most can be propagated from seed. Some, *MM. betonicifolia, grandis, quintuplinervia, punicea* and *simplicifolia* for example, should be sown fresh, overwintering any seedlings that appear in frost-free frames. Others should be stored over winter in cool, dry conditions and sown in spring in a peat-based compost in gentle heat, not exceeding 20°C (68°F). Meconopsis need light for germination so only give the pots of seed the thinnest of dustings of compost. The compost must be kept moist. Sphagnum can be used in the compost mix (see p. 43). Quite a number self-sow and produce quantities of offspring if the conditions are right. A few truly perennial species (e.g. *MM. quintuplinervia* and *grandis*) and many of the hybrids need to be increased vegetatively by careful division in spring. Plant out in a cool position in moist, humus-rich soil and in light shade. (Seed available from some seed merchants but the widest selection comes from the seed exchanges, especially the alpine ones. Seed-collecting expeditions are also a good source of supply.)

Medicago (Leguminosae). Lucerne, Medick. A genus of annuals and perennials mainly grown in the wild-flower garden or meadows. Easily grown from seed sown in spring. Most will self-sow. Plant out in any fertile soil in full sun. (Seed not generally available except from merchants specializing in wild-flower seed.)

Meehania (Labiatae). Japanese Dead Nettle, Meehan's Mint. A small genus of woodland plants easily propagated by dividing the stoloniferous rootstock or by taking basal cuttings from the young shoots, both in spring. They can also be increased from seed, if you can find it, sown in spring. Plant out in a moisture-retentive soil in light shade. (Seed not generally available but more likely to be found in the USA.)

Megacarpaea (Cruciferae). A small genus of perennials of which *M. polyandra* is the most commonly grown. Easily increased from seed sown in spring. Plant out in light, well-drained soil in a sunny position. (Seed and plants difficult to find but the former has been offered in the past by some alpine seed exchanges.)

Melanthium (Melanthiaceae/Liliaceae). A small genus of four species related to *Veratrum*. The only way to increase these plants is by sowing the seed as fresh as possible. Germination takes place the following spring and takes four to five years to reach flowering size. Plant out in a humus-rich soil in part shade or full sun. (The only source of seed seems the occasional appearance in alpine seed exchange lists, especially that of the American Rock Garden Society.)

Melianthus (Melianthaceae). Honeybush. Perennials treated as annuals in colder regions. *M. major* is the main species grown outside. The easiest method of increase is from seed sown in spring under gentle heat. They can also be increased vegetatively by careful division in spring or by summer cuttings. Plant out in a fertile soil in full sun. (Seed available from most seed merchants and seed exchanges.)

Melica (Gramineae). Melick. A large family of grasses easily increased by either dividing in late spring or by sowing seed in spring. Plant out in any fertile soil in either sun or light shade. (Seed not available from commercial sources, except some wild-flower suppliers, but available from HPS and other seed exchanges.)

Melissa (Labiatae). Balm, Lemon Balm. A small genus of which only *M. officinalis* is in general cultivation. Can be grown from seed sown in the spring. Even the golden variegated form *M. o.* 'Aurea' should produce a large percentage of true seedlings. Self-sows. Clumps can also be easily divided in either autumn or spring. Both the foregoing methods are easy and successful but if necessary *Melissa* can also be increased from basal cuttings taken from the young growth in spring. Plant out in any good garden soil, preferably in sun but will take light shade. (Seed not generally available except from those merchants who specialize in wild-flowers or herbs. Also available from HPS and other seed exchanges.)

Melittis (Labiatae). Bastard Balm. A single species (*M. melissophyllum*) genus. The easiest method of increase is by division of the clump in autumn or spring. Basal cuttings can be taken in spring. It can equally be grown from seed sown in spring. Plant out in a woodland soil in light shade. (Seed not generally available from commercial sources but occasionally occurs in seed exchanges.)

Mentha (Labiatae). Mints. A genus of herbs mainly used for culinary purposes. Most are invasive, which means that the easiest method of propagation is by simple division. As anyone who has accidentally left a small piece of root in the ground knows, they will also come from root cuttings taken at any time. Not that it is necessary with the above methods being so easy, but it is also possible to take basal cuttings from the young growth in spring. While it is essential to increase any named forms vegetatively, species can be increased from seed sown in spring. Plant out in any fertile soil in full sun or even light shade. (Seed available from some specialist seed suppliers including wild-flower suppliers. Also available from some seed exchanges.)

Menyanthes (Menyanthaceae). Bog Bean, Buckbean, Marsh Trefoil. A one-species genus consisting of *M. trifoliata*. Can easily be propagated by taking cuttings during the summer from the rhizomes and keeping them in a wet compost. No real need to grow from seed but it is possible if sown in spring in a soil-less compost and kept moist. Plant out in shallow water in spring. (Seed not commonly available but can be found in some commercial outlets, especially those dealing with wild flowers.)

Mercurialis (Euphorbiaceae). Dog's Mercury. A small genus of which one, *M. perennis*, is sometimes grown in a wild-flower or woodland garden, although it is usually considered a weed by most gardeners. It is easily propagated by dividing up the invasive rootstock. It can also be grown from freshly sown seed. Plant out in a moist woodland soil in light shade. (Seed available commercially from seed merchants specializing in wild flowers. Not usually available from seed exchanges.)

Mertensia (Boraginaceae). Bluebells, Virginian Cowslip. The easiest method of increase is by division during autumn or spring. To keep the plants healthy, they should be regularly divided every three or four years. Those with thick fleshy roots can be propagated by taking root cuttings in winter. They will all also come readily from seed either sown fresh or in spring. If they are unlikely to experience frosts, then pre-chilling in a domestic refrigerator may be beneficial. Some, such as *M. virginica*, will self-sow, producing enough seedlings for most uses. Plant out larger species in humus-rich soil in light shade or full sun if soil is not too dry. The smaller and alpine plants need a well-drained soil in full sun. (Seed not generally available from seed merchants but can be found in HPS and other seed exchanges.)

Meum (Umbelliferae). Bald Money, Spignel. A small genus of two species of which *M. athamanticum* is the one generally seen in cultivation. The easiest method of increase is from seed sown preferably fresh, or in spring. Alternatively, if plants are available they can be carefully divided in either autumn or spring, but this method is not as productive as that from sown seed. Plant out in any fertile soil in full sun. (Seed not generally available from commercial sources but can be found in HPS and other seed exchange lists.)

Michauxia (Campanulaceae). A small genus of bell-flowers that are biennials and can therefore only be increased from seed sown either fresh or in spring. Seed can be sown directly into the soil in late spring. Plant out in a well-drained, sheltered position in full sun. (At least one commercial seed merchant supplies seed but they can also be found in HPS and other seed exchanges. Good seed has recently been brought in by seed collecting expeditions.)

Milium (Gramineae). Millet. A small genus of grasses of which M. *effusum*, particularly in its form *aureum*, Bowles' Golden Grass, is the only one in general cultivation. The tufted clumps can easily be divided in late spring. The golden form will also come true from seed, which should be sown in spring. It also self-sows, which generally supplies sufficient seedlings for most uses. Plant out in any fertile soil in a light shade. (Seed available from some specialist commercial sources, as well as seed exchanges.)

Milligania (Asparagaceae/Liliaceae). A genus of four species endemic to Tasmania of which one, M. *longifolia*, is occasionally found in cultivation. They can be propagated by dividing up the leafy clumps or sowing seed in spring. Plant out in a humus-rich soil in full sun. (Seed not generally available but occasionally may be obtained from seed collecting expeditions to Tasmania.)

Mimulus (Scrophulariaceae). Monkey Flower, Musk. A large genus of about 150 species that can be propagated in a number of ways. Most will come readily from seed sown in spring, especially if placed in gentle heat. For early flowering, seed can be sown in autumn and overwintered under glass. Mimulus are promiscuous and great variation is obtained in plants raised from seed. Some will readily self-sow. They can also be increased vegetatively either by division in spring or from cuttings taken in late spring or summer. M. *gemmiparus* is sterile and can only be reproduced vegetatively by gemmules (specialized buds in the axils of the leaves). Many are short-lived and also prone to cold winters, so they should be propagated regularly, and overwintered, to ensure survival of the stock. Plant out in moisture-retentive or moist soil in full sun, or, if necessary, light shade. (Seed available from most seed merchants, but rarer species mainly available from seed exchanges and collecting trips.)

Mindium (Campanulaceae). See **Michauxia**

Mirabilis (Nyctaginaceae). Four O'Clocks, Umbrella Worts. Tuberous plants treated as annuals in colder areas. The tubers can be divided either when lifted in autumn for overwintering, or in spring if left in the ground. They can also be grown from seed sown in spring. Plant out in any fertile soil in full sun. (Seed available from the more specialist commercial sources and more prevalent in the USA. Also available from HPS and other seed exchanges.)

Miscanthus (Gramineae). A genus of about 20 species of which MM. *floridulus*, *sacchariflorus* and *sinensis*, plus all their varieties, are those most frequently met in gardens, although others are becoming available. All are increased by the division in spring of the slowly increasing clumps. Well-established clumps might be difficult to divide without a great deal of force. Regularly divided clumps are easier to deal with. The species can be increased from seed sown in spring. Plant out in a fertile soil, preferably in full sun. (Seed available from specialist commercial sources and seed exchanges.)

Molinia (Gramineae). Moor Grass. A small genus of grasses usually propagated by simple division during the spring. If necessary, species can be grown from seed sown in the spring. (Seed not generally available but may be obtained from commercial sources specializing in wild flowers. Plants readily available.)

Molopospermum (Umbelliferae). Striped Hemlock. A single species genus represented by M. *peloponnesiacum*. Like most umbellifers it is easily increased

143

from freshly-sown seed. Plant out in a well-drained, fertile soil in full sun. (Neither seed nor plants are easy to find but the former occasionally occurs in alpine seed exchanges.)

Moltkia (Boraginaceae). A small genus of perennials and subshrubs. They can all be easily increased by taking cuttings during the summer. Some, in particular the perennial forms such as *M. doerfleri*, can also be increased by division. Most can also be grown from seed sown in the spring. Plant out in a well-drained, fertile soil in a sunny position. (Seed available from the more specialist commercial sources and alpine seed exchanges.)

Monarda (Labiatae). Bee Balm, Bergamot, Oswego Tea. Very readily increased by dividing the spreading (sometimes invasive) rootstock in either autumn or spring. They can also be raised vegetatively by taking basal cuttings in spring. Although not normally necessary as the other methods are so successful, they can also be raised from seed sown in spring, although there is little chance of colours coming true. Seed can be sown in open ground in late spring. Plant out in a moisture-retentive soil in full sun. (Seed available from commercial sources and from HPS and other seed exchanges.)

Monardella (Labiatae). A smaller form of the previous genus. They can be increased either by dividing the creeping rootstock or sowing seed in spring. Plant out in a well-drained soil in a warm, sunny position. (Seed not generally available from commercial sources but can be found in most seed exchanges, especially the alpine ones.)

Moraea (Iridaceae). Butterfly Irises. Cormous plants for warmer areas. They can be increased by division of the offsets in autumn or from seed sown in spring. Plant out in a moisture-retentive soil in a warm, sunny position. (Seed available from the more specialist commercial sources and from seed exchanges.)

Morina (Morinaceae). A genus of about 17 species of which a few are in cultivation, *M. longifolia* being the most commonly met. The easiest method of increase is from seed preferably sown fresh in autumn, but it can also be sown in spring if necessary. Do not plant out the resulting seedlings until they are well established, preferably in their second year. Some species can also be carefully divided immediately after flowering or in spring. Some are also said to come from root cuttings taken in the winter but, although leaves may appear, it can take a long time before roots are established. Plant out in a well-drained but moisture-retentive soil in full sun or a light shade. (Seed available from some specialist commercial sources and from all seed exchanges.)

Muhlembergia (Gramineae). A large genus of grasses of which one, *M. mexicana*, is hardy enough to be grown in Britain and most of the USA as a woodland plant. It can be easily grown from seed sown under gentle heat or by dividing the loose clumps in spring. Plant out in any good moisture-retentive soil in light shade or part sun. (Seed and plants generally difficult to obtain in the UK, easier in the USA.)

Mukdenia (Saxifragaceae). A monotypic genus represented by *M. rossii* (previously *Aceriphyllum rossii*), a creeping woodland plant easily divided in autumn or spring. It can also be grown from seed, but availability of seed may be limited as the plants are self-sterile. Seed should be sown fresh or in spring. Plant out in a woodland-type soil in light shade. (Seed not commercially available and only occasionally occurs in seed exchange lists. Plants available.)

Muscari (Hyacinthaceae/Liliaceae). Grape Hyacinths. A medium sized genus of 50 species of bulbous plants that produce offsets that can easily be divided after flowering or in autumn. Copious seed is produced and this can be sown fresh or in spring. Do not plant out resulting seedlings until their second year. Some species will self-sow, almost invasively. Plant out in any fertile soil in full sun or light shade. (Seed available from specialist commercial sources and most seed exchanges, especially alpine ones.)

Myosotidium (Boraginaceae). Chatham Island Forget-me-not, New Zealand Forget-me-not. A single species genus (closely allied to the next genus) consisting of *M. hortensia*, which is only possible to overwinter in warmer regions. The main means of increase is from seed sown fresh, or germination may be irregular. Do not plant out until at least its second year. Plant out in a cool sheltered spot in a moisture-retentive soil. (Seed offered by one specialist seed merchant and by HPS and other seed exchanges.)

Myosotis (Boraginaceae). Forget-me-nots. A genus of about 50 annual, biennial and perennial species. The most obvious method of increase, especially for the annuals and biennials, is from seed. Many self-sow copiously, indeed so much so that after the initial sowing they are self-perpetuating. Seed can be sown direct in the soil in late spring. In spite of their prolific tendency to self-sow the seed appears to germinate best in total darkness. They can be sown in autumn for early flowering or in spring. Many of the perennials can also be divided, either in autumn or in spring. Cuttings can also be taken in spring. Plant out in any fertile soil in full sun. (Seed generally available from commercial sources, the more specialized species from seed exchanges.)

Myriophyllum (Haloragiedaceae). Water Milfoils. A medium-sized genus of water plants, many totally submerged. They can most easily be increased by taking cuttings during the growing season. Place cuttings in a wet compost or even direct into the mud of a pool. Late cuttings can be overwintered under frost-free glass in a moist compost. Plant out in the bottom of a pond, weighing down if necessary. (Plants commercially available.)

Myrrhis (Umbelliferae). Sweet Cicely. A single species genus consisting of *M. odorata*. The most common method of increase is from seed sown preferably fresh or in spring. This can also be sown in the open ground in late spring. It will self-sow but any required seedlings should be moved when they are still young as the plants have large tap roots. Do not leave pot-grown plants in pots too long for the same reason. It is also possible to increase by very careful division of the roots in autumn or spring. Plant out in any fertile soil in light shade or full sun. (Seed is generally available from seed merchants or any of the seed exchanges.)

Narcissus (Amaryllidaceae). Daffodils. A bulbous genus of small species and large hybrids. The species can all be grown from the offsets that are usually produced. Division can be after flowering or in early autumn. They can also be grown from seed, preferably sown fresh, or in spring if necessary. Do not plant out seedlings until large enough, usually in their second or even third year. The larger hybrids will only come true if they are increased vegetatively. This usually means splitting off the offsets after flowering or in early autumn. Clumps of both should be regularly split up every three to four years. Rare bulbs can be multiplied quickly by twin scaling (see p. 69). Plant out in a fertile soil in full sun or light shade. (Seed offered by some seed merchants but the main source is seed exchanges, especially the alpine ones and the RHS Lily Group.)

Nardus (Gramineae). Mat Grass. A single species genus consisting of *N. stricta*. Along with most grasses it can either be increased by division in spring or from seed sown at the same time of year. Plant out in any fertile soil in full sun. (Seed not generally available but can be found in the catalogues of some wild-flower specialists.)

Narthecium (Liliaceae). Bog Asphodel, Yellow Grass. A small genus of creeping plants for the bog garden, which can easily be propagated by division in spring. They can also be increased from seed sown fresh or in spring. Keep young plants and seed compost moist. Plant out in a moist or boggy ground in full sun. (Seed available from specialist commercial sources, especially those dealing in wild flowers. Occasionally available from some seed exchanges, especially alpine ones.)

Nectaroscordum (Alliaceae/Liliaceae). Once part of *Allium*, this one or two species genus (depending on which taxonomist you follow) is very closely allied to the onions and can be propagated in the same way. They can easily be grown from seed sown either fresh or in spring. Seedlings come perhaps too easily in this genus as they tend to self-sow everywhere, producing deep-rooted bulbs often in the middle of other plants, making them difficult to eradicate. These seedlings supply more than enough surplus plants for most needs. They can also be increased by removing the offsets produced around the parent bulb. Plant out in any fertile garden soil that is not too moist and in either a sunny position or in light shade. (Seed available from some specialist commercial sources and all seed exchanges.)

Nelumbo (Nelumbonaceae). Lotus. Pond lilies for warmer areas. The easiest method of increase is by splitting off parts of the rhizomatous rootstock, each with a bud, and potting up in a wet soil-less compost. They can also be increased from seed, which may need scarification either with sand, knife or file. It should be sown in spring in gentle heat. Keep compost moist. Young seedlings and divisions should be kept under water with the leaves just floating, gradually increasing the depth as the plants grow. Plant out in warm weather in late spring in a warm sunny pool, either direct in the mud or in baskets. (Seed not generally available in the UK, although more widespread in the USA. Plants are available.)

Nepeta (Labiatae). Catmint. A large genus of some 250 species. On the whole they are very easy to increase by a variety of methods. The plants can be divided without much difficulty, preferably in spring but also in autumn. Another vegetative method is to take basal cuttings from the young shoots in spring. They can also be grown from seed although some named forms will not come true. Seed can be sown directly into the open ground if necessary. Many will self-sow, providing a ready source of young plants. Plant out in a fertile, well-drained soil in full sun, although *N. govaniana* will tolerate some shade. (Seed available from some seed merchants as well as HPS and other seed exchanges.)

Nephrophyllidium (Gentianaceae). Deer Cabbage. A single species genus consisting of *N. crista-galli*. A clump-forming plant easily divided in spring. It can also be grown from seed sown in spring. Plant out in a moist, even boggy, soil. (Seed not very easy to find.)

Nerine (Amarydillaceae). A bulbous genus that produces offsets easily divided after flowering. A large number of plants can be created by scaling in the same way as for lilies. They can also be grown from freshly-sown seed. Although germination is often quick (sometimes before the seed leaves the seedhead!) it takes some years for the large species to reach flowering size. Only lightly cover the seed. Do not plant out until they have reached a reasonable size. Plant out in well-drained but humus-rich soil in a warm, sunny position. Bulbs should have the their tips showing above the soil. (Seed not generally available from commercial growers but can be found in seed exchanges, particularly alpine ones and the RHS Lily Group.)

Nicotiana (Solanaceae). Tobacco plants. A genus of about 70 species of annual and perennial plants. Many of the perennials are tender and are treated as annuals in colder regions, although the rootstock will persist below ground. They are all easily propagated from seed, which is produced in copious quantities. Only cover the seed with a very thin layer of compost as light is required for germination. Many will self-sow. Plant out in a well-drained, but moisture-retentive, soil in full sun. (Seed generally available from most seed merchants, particularly the 'annual' forms. Rarer species available from seed exchanges.)

Nierembergia (Solanaceae). Cupflower. Perennial herbs and subshrubs often treated as annuals in colder districts. Easily propagated by taking cuttings in spring, often rooted portions of stem can be directly potted up. They can also be divided in spring. Alternatively, they can be grown from seed sown in the spring under gentle heat. If treated as annuals sow under glass in gentle heat in mid-winter. Plant out in fertile, well-drained soil in full sun. (Seed available from some specialist commercial sources and some seed exchanges.)

Nigella (Ranunculaceae). Love-in-a-mist. A small genus of annual plants included here as they are a constituent part of many herbaceous borders. Being annual they can only be grown from seed, which can be sown in pots, or better still, scattered where they are to grow, either in autumn or spring. Once established they will self-sow. They come so readily from direct soil-sowings that there is rarely any need to sow in pots. Sow in any garden soil, in full sun. (Seed available both commercially and from seed exchanges.)

Nipponanthemum (Compositae). See **Chrysanthemum**

Nomocharis (Liliaceae). Closely related to the lily these bulbous plants can be propagated in the same manner. Seed can be sown either fresh or in spring. Plants should not be planted out too soon, preferably during the spring of their second year. They need not be pricked out but sown thinly in a pan and the whole lot planted out without disturbance. Seedlings can take several years to reach flowering size. The bulbs consist of a few scales, which can be used for increase in the same manner as for lilies (see p. 67). Plant out in a well-drained but moisture-retentive soil in a cool, moist atmosphere as found in West Scotland. (Seed not generally available commercially but can be found in seed exchanges, especially alpine ones and the RHS Lily Group.)

Notholirion (Liliaceae). Another genus closely related to *Lilium* and propagated and treated in the same manner as *Nomocharis*. The main bulb dies after flowering leaving innumerable rice grains to grow on into new bulbs. These can take several years to reach flowering size. (Seed availability as for *Nomocharis*.)

Nothoscordum (Alliaceae/Liliaceae). A medium-sized genus of bulbs related to the onions. Some, *N. gracile* for example, are terribly invasive, producing masses of bulblets that manage to get everywhere. Splitting up the clumps of bulblets or offsets while dormant (the time of which varies from species to species) is the easiest method of propagation of all species. They can also be readily increased from seed sown fresh or in spring. Plant out in a well-drained soil in full sun. (Seed available from some specialist seed firms and from seed exchanges.)

Nuphar (Nymphaeaceae). Brandy Bottle, Spatterdock, Yellow Pond Lilies. A genus of up to 25 pond lilies best propagated by dividing the spreading rhizomes in late spring and replanting either directly back in the pool or in compost kept below water. Plant out either directly into rich soil at the bottom of a pond, anchoring down the plants if necessary, or in lattice pots. Place in a warm position in full sun. (Plants commercially available.)

Nymphaea (Nymphaeaceae). Water Lilies. The hardy species are rhizomatous and can be easily propagated by division, planting directly back into the pool or by placing in a pot of compost kept below water. Some of the more tender forms are viviparous and can be propagated by placing leaves carrying adventitious buds on pots of wet compost. These forms can also be increased by sowing fresh seed on wet compost, putting the seedlings into progressively deeper water. Plant out directly into rich soil in the bottom of the pool, anchoring plants down if necessary, or plant in baskets. They should be in a warm, sunny position. (Seed not readily available but some specialist commercial firms stock a few.)

Nymphoides (Menyanthaceae). Water Fringe. Mainly tender annual and perennial water plants but one, *N. peltata*, is grown in cooler areas. Propagation is carried out vegetatively and can be easily achieved by separating the rooted runners from the parent plants. Plant out direct into the bottom of the pond or into pots kept below water. (Plants commercially available.)

Oaksiella (Convallariaceae/Liliaceae). See **Uvularia**

Oenothera (Onagraceae). Evening Primroses. A large genus of which quite a number are in cultivation. The principle method of increase is from seed sown in spring, which tends to be copiously produced by most species. Seed can also be sown in the open ground in spring. Many will in fact self-sow, providing enough seedlings for most uses. The hard oenothera seed pods are very difficult to open but soaking in water overnight will readily allow the seed to be extracted. The perennial species can also be increased vegetatively by division of the running rootstock in spring. Others, for example *O. missouriensis*, can have cuttings taken from their underground stems, which are extended annually from the central woody rootstock. Cuttings can also be taken from young basal shoots in spring. Alternatively, some, for example *O. glaber*, can be increased from stem cuttings taken in early summer. Sections of the flowering stem, each containing a leaf, are placed in compost in a pot or tray, with the leaf just resting on the surface. Young plants form at the nodes. Most evening primroses are short lived and need regular propagation. Plant out in a well-drained soil in full sun. (Seed available from commercial seed merchants and most seed exchanges.)

Omphalodes (Boraginaceae). Creeping Forget-me-not, Navelworts. A medium-sized genus of annual and perennial plants. The annuals, of course, need to be increased from seed and readily come from both autumn- and spring-sown seed. Most will self-sow, providing a ready supply of seedlings. Perennials can also be grown from seed but many have a creeping rootstock easily divided preferably in autumn or, if necessary, in spring, to provide more plants. Most annual species and some perennials prefer a well-drained soil in full sun. The woodland perennials, such as *O. verna* or *O. cappadocica*, need to be planted out in a moisture-retentive soil in light shade. (Seed available from some commercial firms and most seed exchanges.)

Omphalogramma (Primulaceae). A small genus of Chinese perennial plants. They are clump forming and the best method of propagation is by division of these clumps in the spring, after flowering, or later in the autumn. They can also be grown from freshly-sown seed but this is not very easy to obtain. Plant out in a woodland-type soil in light shade. (Seed rarely available from either commercial sources or seed exchanges, but plants occasionally obtainable.)

Onoclea (Aspleniaceae). Sensitive Fern. A single-species genus consisting of *O. sensibilis*. As with most ferns, this one can be either divided in spring or grown from spore sown when fresh. (Spore may be available from pteridological societies. Plants generally available.)

Ononis (Leguminosae). Rest Harrow. A large genus of annuals, biennials and perennials, some of which are of shrubby growth. All can be sown from seed sown fresh or in spring. Best grown in pots but if sown in open ground, any transplanting should be undertaken when they are still small as they dislike being moved. The shrubby forms come quite easily from cuttings taken in spring or late summer. Again, plant out before the root gets too big. Plant out in any fertile, well-drained soil in full sun. (Seed available from at least one specialist seed merchant and possibly also others specializing in wild flowers. Seed generally available from most seed exchanges.)

Onopordum (Compositae). Cotton Thistle, Scotch Thistle. A genus of biennials that often make an appearance in an herbaceous border. They are simply grown from seed in spring either in pots or directly into the ground. In either case light seems to be beneficial to germination, so do not cover too deeply. Self-sowing will sometimes provide enough seedlings for most use; transplant when plants are still quite small. Wear leather gloves when collecting seed. Plant out in a well-drained soil in full sun. (Seed widely available from seed merchants and seed exchanges.)

Onosma (Boraginaceae). A large genus of plants of which quite a number are suitable for a large rock garden or front of border position. Propagation is most easily carried out by sowing seed in spring. Copious seed is produced and many will self-sow providing sufficient seedlings for most uses. They can also be increased vegetatively by taking cuttings in spring. Plant out in a well-drained soil in full sun. (Seed available from at least one seed merchant. A greater range is offered by seed exchanges, particularly the alpine ones.)

Ophiopogon (Convallariaceae/Liliaceae). Lilyturf. These plants divide easily in the spring. The points where they will divide can be clearly seen and felt. They should be split using fingers and thumbs, pulling and shaking the divisions apart. The nodules on the roots may sometimes make the entanglement of roots difficult to separate, doing it in a bucket of water will help. Be warned that *O. japonicum* puts out stoloniferous roots that closely resemble couch grass and can cause panic when first spotted. The tips turn up some way from the parent producing new plants that can easily be split off. Plants need regular splitting every three or four years to keep in prime condition. Can also be grown from seed sown in spring although named forms should be vegetatively propagated. *O. planiscapus nigrescens* will produce a number of black seedlings as well as some that have reverted back to the green of the species. Plant out in any fertile soil in part shade or full sun. (Seed not generally available from commercial sources but can be obtained from most seed exchanges.)

Ophrys (Orchidaceae). Bee Orchids. A very difficult genus to cultivate out of doors. Better chances of success will be had by growing in pots. They are equally difficult to propagate. In cultivation increase from seed is virtually impossible and if attempted fresh seed must be used. If seed is available it might be worth scattering it on a lawn in the hope that one may germinate, but care should be taken in mowing during the growing season or treating the lawn subsequently with chemicals as these will soon kill off any plants that are becoming established. With skill they can be increased vegetatively if you are lucky enough to have plants that form tuberous offsets. As the flowers begin to shrivel remove the new tuber that is formed on the old plant. Repot the latter keeping it in growth for as long as possible, preventing it from forming seed. The new tuber should be potted up and left dormant, without water, until it is time for normal growth to resume. Do *not* dig up plants in the wild in an attempt to establish them. If an attempt is made to grow these outside, a well-drained, preferably alkaline soil in full sun is needed. (Seed sometimes seen in seed exchanges lists but their viability is extremely doubtful.)

Orchis (Orchidaceae). A number of the species have been moved out of this genus and placed in *Dactylorhiza*. Those remaining are not so easy to cultivate and propagate as those that have departed so if the choice is not critical go for *Dactylorhiza*. *Orchis* are almost as difficult to establish in cultivation, in particular outside, and to propagate as the *Ophrys*. The methods and comments under that entry equally apply to this.

Origanum (Labiatae). Marjoram, Oregano. A genus of herbs and decorative plants for the border and rock garden. The easiest method of increase is by taking basal cuttings in spring or more mature cuttings in summer. Cuttings can be prone to rotting so dip in or spray with a fungicide. Alternatively, some plants can be divided in spring. Seed is a reasonable alternative, except for some reason it is not very easy to come by, which is surprising as some plants, such as *O. laevigatum*, are quite happy to self sow in a mild way. Named forms must be increased vegetatively. Plant out in well-drained soil in full sun. (Seed occasionally found in commercial catalogues and some seed exchanges, mainly the alpine ones.)

Ornithogalum (Hyacinthaceae/Liliaceae). Star-of-Bethlehem. A large genus of bulbous plants generally not too difficult to propagate, indeed some, such as *O. umbellatum*, can become quite invasive. Most produce numerous offsets and these can easily be divided at any time during dormancy. All clumps should be divided every three or four years as they can become congested and cease flowering. They can also be grown from seed sown either fresh or in spring. It is best to leave young seedlings in their pots until they are large enough to plant out, which is not before their second year. Plant out in a fertile well-drained soil in a sunny position. (Seed available from at least one commercial source and from most seed exchanges, especially the alpine ones.)

Orobanche (Orobanchaceae). Broomrapes. A large genus of parasites often very difficult to propagate. The only way of succeeding is to sow the seed round the roots of one of the known host plants either in a pot or in the open ground, preferably while the seed is still fresh. Success is not always assured but broomrapes are usually generous in the amount of seed they produce, so plenty can be sown. *O. hederae* will readily germinate (even old seed) when spread around the roots of ivy (*Hedera helix*). Careful study must be made of the host plants for each individual species. Plant out in soil and position relevant to the host, which must be included in the planting. Once established, more success is likely and it may be possible to transplant the parasite along with its host. (Seed generally not available although *O. hederae* is offered by one seed merchant and quite a number of other species have been offered in the past by alpine seed exchanges.)

Orontium (Araceae). Golden Club, Water Dock. Monospecific aquatic genus of which *O. aquaticum* is the only species. Can be propagated from the seed, which must be freshly collected, and sown in compost kept permanently wet. It will also self-sow, providing quite a number of seedlings. It is also possible to divide the rhizomes in spring, planting either directly back into the pool or in pots of compost kept under water. Plant out in the bottom of the pool either directly or in baskets in a sunny position. (Because of the necessity to have fresh seed, it is not available from either commercial or seed exchange sources. Plants, however, are available.)

Orostachys (Crassulaceae). A small genus of about 20 species of succulent plants only hardy in the warmer areas. They can easily be increased by removing the offsets produced round the main rosette. They can also be grown from seed although this is not easy to find. Plant out in a well-drained soil in full sun. (Seed not generally available although it occasionally occurs in alpine seed exchanges.)

Orthrosanthus (Iridaceae). Morning Flag, Morning Flower. A small genus of tender species that can only be grown outside in warmer areas. It is very closely related to *Sisyrinchium* and, like that genus, can easily be increased by division of the tufted rootstock in spring. They can also be readily increased from seed sown in spring under gentle heat. Plant out in a moisture-retentive soil in light shade. (Seed not generally available from commercial sources but occasionally obtainable from HPS and alpine seed exchanges.)

Osmunda (Osmundaceae). Royal Fern. A genus of about ten species of which *O. regalis* is the best known, although several others are becoming available. As with most ferns, they can either be divided in spring or grown from spores. The latter should be sown as fresh as possible as they rapidly lose viability, usually within three days. Plant out in a moist, humus-rich soil in light shade. (Spores have such a short viability that they can only really be obtained direct from the plant. Plants, however, are available.)

Osteospermum (Compositae). Star of the Veldt. A genus of 70 species that are mainly tender except in warmer areas; they can be overwintered in colder areas as cuttings. The most common method of increase is from cuttings taken at any time during the growing season. The named forms are best treated in this fashion. The plants are clump forming and can easily be divided or root-bearing cuttings taken, both in spring although the cuttings can be taken in autumn and overwintered under glass. They can also be sown from seed in spring, preferably under gentle heat. Do not cover too deeply as light is beneficial for germination. The annuals sold by most seed merchants are best treated this way. Plant out in a well-drained soil in full sun. (Seed available from commercial sources, especially annual seed; others are obtainable from seed exchanges.)

Ostrowskia (Campanulaceae). A single species genus, namely O. *magnifica*. There are two ways of propagating this magnificent plant. Probably the easiest is from seed that should be sown preferably fresh or, if necessary, in spring. The seedlings should be planted out as soon as possible as the deep-rooted plants resent disturbance. They take up to four years to reach flowering size. They can also be increased from root cuttings taken during the winter months. These will flower in a shorter time. Plant out in a deep, rich soil in a warm, sunny position. (Seed rarely offered commercially but does occasionally occur in seed exchanges. Some nurseries specializing in Campanulaceae may be able to supply plants or seed.)

Ourisia (Scrophulariaceae). Although mainly considered for use in the rock garden, one or two (in particular OO. *macrophylla* and *macrocarpa*) are large enough for the border. Increase by dividing the mat-forming plants in spring, after they have finished flowering. They can also be increased from seed sown in spring. Plant out in a moisture-retentive soil in light shade or full sun. (Seed available from at least one commercial source and from seed exchanges, in particular alpine ones.)

Oxalis (Oxalidaceae). Wood Sorrel. A very large genus of over 800 species, consisting of low plants mainly grown in the rock garden, although some appear in borders (often uninvited) and one, O. *acetosella*, is frequently seen in woodland gardens. Some of those that are grown in borders are bulbous in character and several have the nasty habit of producing lots of offsets that are distributed far and wide at the slightest disturbance of the ground. O. *corymbosa* is a particular problematic plant in this respect. Not all oxalis are invasive and a number can be increased without fear of filling the garden with them. Other oxalis are rhizomatous and can become equally pestilent, O. *corniculata* being an example of this. But again there are many that are more restrained and can be safely increased by division of the rhizome. O. *acetellosa* is rhizomatous and can be a pest in the wrong place. It can easily be divided. Seed is also an option and should be sown in spring. Seed is difficult to collect as it is dispersed by an explosive mechanism. Plant out in a well-drained soil in full sun, except for the woodland species, which prefer a moisture-retentive soil in light shade. (Seed available from some commercial seed firms and most seed exchanges; the alpine ones providing the largest range.)

Oxtropis (Leguminosae). Locoweed. A large genus allied to *Astragalus*. Increased from seed sown in spring. Transplant the young plants as soon as possible to their final positions as their long tap roots resent disturbance. Plant out in a well-drained soil in a sunny position. (Seed not available from commercial sources but can be found in seed exchanges, especially alpine ones.)

Paeonia (Paeoniaceae). Peonies. A medium-sized genus of perennials and shrubby plants. The commonest method of increase is by division. Clean off soil and carefully divide the plant, making certain that each division has one to several eyes, depending on the number of divisions it is intended to make. This should be done in autumn or early winter, preferably as early as possible. Divisions with more than one eye or bud can be cut up, in a form of root cutting, each bud having about 1.25 cm (½ in) of rootstock with it. The eyes can be 'sown' in open ground with the tip of the shoot just below the soil level. They should be left for two years before planting in their final positions. The thicker the rootstock the better. The species can also be grown from seed, which should be sown fresh in the autumn. If seed is allowed to dry out, germination will take a long time, often two or three years. Pots of ungerminated seed should not be thrown away for at least four years, keeping them moist all the time. Germination can be speeded up by one or two periods of pre-chilling, with a warm period between if two are used. Preferably sow only one seed per pot. Plant out in a humus-rich soil in autumn in a sunny position. (Some seed available from commercial sources but a wider range is to be had from seed exchanges.)

Paesia (Dennstaedtiaceae). A small genus of ferns of which *P. scaberula* is occasionally grown. It has a rhizomatous, creeping habit and so can easily be divided in spring. It can also be grown from spore sown fresh. Plant out in a woodland-type soil in light shade. (It is doubtful if spore are available but plants are commercially available.)

Pancratium (Amaryllidaceae). A small genus of bulbous plants for warmer areas. The bulbs slowly produce offsets, which can be divided when the plants are dormant. They can also be grown from seed sown in spring, and require a minimum night-time temperature of about 13°C (55°F). Keep seed pans under glass as the compost should not be allowed to get too wet until seedlings appear. Plant out in a free-draining soil in a warm sunny position. (Seed not available commercially but may be found in some seed exchanges, especially the alpine ones.)

Panicum (Gramineae). Panic Grass, Switch Grass. A large genus of grasses, a few of which are in cultivation. As with most grasses, these can be divided in spring or grown from seed sown at the same time of year. (At least one commercial source stocks some seed, but seed exchanges are a better bet.)

Papaver (Papaveraceae). Poppies. A large genus of annual and perennial plants, some of the latter short-lived. Many of the perennials are cultivars or hybrids and can only be increased vegetatively. Some can be divided but the general method of increase is by root cuttings taken in early winter and placed vertically in pots. These should be ready for planting out the following autumn. Cuttings can be extracted without disturbing the plants by digging down one side and removing a few roots. A cruder way of increase can be by digging out the bulk of the plant in autumn and transplanting it, at the same time leaving a number of severed roots in the ground, each of which will start a new plant. Annuals and species perennials can also be sown from seed, which is usually prolifically produced. This can be sown in autumn or spring, either in pans or, in spring, direct in their flowering position. Do not cover as light is beneficial for germination. Many are self-sowers; seedlings thus produced should be moved to their flowering positions at an early stage as poppies generally do not transplant very well. The best time for planting out is in autumn. Plant out in a well-drained soil in a sunny position. (A wide range of seed available from most commercial growers but the seed exchanges provide a better source for species.)

Paradisea (Asphodelaceae/Liliaceae). St Bruno's Lily. A two species genus. These clump-forming plants can be increased by division, preferably in autumn but also in spring if necessary. Alternatively, they can easily be grown from seed sown either in autumn or spring. Plant out in a well-drained soil in a sunny position. (Seed available from the specialist commercial merchants and most seed exchanges.)

Paris (Trilliaceae). A small genus of mainly woodlanders. They are rhizomatous plants and can be increased by careful division in autumn after the foliage has died down. Can also be grown from seed, preferably sown fresh, but are slow to germinate with the roots being formed before anything appears above ground. The plants take several years to reach flowering size. Plant out in a humus-rich soil in light shade. (Seed only sparingly available from specialist commercial sources but more readily so from HPS and alpine seed exchanges.)

Parnassia (Saxifragaceae). Grass-of-Parnassus. A medium-sized genus of plants that like a moist position, *P. palustris* being the commonest in cultivation. Propagation is from seed sown either in autumn or spring, keeping the seed pan moist. They can also be increased vegetatively by division in spring. Plant out in a moist, lime-free soil in sun or light shade. (Seed available from specialist commercial sources and most seed exchanges.)

Parochetus (Leguminosae). Shamrock Pea. A one-species genus, namely *P. communis*. This mat-forming plant is very easy to increase by dividing off rooted pieces in spring. As it is only marginally hardy it is worth overwintering potted-up rooted divisions. It will also come from seed sown in spring. Soaking the seed overnight in warm water is beneficial. Plant out in any good garden soil in a sunny position. (Seed not available commercially but can be found in seed exchanges.)

Patrinia (Valerianaceae). Rhizomatous or stoloniferous perennials that can be increased by division in autumn or early spring. They can also be grown from seed sown in spring. Plant out in a moisture-retentive, but well drained soil in a light shade. (Seed available from at least one specialist commercial source and from most seed exchanges.)

Pelargonium (Geraniaceae). A genus of somewhat tender species and hybrids of which the latter are particularly popular. The most common method of propagation is from cuttings taken at any time, but especially in autumn for over-wintering plants in colder areas. Cuttings can be taken from any part of the plant although tip cuttings generally make quicker and better plants. It has always, of course, been possible to grow species from seed, but it is now increasingly possible to grow the hybrids from seed. Seed should be sown in either autumn for early flowering or early spring for later flowering. They are best grown under glass in gentle heat of around 22°C (74°F). Light is not essential but speeds up germination, so only cover the seed with a thin layer of compost or fine grit. Plant out in a fertile but free-draining soil. (Seed of the hybrids are available from all commercial sources. Some of the species can be found in specialist commercial catalogues and seed exchanges.)

Peltandra (Araceae). Arrow Arum. A small genus of bog-loving plants. The easiest way of increase is by dividing the rhizomes in early spring. They can be planted directly back into the ground or potted up; in the latter case the pots should be kept wet. They can also be grown from seed sown fresh. Again, the seed pots should be constantly kept wet. Plant out in a wet, even boggy, soil near water in sun or part shade. (Seed not generally available although it does occasionally occur in seed exchanges. Plants, however, are available.)

Peltiphyllum (Saxifragaceae). See **Darmera**

Pennisetum (Gramineae). Fountain Grass. A moderately large genus of grasses. The easiest method of propagation for the perennials is by making divisions in spring. Both annuals and perennials can also be grown from seed sown in spring, preferably under glass as the seedlings are not fully hardy. Plant out in a well-drained soil in full sun. (Some seed available from commercial sources including those specializing in wild flowers. It can also be found in seed exchanges.)

Penstemon (Scrophulariaceae). A large genus of plants suitable for both the herbaceous border and the rock garden. The easiest method of increase is by taking cuttings at any time during the growing season, although it is often best to take some in autumn in order to overwinter them in case of losses, especially in colder areas. Penstemons are one of the easiest of plants to root and an ideal plant for beginners to acquaint themselves with the techniques of taking cuttings. The species can also be easily raised from seed sown in autumn or spring, the former being particularly important for plants needed for bedding schemes. Some species will self-sow, providing sufficient seedlings for most purposes, although they can cross and produce hybrids. Cultivars, if they do provide seed, are unlikely to come true. Plant out in a fertile, well-drained soil in full sun. (Seed available from some commercial seed merchants and from seed exchanges, especially alpine ones.)

Pentaglottis (Boraginaceae). A single species genus, namely *P. sempervirens*. Like most of the borage family this will come readily from seed sown in spring. Plant out in a moisture-retentive soil in light shade. (Seed not generally available from commercial sources, although it may appear in wild-flower catalogues. It does, however, occur in HPS and other seed exchange lists.)

Perezia (Compositae). A medium-sized genus of annuals and perennials. The latter can be propagated by dividing in autumn or spring, or by taking basal cuttings in spring. Both annuals and perennials can be increased from seed sown preferably fresh or in spring if necessary. Plant out in a well-drained soil in full sun. (Seed not available from commercial sources but can be found in alpine seed exchanges and occasionally on private collectors' lists.)

Perovskia (Labiatae). A small genus of subshrubs and shrubs frequently grown in the herbaceous border. The best method of increase is by taking basal cuttings in spring. Some authorities claim that they can be divided but this looks difficult and, with cuttings such an easy method, should only be carried out as a last resort. All except named forms can also be grown from seed sown in spring. A few self-sown seedlings can occasionally be found. Plant out in a fertile, well-drained soil in full sun. (Seed not available from commercial sources but occasionally can be found in exchange lists. Plants widely available.)

Persicaria (Polygonaceae). Knotweeds. Many of the *Polygonum* have been moved into this genus. Most persicaria are spreading plants, some slightly invasive. This means that propagation can easily be achieved by simply dividing off part of the parent plant without even lifting it. This can be done during autumn or spring. The species can also be grown from seed although division is so easily achieved there seems little advantage in it except that there might be the possibility of raising better or different forms. Seed can be sown in spring. Plant out in any fertile soil in sun or light shade. (Seed available from some specialist seed merchants and from seed exchanges.)

Petasites (Compositae). Butterbur, Coltsfoot. A small genus of invasive plants for the wild garden. They spread quickly and are easily divided if yet more plants are required. Doubtless they can be grown from seed although I have not come across anybody who has bothered mainly, I imagine, because the plant is dioecious and the majority in cultivation are male. Plant directly back in a moist soil in either sun or light shade. (Seed does not appear to be available from any sources except suppliers of wild-flower seed.)

Peucedanum (Umbelliferae). A large genus of mainly perennial plants, a few of which are in cultivation, the best known being the parsnip. They all have the thick taproot of the vegetable and thus the only way of raising new plants is by sowing seed, preferably in autumn or, possibly, in spring. Some will self-sow producing enough seedlings for most uses. These should be moved while young. Plant out in any fertile soil in sun. (Apart from parsnip, seed not generally available.)

Phanerophlebia (Aspleniaceae). This genus of ferns now includes members of *Cyrtomium*. They are increased in the normal way of propagating ferns, namely from spore collected in autumn. Plant out in any good enriched garden soil in light shade. (Spore may be available from pteridological societies exchanges. Plants commercially obtainable.)

Phlaris (Gramineae). Canary Grass, Gardener's Garters, Ribbon Grass. A small genus of grasses, most of which are invasive. The spreading rhizomes can easily be divided, if necessary without moving the parent plant. This is best done in spring, although large clumps, with plenty of earth round them, can be dug up at any time of year. Annuals and species can also be grown from seed sown in spring. Plant out in any soil in sun, although they will take some shade. (Seed not generally available although it does occasionally crop up in seed exchanges.)

Phleum (Gramineae). Cat's Tail, Timothy Grass. A small genus of annual and perennial grasses. The latter can be easily increased by dividing the plants in spring. Both can be grown from seed sown in spring. Plant out in any fertile soil in sun. (Seed mainly available from wild-flower seed merchants although some other specialist seed merchants may carry it.)

Phlomis (Labiatae). Jerusalem Sage. A large genus of perennial and shrubby plants. The herbaceous members are mainly clump forming and can easily be divided in spring. Those that are woodier, i.e. subshrubs and shrubs, can also be propagated from cuttings taken in spring. They can all also be grown from seed sown in spring. Plant out in a fertile, well-drained soil in full sun. (Seed available from the more specialist commercial sources and from seed exchanges.)

Phlox (Polemoniaceae). A moderately large genus of valuable garden plants that can be split into several types. The tall border phloxes based on *P. paniculata* can most easily be increased by dividing the spreading clumps, preferably in autumn, although the operation can be carried out in spring. Basal stem cuttings can also be taken in spring. Both these methods, unfortunately, transmit eelworm (nematodes), which cause distorted and weakened plants. A safer, but slower way that produces clean stock is to take root cuttings in early winter. Species, but not named forms, can be increased from seed sown in spring, which, of course, also avoids transmission of the eelworm. Pre-chilling in a domestic refrigerator may help to break dormancy. The low-growing, mat-forming species and cultivars such as *PP. subulata* and *douglasii* can best be increased by taking cuttings in summer after flowering. Choose young shoots as the older ones are more difficult to root. Sheering over will produce new growth suitable for cuttings. The stems of these mat-forming plants often root where they touch the soil and these can be removed as rooted cuttings and potted up. The species will, of course, come from seed. The dwarf species, of which *P. divaricata* is typical, can be increased by dividing after flowering. They can also be propagated by taking cuttings in spring. Again, the species can be increased from seed. The tall species require a moisture-retentive soil in full sun, the mat-forming need a well-drained soil also in full sun and the dwarf forms need a humus-rich, woodland soil in light shade. (Seed available from some commercial sources and most seed exchanges, especially alpine ones.)

Phormium (Agavaceae/Phormiaceae). New Zealand Flax. A small genus of only two species although there are numerous cultivars and hybrids, which indicate that vegetative propagation is going to be the main method of increase. This is undertaken by division in spring. Mature plants are big and cumbersome to deal with, younger plants are easier to handle. If a lot of plants are required, divide off individual clumps as indicated by fans of leaves. If only a few are required, then make the portions larger with several fans per division. Divisions are likely to be without roots but these quickly form. Phormium can also be grown from seed but the results can be variable. Seed can be sown in pans in spring or in the open ground in late spring. Plant out in a rich, free-draining soil in sun or even light shade. (Seed available from specialist commercial sources as well as HPS and other seed exchanges.)

Phragmites (Gramineae). A small genus of very invasive grasses or reeds suitable for large ponds and lakeside plantings. Propagation can simply be executed by digging up a section and transplanting it in spring. Plant out in a moisture-retentive soil or wet pondside in sun. They provide so much vegetative material that it barely seems worth growing from seed but this can be achieved, doing so in spring. (Seed available from some commercial sources.)

Phuopsis (Rubiaceae). A single species genus, namely *P. stylosa* (formerly known as *Crucianella stylosa*). In some situations it can become invasive, its rhizomatous rootstock providing ample satellite plants for divisions, which can be undertaken in spring or autumn. It can be divided without disturbing the parent plant. It can also be grown from seed sown in spring. Plant in a well-drained soil in sun or light shade. (Seed available from some specialist commercial sources and most seed exchanges.)

Phygelius (Scrophulariaceae). Cape Figwort. A small genus of two species of subshrubs, with many names forms including hybrids. The easiest way of increasing these plants is by taking cuttings in summer. They can also be propagated by division of the underground stems in spring. Seed is another method, but the named forms are unlikely to come true and is only recommended for the species, unless potential new forms are being sought. Seed should be sown in spring. Germination is helped by a little warmth. They should be planted out in spring in a sunny, sheltered position in a well-drained, but moisture-retentive soil. (Seed available from HPS and alpine seed exchanges, and more specialist commercial sources.)

Phyllitis (Polypodaiaceae). See *Asplenium*

Phyllostachys (Gramineae). Golden Bamboo. A medium-sized genus of bamboos, a number of which are in cultivation. Normally the only way to propagate them is by division of the two- to five-year-old rhizomes in spring just before growth begins, planting them out in open ground. With some species it may be found easier to take younger growth and pot these up rather than dividing direct into open ground. Occasionally phyllostachys flowers (and then dies) providing some seed. This seed should be sown in spring (in open ground if required) and the resulting seedlings planted out in their permanent positions, after two or three years, in spring. Plant out in rich soil in either sun or light shade. (Seed very difficult to come by as they rarely flower.)

Physalis (Solanaceae). Chinese Lanterns, Winter Cherry. A surprising large genus of plants of which only one, *P. alkekengii*, is in general cultivation. It is easy to propagate as its stoloniferous rootstock can easily be divided, usually without the need to disturb the parent plant, in autumn or spring. It can also be propagated from seed sown in autumn or spring. Germination can be erratic and pre-chilling may help if the seed pans are not exposed to any frosts. Plant out in any soil in full sun or part shade. (Seed available from some commercial sources and occasionally from seed exchanges.)

Physostegia (Labiatae). Obedient Plant. A small genus of which *P. virginiana* is the main species in cultivation. The species and its cultivars have a rhizomatous growth making large clumps of plants that can be easily increased by dividing in the spring. Basal cuttings from the young growth can be taken in spring. The species can also be grown from seed sown at the same time of year. Plant out in a moisture-retentive soil in full sun. (Seed available from some specialist commercial sources and from HPS and other seed exchanges.)

Phyteuma (Campanulaceae). Horned Rampions. A medium-sized genus of perennials. The normal method of propagation is by sowing seed in spring. The clump-forming plants can also be divided in spring. Plant out in any well-drained soil in sun or light shade. (Seed available from specialist commercial sources or from most seed exchanges, especially alpine ones.)

Phytolacca (Phytolaccaceae). Pokeberry, Pokeweed. A genus of large plants, some perennials, others shrubs. The main method of propagation is by sowing fresh seed in autumn or spring under glass. They can also be divided in spring if you are strong enough. Plant out in a moisture-retentive soil in sun or light shade. (Seed available from specialist commercial sources and occasionally from seed exchanges.)

Pimpernella (Umbelliferae). Anise. A large genus of which only *P. major* is in general cultivation and this usually in the form 'Rosea'. The species can best be increased from seed sown fresh. *P. m.* 'Rosea' and any other special forms that need increasing will have to be carefully divided in spring. Plant out in any fertile soil in full sun. (Seed not generally available from commercial sources but can occasionally be found in seed exchange lists.)

Plantago (Plantaginaceae). Plantain. A large genus of plants, many of which are considered weeds, which few gardeners would want to propagate. However, there are a few garden-worthy species and forms. The majority can be divided in spring and this is the best way of increasing them, especially the named forms. As most gardeners know, they will also come very readily from seed sown in either autumn or spring. Some of the named forms will produce a few seedlings close in appearance to their parent. Plant out in any garden soil in sun or light shade, the former for coloured forms. (Seed available from at least one commercial source and from HPS and other seed exchanges.)

Platanthera (Orchidaceae). Butterfly Orchids. Like all orchids these are difficult to grow and even more difficult to propagate unless you are a specialist in the field. If you want to try to grow them the best bet is to buy plants (*never* dig up from the wild) from specialist nurseries. A woodland-type soil in light shade is the best position to grow these plants outside. (Seed occasionally seen offered but its viability is very doubtful and chances of germinating it negligible.)

Platycodon (Campanulaceae). Balloon Flower. A single species genus, namely *P. grandiflorus*, although there are several named cultivars. They are clump forming and can all be increased by division in spring, although they are not too happy about being disturbed. They can also be increased vegetatively by taking basal cuttings of the young growth in spring. They can, of course, be grown from seed sown in spring but the results will be variable, although the form 'Mariesii' comes reasonably true from seed (but the resulting seedlings should not bear the cultivar name). Plant out in any fertile soil in full sun. (Seed available from some specialist commercial sources and from HPS and other seed exchanges.)

Plumbago (Plumbaginaceae). A small genus of annuals perennials and shrubs (of which *P. larpentae* has been moved to *Ceratostigma plumbaginoides*). They can all be raised from seed sown in spring. All except the annuals can also be increased by taking rooted cuttings from the base of the plants or by taking semi-ripe cuttings in summer. Plant out in a well-drained soil in a sunny position. (Seed available from specialist commercial sources and seed exchanges.)

Poa (Gramineae). Blue Grass, Meadow Grass. A very large genus of annual and perennial grasses. They can all be raised from seed sown in spring. The perennials can also be increased by division in spring. Plant out in any fertile soil in the sun. (Seed not generally available although some wild-flower specialists distribute it.)

Podophyllum (Podophyllaceae). A small genus of clump-forming perennials. This habit means that, with care, they can be divided in spring. They can also be grown from seed, best sown as soon as harvested. If sown when unlikely to receive frosts, then a period of pre-chilling in a refrigerator may help. Keep the compost moist. In a favourable position they will self-sow, producing seedlings that can be transplanted if needed. Plant out in a humus-rich, woodland-type soil in light shade. (Seed available from some specialist commercial firms and from HPS and other seed exchanges.)

Polemonium (Polemoniaceae). Jacob's Ladder. A medium-sized genus of clump-forming perennials that can be divided in autumn or spring. Sow seed fresh in autumn or spring. They can also be increased from seed, which is copiously produced. Many are self-sowers and will produce enough seedlings for most purposes. Plant out in any fertile soil, preferably in full sun although they will take a little light shade. (Seed available from specialist commercial sources and from HPS and other seed exchanges.)

Polygonatum (Convallariaceae/Liliaceae). Solomon's Seal. A medium-sized genus of creeping rhizomatous plants. This tendency makes the plant easy to divide, without disturbing the main clump if necessary. Division should preferably be in autumn. The species can also be grown from seed, which should be sown fresh. They can take several years to reach flowering size from seed. Plant in a moisture-retentive, woodland-type soil in light shade. (Some seed available from specialist commercial sources, more listed in the various seed exchanges.)

Polygonum (Polygonaceae). Not a great deal has been left under this genus. Most has been recently moved to either *Persicaria* or *Fallopia*; the taller, more rampant forms generally going to the latter. Irrespective of where they were and where they have ended up most, because of their spreading nature, can be easily divided in autumn or spring. The species can also be grown from seed sown in spring but since they come so readily from divisions this method is not frequently employed. Plant out in any fertile soil in sun or light shade. (Seed available from some specialist seed merchants, also listed by most seed exchanges.)

Polypodium (Polypodiaceae). Polypody. A very large genus of ferns that tend to be rhizomatous, which means that they can be easily divided in late autumn or spring. Some produce hairy bulbils on the lower part of the fronds, which can be used to produce new plants. Peg a frond down onto a tray of soil-less compost and keep moist until roots have developed on the bulbils. Transfer these to individual pots until large enough to plant out. They can also be grown from spore sown fresh. Plant out in a humus-rich soil in light shade. (Spore may be available from pteridological societies, plants readily obtainable.)

Polystichum (Aspleniaceae). Shield Ferns. Division in spring is the easiest method of increase from this rhizomatous genus. Some, *P. setiferum acutilobum* and *P. s. divisilobum* in particular, can be grown from bulbils that can be found at the lower end of some pinnae. In autumn peg down such a frond and keep moist until the bulbils have developed roots. Pot up individually in late spring and grow on until they are large enough to plant out. *P. a. pulcherrimum* 'Bevis' can be increased by taking the offsets. As with other ferns, many can also be grown from fresh spore. Plant out in humus-rich soil, in light or full shade. (Spore may be available from pteridological societies.)

Pontederia (Pontederiaceae). Pickerel Weed. A small genus of aquatic marginal plants. The quickest method of increase is by dividing the crowns in late spring. Do this after the plant is seen to come into growth as wounded plants will rot if still dormant. It is also possible to take cuttings from the stolons in summer. They should be kept in a wet soil-less compost. Alternatively, they can be grown from seed but it must be sown fresh. Germination of some seed is erratic. Plant out in shallow water in sun. (Seed not generally available but plants can be readily found.)

Pontamogeton (Pontamogetonaceae). Pondweed. A large genus of submerged aquatic plants with floating leaves. They can be increased by taking cuttings in late spring or early summer. These can be placed in containers and submerged or planted directly into the soil at the bottom of the pond. They may need anchoring down to make certain they do not float away. Alternatively, they can be divided and replanted directly into the base of the pond. If cuttings or division are to be potted up then submerge the pots in water. Plant in reasonably deep water in sun. (Seed not available but plants readily obtainable.)

Potentilla (Rosaceae). A very large genus of annuals, perennials and shrubs. For most perennial species and named forms the easiest method of increase is by division in either autumn or spring. Some produce plantlets on runners, which can easily be detached from the parent plant. The shrubby species and their varieties can be propagated by taking semi-ripe cuttings during summer. All non-named forms can be grown from seed sown in spring. Some growers find that some species require light for germination so it may be advantageous not to cover the seed too deeply. Plant out in any well-drained, fertile soil in full sun. (Seed available from both specialist commercial sources and seed exchanges.)

Preslia (Labiatae). A genus of a single species, namely *P. cervinia*, grown as a marginal plant for ponds. It is a prostrate plant that can easily be divided. It can also be easily increased from cuttings taken in spring and kept in very wet compost. Plant out in very moist soil or very shallow water. (Seed not generally available although plants can occasionally be found.)

Primula (Primulaceae). Polyanthus, Primulas, Primroses. A very large genus of low plants of which a surprising number are in cultivation. For the open border only the easiest species and forms are normally grown and these can generally be best increased by division after flowering or in autumn. This can usually be easily achieved as, once the soil is removed the plants will naturally fall into several crowns. One, namely *P. denticulata*, is also commonly grown from root cuttings taken while the plant is dormant. Seed is the other main source of plants, but this must be sown fresh. Keep the compost moist and do not keep it in too warm an atmosphere, in a greenhouse for example. Maximum temperatures should not exceed 20°C (68°F). Seed can be sown in spring if it has been stored in a refrigerator. Many will self-sow and seedlings can be pricked out direct from the soil. This is important in drier areas as the seedlings are likely to die if left in the open ground. Many of the smaller and more difficult plants are grown on rock gardens or in pots and specialist publications should be consulted as to their propagation and cultivation. Plant out in a moisture-retentive soil in sun or light shade, many preferring the latter but will survive in sun if the soil is moist enough.

(Seed available from a wide selection of commercial sources, but a better selection of species is available from seed exchanges, especially alpine ones.)

Prunella (Labiatae). Self-heal. A small genus of clump-forming plants easily divided in autumn or spring. Vegetative propagation can also be achieved by taking basal cuttings from the young growth in spring. Rooted cuttings can be taken at any time as long as they are kept moist until established. Species can be increased from seed sown in spring but this method should not be trusted for named forms. Plant out in any fertile soil in full sun or light shade. (Seed available from some seed merchants and seed exchanges.)

Pteridium (Dennstaedtiaceae). Bracken. A single species genus, namely *P. aquilinum*, that is considered by most gardeners as a pestilent weed but is included here just in case any one wants to introduce it, possible in a woodland garden for example, where it can look very graceful. Although it is a rhizomatous plant it is not very easy to establish by division, although if a large enough clump is taken it might be successful. The best method is to sow fresh spore. If you have to plant it out do so in any light soil in either full sun or light shade. (It is extremely doubtful whether anyone supplies spore or plants, except for the occasional special form, but this is one plant that the occasional shoot removed from the countryside would probably not be frowned on.)

Pteridophyllum (Fumariaceae). A genus with only a single species, namely *P. racemosum*. It can be increased by sowing seed in spring or, alternatively, the plant can be divided in autumn, but it dislikes disturbance and transplanting. Plant out in a woodland-type soil in light shade. (Seed not available from commercial sources but is occasionally available from seed exchanges, especially alpine ones.)

Pulmonaria (Boraginaceae). Lungwort. The main way of increase is from division in spring, after flowering. Washing off the soil should make division very easy, the plants often falling into natural divisions. Cut off the old rootstock leaving the fresh, young roots. The foliage can also be reduced by trimming 7.5–10 cm (3–4 in) above the crown. They will also come very easily from seed but there is no telling what the results will be as they readily hybridize. Self-sown seedlings will often appear in a border that bear no colour resemblance to their parents nearby. Thus within *P. officinalis* 'Sissinghurst White' there will often be seen blue seedlings, which should, of course, be rogued out if you want to keep the clump pure. Seed can be used as a method of reproducing species as long as they have been isolated or hand pollinated. It can also be used to raise new cultivars and hybrids but selection should be very keen as many insignificant plants have been given names in recent years. The new plants can be replanted in the open or in pots. Plant out in moisture-retentive soil in light shade, although they will grow in full sun if moist enough. (Seed does not appear to be available from commercial sources but is regularly listed in HPS and alpine seed exchanges.)

Pulsatilla (Ranunculaceae). Pasque Flower. A small genus of desirable border plants. The easiest way of increase is by sowing seed. Sown fresh it comes up like the proverbial mustard and cress, left until spring germination is very poor and erratic. Most colour forms will produce some seedlings close to the original colour. Some authorities advocate cutting the silken 'tails' off the seed but this is unnecessary if the seed is covered with a layer of fine grit. Special forms of *P.*

vulgaris are sometimes increased by root division taken in early winter. Plant out in any well-drained, fertile soil in full sun. (Seed available from most sources but the more obscure species only from seed exchanges, particularly alpine ones.)

Puschkinia (Liliaceae). A small genus of only one or two species, *P. scilloides* being the main one grown in gardens. This is most easily propagated by lifting the bulbs and removing any offsets, although they are not too keen on being disturbed and it should be undertaken when the bulbs are dormant, after the leaves have died down. They can also be raised from seed sown in spring. Plant out in a cool, well-drained, but moisture-retentive soil. (Seed not available commercially but occurs in seed exchanges. Bulbs easily purchased.)

Puya (Bromeliaceae). A large genus of tender plants of which a few can be grown in warmer areas. Increase by dividing the offsets or suckers from the parent plant. They can also be grown from seed sown in gentle heat in spring. They take several years to reach flowering size from seed. Plant out in a well-drained soil in a warm sunny spot. (Seed not widely available but may be obtained from specialist societies.)

Pyrethrum (Compositae). See ***Tanecetum***

Ranunculus (Ranunculaceae). Buttercups. A large genus of plants, some of which are weeds and should be avoided, but quite a number of species are grown in gardens. Apart from named varieties, most can be grown from seed, which should be sown fresh. Seed sown while still green is liable to germinate immediately, whereas seed that has turned brown or black can take several years before seedlings appear. *R. calandrinioides* often needs cross pollination to achieve a viable seed set. As most gardeners know, buttercups have a tendency to self sow and many cultivated forms do likewise. Some produce runners and the new plants thus formed can easily be divided off. Others clump up and again can be divided, either in autumn or spring, the former for spring-flowering species. *R. ficaria* produces storage organs below ground (tubers) that can also be divided. This plant does not set much seed but does produce bulbils in the leaf axils and these can be sown and will come true to the parent plant. Plant out in any fertile soil that is not too dry, in sun or light shade. (Seed available from some commercial seed merchants and all seed exchanges.)

Ranzania (Podophyllaceae). A single species genus, namely *R. japonica*. This is a plant with branching rhizomes that can easily be divided, preferably in autumn as this is a spring-flowering plant. It can also be grown from seed sown in spring, although it will take three or four years to reach flowering size. Plant out in a woodland-type soil in light shade. (Seed not generally available although it does occasionally occur in a seed exchange list, particularly alpine ones.)

Ratibida (Compositae). Mexican Hat, Prairie Coneflower. A small genus of annual and perennial plants of which *R. columnifera* is the most frequently grown. They are most easily increased from seed sown, preferably fresh, in autumn or spring. They can also be divided in spring. Plant out in a well-drained, fertile soil in a sunny position. (Seed available from specialist seed merchants and occasionally HPS and other seed exchanges.)

Rehmannia (Gesneriaceae/Scrophulariaceae). A small genus of tender or marginally tender species rather intolerant of winter wet. All come reasonably easily from seed sown in spring. They have taproots, which make vegetative propagation difficult, the only method being root cuttings taken in late autumn or early winter. Although perennial, some act as biennials and die after flowering. Their natural growing place is in old walls, rock crevices and cliffs, and these free-draining positions are the best place to set out the plants in spring. (Seed available from alpine seed exchanges.)

Reineckia (Convallariaceae/Liliaceae). A genus of one species, namely *R. carnea*. This is a spreading, rhizomatous plant easily divided in autumn or spring. It can also be grown from seed, but this is not often formed in Britain. Plant out in a woodland-type soil in light shade. (Seed not generally available although it does occasionally appear in seed exchange lists.)

Reynoutria (Polygonaceae). See *Fallopia*

Rhazya (Apocynaceae). A two-species genus, of which *R. orientalis* is the only one usually grown. They are clump forming and can be propagated by division in spring. They can also be increased vegetatively by taking basal cuttings in spring. Alternatively, they can be grown from seed sown in spring. Plant out in any fertile, well-drained soil in a sunny position. (Seed does not appear to be currently available from commercial sources but can be found in HPS and other seed exchange lists.)

Rheum (Polygonaceae). Rhubarb. A medium-sized genus of large-sized plants. Increase is by division in autumn or spring if you can cope with the size of the plant. Make certain that each division has an eye. A less strenuous method is to sow seed in spring. Plant out in a rich humus-fed soil in sun or light shade. (Seed available from some specialist seed merchants and from seed exchange lists.)

Rhexia (Melastomaceae). Deer Grass, Virginia Meadow Beauty. This smallish genus is mainly represented by *R. virginica* in gardens. It can be propagated by the division of its tuberous rootstock or from seed, both in spring. Plant out in a moisture-retentive soil in a sunny position. (Seed not generally available in Britain but several species do occur in AGS and American seed lists.)

Rhodiola (Crassulaceae). Roseroot. A medium-sized genus of succulent plants, closely allied to *Sedum*, some of which can be used in front of a border, others on rock gardens. Propagate from cuttings taken in spring. Can also be grown from seed sown in spring. Some species (*RR. heterodonta* and *rosea* for example) are dioecious and therefore require both male and female plants to produce seed. Plant out in a well-drained soil in full sun. (Seed not generally available from commercial sources but can be found in seed exchange lists. Check under *Sedum* in catalogues and lists as species are often listed under this genus.)

Rhodochiton (Scrophulariaceae). A single-species genus (*R. atrosanguineum*) that has recently become popular. It is a climbing plant that is on the tender side but can be grown in warmer areas. It is propagated from seed sown in gentle heat in spring. Plant out in a well-drained soil in a sunny position. (Seed available commercially and from seed exchanges.)

Riccia (Ricciaceae). A large genus of aquatic liverworts of which *R. fluitans* is used in ponds. It can simply be divided and replaced in the water. (Plants available.)

Rigidella (Iridaceae). A small genus of bulbous plants for warmer areas. The easiest method of propagation is to lift and divide after they have died down. Alternatively, can be sown from seed, preferably fresh or in spring. Plant out in a well-drained soil in a warm, sunny position. (Seed not available commercially but can occasionally be found in seed exchange lists, especially those of alpine and specialist groups.)

Rindera (Boraginaceae). A medium-sized genus, a few of which are occasionally seen in gardens. The easiest method of propagation is from seed sown in spring. Being related to *Cynoglossum* it is likely that they can be propagated from root cuttings taken in early winter. Plant out in a well-drained site in a sunny position. (Seed not available commercially and only occasionally occurs in seed exchanges.)

Rodgersia (Saxifragaceae). A small, colony-forming, genus of plants, all of which are in cultivation. The main method of increase is by division of the rhizomatous root stock either in autumn or spring. They can also be grown from their fine seed, sown in spring. Plant out in a rich, moisture-retentive soil in light shade or sun if the soil is kept moist. (Seed available from some commercial sources and from HPS and other seed exchanges.)

Romneya (Papaveraceae). Californian Tree Poppy. A one (or two depending which taxonomist you follow) species genus. The main method of increase is by taking root cuttings in early winter and individually potting these up. There is a greater take rate if the sections of root are laid horizontally in the compost. It is also possible, with care, to divide the running rootstock in spring but this is not always a successful method as the plants greatly resent disturbance. They can be successfully grown from seed sown in spring. Some gardeners sow seed singly in individual pots, again to prevent disturbance. Plant out in a moisture-retentive soil in full sun. (Seed available from at least one commercial source as well as seed exchanges.)

Roscoea (Zingiberaceae). A small genus of clump-forming plants of increasing popularity. The main method of propagation is by division of the tubers in spring. Alternatively, they come quite readily from seed, particularly if sown fresh. Plant out in a moisture-retentive soil in light shade or sun. (Seed available from specialist commercial sources but a better selection is found in the seed exchanges. Seed collecting expeditions often list interesting species.)

Rudbeckia (Compositae). Coneflower. A medium-sized genus of annuals and perennials. Most of the perennials are spreading and can easily be divided in autumn, after flowering, or in spring. Alternatively basal cuttings can be taken from the young growth in spring. Rooted cuttings, with a few roots attached, can also be taken later in the year. The annuals and the species, but not the named forms, can also be grown from seed sown fresh or, if necessary, in spring. Some growers find a period of pre-chilling helps germination. Plant out in any fertile soil that does not dry out too much, preferably in sun, although they will take light shade. (Seed available from commercial sources and seed exchange lists.)

Rumex (Polygonaceae). Docks. A large genus of plants regarded as weeds in the garden. But some, *R. hydrolapathum* for example, have their place, in this case in the water garden. They can be grown from seed sown in spring. Alternatively, some can be divided just as growth begins in spring. As most gardeners know to their cost, the thick-rooted forms can also be increased by root cuttings taken in early winter. Plant out in any fertile soil in sun or light shade. (Some seed available commercially and from HPS and other seed exchange lists.)

Ruta (Rutaceae). Rue. A medium-sized genus of which *R. graveolens* is the main species grown in gardens. They can easily be increased from cuttings taken at any time during the growing season, although cuttings taken in late summer root the most rapidly. Some people are allergic to rue and contact with the skin should be avoided. Non-named forms can also be grown from seed sown in spring. Plant out in a fertile soil in sun. (Seed available from some commercial sources and from seed exchanges.)

Sagittaria (Alismataceae). Arrowhead. A genus of aquatic plants for marginal plantings. The plants can be divided during summer and replanted directly into shallow water. Alternatively the plants can be lifted in early spring and sections of the rhizome, each with a bud, cut off and either replanted or potted up. The pots should be stood in water. They can also be grown from seed sown fresh in pots, which are, again, stood in water. Some self-sow. (Seed available from at least one commercial source and occasionally from seed exchanges.)

Salvia (Labiatae). Sage. A very large genus of annuals, perennials and shrubs. All, apart from named clones, can be grown from seed sown fresh in autumn or spring. Wait until spring for the more tender species such as *S. patens*. Some, such as *SS. sclarea* or *haematodes*, self-sow and provide sufficient seedlings for most purposes. The perennials and woodier plants can be increased by cuttings taken in spring. Some will also lend themselves to division in either autumn or spring. A few, such as *S. patens*, form underground tubers, somewhat similar to dahlias, and should be lifted in autumn in colder areas as they are somewhat tender. These can be divided in spring before replanting. Plant out in a well-drained soil in a sunny position. (Seed available from most commercial sources as well as seed exchange lists.)

Sambucus (Caprifoliaceae). A medium-sized genus of woody plants of which there is one garden plant that is herbaceous, namely *S. ebulus*. It is easy to increase by either division, cuttings or seed, all accomplished in spring. Plant out in any fertile soil in sun. (Seed not generally available, but plants can be obtained.)

Sanguinaria (Papaveraceae). Blood Root. A genus of a single species, namely *S. canadensis*. This woodlander has spreading rhizomes, which can be easily divided while they are dormant. The single-flowered type-plant can also be grown from seed as long as it is sown fresh. Plant out in a humus-rich, woodland-type soil in which it can run about in light shade. (Seed not available commercially but may be found on seed exchange lists, although germination of seed from these sources will be slow and erratic.)

Sanguisorba (Rosaceae). Burnet, Salad Burnet. A small genus of spreading plants easily divided either in autumn or spring. They can also be grown from seed sown in spring. Some will self-sow producing a few plants for use. Plant out in a moisture-retentive soil in full sun. (Seed available from some specialist commercial sources, including those dealing with wild-flower seed, and seed exchanges.)

Sanicula (Umbelliferae). Sanicle. A medium-sized genus of which one, *S. europaea* is grown in woodland gardens. The main method of propagation is from seed sown fresh. Plant in a woodland-type soil in light shade. (Seed not generally available but is supplied by those dealing with wild-flower seed.)

Santolina (Compositae). Lavender Cotton. These are really shrubs but are frequently grown in herbaceous borders. They are easily propagated from soft cuttings taken at any time during the growing season. Doubtless they are also grown from seed but with increase from cuttings so easy this is hardly worthwhile unless there are no plants to hand. Sow seed either fresh or in spring. Plant out in a well-drained soil in a sunny position. (Seed available from some specialist commercial sources, more species occasionally available from seed exchange lists.)

Saponaria (Caryophyllaceae). Soapwort. A medium-sized genus of which a couple are tall enough for the open border. They can all, including smaller ones for rock gardens and front of border, be increased from cuttings taken in spring or seed sown at the same time of year. A period of pre-chilling is often beneficial. Those with a running habit, such as *S. officinalis*, can be increased by division either in autumn or spring. Plant out in any fertile soil in full sun or even light shade. (Seed available from commercial sources and seed exchanges.)

Sarracenia (Sarraceniaceae). Pitcher Plants. A small genus for the bog garden in warmer areas. Can be increased by careful division or from seed sown onto chopped-up sphagnum moss over a soil-less compost that is kept wet. Plant out in a sphagnum bog or a mixture of sphagnum and peat. (Seed available from specialist commercial sources and seed exchanges, in particular specialist ones.)

Sasa (Gramineae). Dwarf Bamboo. A large genus of bamboos best increased by division of their rhizomatous rootstock in spring just as growth begins. Rarely seed becomes available and it can also be increased from this. Plant out in any fertile soil in light shade or sun. (Seed rarely available.)

Satureja (Labiatae). Savory. Annual or perennial herbs and subshrubs. They can all be increased from seed sown in spring. The perennials can also be easily increased from cuttings in spring. Rooted cuttings, containing a few roots, can be taken at any time while the plant is in growth. Many have a creeping habit and can also be divided in spring. Plant out in a well-drained soil in a sunny position. (Seed available from some commercial sources and from seed exchanges.)

Sauromatum (Araceae). A small genus of tropical aroids of which one, *S. venosum*, is sometimes grown in warmer areas. It is best increased by division of its tubers in autumn or spring. It can also be increased from seed, sown fresh, if it can be found. Plant out in a moisture-retentive soil in a warm, sunny position. (Seed not generally available, but plants can be obtained.)

Saururus (Saururaceae). Lizard's Tail. A small genus of aquatic plants for shallow water. The easiest method of increase is by division in spring. They can also be grown from seed sown fresh. Plant out in shallow water or a boggy area that is kept wet. (Seed not generally available, but plants can be obtained.)

Saussurea (Compositae). A large genus of plants that have been increasing in popularity recently, particularly the fascinating ones from the Himalaya. They can be grown from fresh seed. They are also reputed to be able to be increased vegetatively from root cuttings taken in early winter, and by division in spring. Plant out in a well-drained soil in sun. (At least one species is offered by a commercial source and others occur in seed exchanges, especially alpine ones. Seed also often available from seed-collecting expeditions.)

Saxifraga (Saxifragaceae). A large genus of plants mainly for the rock garden but there are a few for the border or woodland garden. The easiest method for these groups is by division in spring of the clumps or new plants formed on stolons. The mat- and cushion-forming plants can be readily increased from cuttings taken in spring. They can also be grown from seed sown in spring. Plant out in a moisture-retentive soil in a cool position in light shade. (Seed available from specialist commercial sources and seed exchanges.)

Scabiosa (Dipsacaceae). A large genus of annual and perennial plants. Both, apart from named clones, can be grown from seed sown in spring. The perennials can also be increased by division in spring, but dislike disturbance and basal cuttings, also taken in spring, may be considered a better method. Plant out in well-drained, fertile garden soil in a sunny position. (Seed available from most seed commercial merchants and from HPS and other seed exchanges.)

Schizostylis (Iridaceae). Kaffir Lily. A two-species genus of which *S. coccinea* has become a popular autumn-flowering plant. It clumps up well and can easily be divided after flowering in autumn or spring. They need to be divided every three years to prevent congestion. It can also be grown from seed, although the results will be variable. Plant out in a rich, moisture-retentive soil in sun. (Seed available from some specialist seed merchants and from HPS and other seed exchanges.)

Scilla (Hyacinthaceae/Liliaceae). Squills. A popular genus of short spring and autumn bulbs. They clump up quite quickly and can be divided during their dormant season. They can also be grown from seed, preferably fresh. Many will self-sow. Plant out in most soils in light shade or sun. Some, such as *S. peruviana*, need well-drained soils in full sun. (Seed available from some commercial sources but a better range of species is available from the alpine seed exchanges.)

Scirpus (Cyperaceae). Bulrushes, Rushes. A large genus of rhizomatous plants used mainly as marginal plants for ponds. They spread quickly and can be easily divided as they come into growth in spring. If necessary they can also be grown from seed sown in spring in a pot of soil-less compost standing in a tray of water. Plant out in shallow water on the margins of ponds in sun. (Seed available from at least one commercial source and occasionally from seed exchanges.)

Scoliopus (Trilliaceae/Liliaceae). A two species genus, of which *S. bigelovii* is occasionally grown. The easiest method of increase is by division in autumn or from seed sown fresh. The problem with the latter is that seed does not seem to set readily in cultivation. Plant out in a woodland-type soil in light shade. (Seed rarely available but occasionally occurs in alpine seed exchanges.)

Scopolia (Solanaceae). A small genus of which *SS. carniolica* and *lurida* are occasionally grown in gardens. The usual method of propagation is by division in autumn (they flower in early spring). They can also be grown from seed if any can be found. Plant out in any fertile soil in light shade or sun. (One seed merchant supplies seed and it occasionally occurs in seed exchange lists. Plants available.)

Scorzonera (Compositae). Salsify. A large genus of plants of which *S. purpurea* is grown as a vegetable but it also is very attractive in flower. They can easily be grown from seed sown in the spring, flowering in their second year. They can also be increased by taking root cuttings in winter, and in some cases by division in spring. Plant out in any fertile soil in a sunny position. (Seed available from vegetable seed merchants, but other forms and species are difficult to find, although some plants are available.)

Scrophularia (Scrophulariaceae). Figwort. A large genus of biennials, perennials and subshrubs, several of which are grown in gardens. The commonest is the variegated form of a British weed, *S. auriculata* (syn. *S. aquatica*). It is best increased by taking cuttings in late summer, but do not cover too closely. The clumps can also be divided in autumn or spring. Avoid letting it seed as the resulting plants will not be variegated. Species, however, can be grown from seed sown in spring. Some are rather rampant self-sowers. Plant in a moisture-retentive soil in sun or light shade. (Seed available from at least one seed merchant and from HPS and other seed exchanges.)

Scutellaria (Labiatae). Skullcaps. A large genus of plants of which only a few are in cultivation. The easiest method of propagation is by division in spring. Alternatively, basal cuttings can be taken from the young growth or seed sown in spring. Some prefer a well-drained soil in a sunny position, others a moist one in light shade. (Seed available from specialist seed merchants and seed exchanges.)

Sedum (Crassulaceae). Stonecrops. A very large genus of which many are in cultivation. They are amenable to most methods of propagation. Many form clumps that can easily be divided either in autumn or spring. They are the classic plants for taking leaf cuttings as many will easily take root from a leaf stuck with its lower (stem) end into a cutting mixture at virtually any time during the growing season. It is more usual, however, for the larger, border forms to be struck from young shoots taken in the spring, but do not make the conditions too close otherwise they might damp off. The species can also be grown from seed sown in spring. Plant out in a well-drained soil in full sun, although many will take a bit of shade, although they will be shy flowering. (Seed available from specialist commercial sources and seed exchanges.)

Selinum (Umbelliferae). A small genus of which *S. tenuifolium* (*S. candollei*) is the main one grown. The easiest way to propagate this is from seed sown either fresh or in spring, although it will take three years to reach full size. It can also be increased by careful division in spring. Plant out in any fertile soil in a sunny position. (Seed not available commercially but is listed by HPS and other seed exchanges.)

Semiaquilegia (Ranunculaceae). A small genus very closely related to *Aquilegia*. As with that genus, they are best grown from seed as long as it is pure. They self-sow and usually provide enough seedlings for most purposes. Plant out in a well-drained soil in full sun. (Seed available from some specialist seed merchants and from HPS and other seed exchanges.)

Sempervivum (Crassulaceae). A medium-sized genus of succulents with many garden forms. They are very easy to propagate as the offset rosettes can be readily detached and potted up or planted out individually. There is little reason to propagate from seed as the majority of plants are hybrids or cultivars but species (and new forms) can be grown from seed sown in spring. Plant out in a well-drained soil in full sun. (Seed available from specialist seed merchants and seed exchanges.)

Senecio (Compositae). Ragworts. A very large genus of up to 3,000 species of which only a comparative few are in cultivation. Some, such as *SS. vulgaris* (groundsel) and *jacobaea* (ragwort) are weeds and should be avoided. These weeds propagate themselves all too easily around the garden but it is an indication that the family as a whole increases well from seed, especially if sown fresh. In some species it may be possible that light is beneficial to germination, so if difficulty is experienced resow allowing light to reach the seed. Many can also be increased vegetatively, usually by division but some can also be propagated from cuttings taken in spring or summer. Division is particularly easy with the rhizomatous species such as *S. tanguticus*. *S. pulcher* can be increased from root cuttings taken in winter. When taking cuttings of the silver *S. bicolor cineraria* (formerly *S. maritima*) avoid keeping it in too close an atmosphere. Plant out in any fertile garden soil in full sun or light shade. (Surprisingly few are available from either commercial or seed exchange sources although alpine exchanges offer more.)

Seriocarpus (Compositae). A small North American genus akin to asters. They can be grown from seed, preferably sown fresh. They can also be increased vegetatively either by dividing the clumps in autumn or spring, or by taking basal cuttings from the young shoots in spring. Plant out the young plants in any fertile soil in a sunny position. (Seed not generally available but does occasionally occur in a seed exchange list.)

Serratula (Compositae). Saw-worts. A large genus of which only *SS. seoanei* (*S. shawii*) and *tinctoria* are generally grown. The easiest method of increase is division, which can be carried out in late autumn after flowering or, preferably, in spring. Can also be grown from seed sown fresh or in spring. Plant out in any fertile soil in full sun. (Seed only available from one commercial source but can be found in seed exchanges.)

Sesleria (Gramineae). Moor Grass. A small genus of grasses that can be increased by dividing the clumps in late spring or from seed sown a little earlier. Plant out in any good soil in an open, sunny position. (Seed not generally available.)

Shortia (Diapensiaceae). A small genus mainly increased vegetatively. It is possible to grow from seed but this is difficult. Seed should be sown fresh and on a peaty compost that is kept moist. It may well be worth trying to germinate them on sieved sphagnum moss. A period of pre-chilling in a refrigerator before sowing may be beneficial. Vegetatively they can be propagated by very careful division of the mature clumps or by potting up the young plants formed on the spreading stolons. The latter is preferable as it does not disturb the main plant, which resents being moved. Plant out in a humus-rich, peaty soil (avoid alkaline soils) that is kept moist and in a light shady position. (Seed not often seen in cultivation and is mainly available from the alpine seed exchanges.)

Sidalcea (Malvaceae). A small genus of plants of which some species and cultivars have become popular garden plants. In order to perpetuate the most popular forms they must be increased vegetatively, which can be easily achieved by division in spring or autumn. Species can also be grown from seed sown fresh in autumn. Some colour forms will come true from seed but inferior forms must be rigorously weeded out. Plant out in a humus-rich soil in full sun. (Seed available commercially and from seed exchange lists.)

Sideritis (Labiatae). A large genus of species with only a few in cultivation. They can be increased from seed sown in either autumn or spring, or vegetatively from basal cuttings taken in spring or harder cuttings taken later in the year. Many are also suitable for division in the spring. Plant out the young plants or divisions into a well-drained, sunny position. (Seed not available commercially but can occasionally be found in seed exchanges, especially alpine ones.)

Silene (Caryophyllaceae). Campions. This large genus tends to produce copious amounts of seed and use of this is the main method of increase. It can be sown fresh or in spring. If required, it can be sown directly into open ground. They are amenable plants and most can also be increased by division in autumn for the spring-flowering forms. Cuttings from young growth can also be taken in spring. Plant out in any good soil in either sun or light shade. (Seed of some species available commercially, more can be found on seed exchange lists.)

Silphium (Compositae). Compass Plant, Cup Plant, Prairie Dock, Rosinweed. A small genus of about 20 species of which only two or three are in cultivation. They can be increased from seed, preferably sown fresh in autumn or, more commonly, by division in autumn or spring. Plant out in any good garden soil in full sun. (Seed not generally available although *S. lanciniatum* is stocked by a specialist commercial supplier and others occasionally occur in seed exchange lists.)

Silybum (Compositae). A genus of two species of which *S. marianum* is commonly grown in borders. It is biennial and comes readily from seed, which can be sown directly into the open ground if desired. It will self-sow prodigiously, which can be a boon as collecting seed from the seed-head can be a prickly business. Sow fresh in autumn or in spring, if necessary. Do not keep too warm as heat may slow down germination. Plant out in any garden soil in a sunny position. (Seed available from commercial sources and seed exchanges.)

Sisyrinchium (Iridaceae). A large family of interesting, although sometimes weedy plants. They all tend to come very readily from seed, often self-sowing with sufficient profusion to supply enough plants for most uses. The plants can also be divided in early autumn, a particularly important method for the variegated form of *S. striatum*, 'Aunt May'. Plant out in any good soil in a sunny position. (Seed available commercially and from seed exchanges.)

Smilacina (Convallariaceae/Liliaceae). Woodland plants with a creeping habit that makes them easy to divide. This should be undertaken after the plants have flowered, from early summer to autumn. They can also be grown from freshly-sown seed, but can take several years to reach a decent flowering size. If the seed pan is unlikely to receive a frost than a period of artificial pre-chilling in a refrigerator may help germination. Plant out in a humus-rich, woodland-type soil in a light shade. (Seed available from some specialist commercial sources and from HPS and other seed exchanges.)

Smyrmium (Umbelliferae). A small genus of biennial plants of which *S. perfoliata* is often grown in woodland gardens. They can be easily grown from seed sown in spring and, once established, will continue to self-sow. Plant out in any garden soil in light shade. (Seed available from specialist commercial sources and seed exchanges.)

Solidago (Compositae). Goldenrod. A large genus with very few in cultivation. The majority are hybrids and cultivars, so that the best method of increase is by division, either in autumn or spring. They can also be increased by rooted cuttings in summer or from cuttings of basal shoots in spring. Species can be grown from seed, preferably sown fresh or in spring. Plant out in a rich, moisture-retentive soil in full sun or partial shade (although here they will not flower very well). (Seed available from specialist commercial sources and seed exchange lists.)

× *Solidaster* (Compositae). A bigeneric hybrid between a *Solidago* and *Aster ptarmicoides*, so must be increased vegetatively, either by division or by basal cuttings, both in spring. Seed is set but results are unreliable. Of course seed could be used if the cross were repeated, but in such a case new forms would be raised. Plant out in a moisture-retentive soil in a sunny position. (Seed not available commercially although it can be found in seed exchange lists. Preferable to increase vegetatively.)

Sonchus (Compositae). Sow Thistles. A large family of mainly weeds, some pestilent. Occasionally grown in gardens, in particular *S. palustris*. Increase can either be by seed sown fresh or in spring, or by division in spring. Plant out in any garden soil in sun, but beware of invasiveness. (Seed not generally available.)

Sophora (Leguminosae). A medium-sized genus of woody plants that contains a few herbs and sub-shrubs that can be treated as herbaceous, *S. flavescens* for example. The easiest way of increase is to sow seeds in gentle heat in spring. It may also be possible to take cuttings if they are taken early enough in the season. (Seed not generally available.)

Sorghum (Gramineae). A small genus of grasses, which are mainly annual although the perennial *S. halepense* is sometimes grown. It is a creeping, rhizomatous plant easily divided in spring. It can also be increased from seed sown in spring. Plant out in a moist soil in sun, but beware of its invasiveness. (Seed not generally available.)

Sparaxis (Iridaceae). Harlequin Flower, Wandflowers. A small genus of South African bulbous plants that can be grown in warmer areas. The corms can be divided during the dormant season. The species, but not the many varieties, can also be sown from fresh seed or in spring. Plant out in a warm, well-drained soil in full sun. (Seed not generally available but does occasionally occur in seed exchange lists. Corms are more readily available.)

Sparganium (Sparganiaceae). Bur-reeds. A small genus of plants for water-margins. They have a tendency to creep, sometimes invasively so, and can thus be easily divided, preferably in spring. They can also be sown from seed sown in spring. Plant out in the shallow water at the edge of ponds and streams. (Seed available from at least one specialist commercial source.)

Spartina (Gramineae). Prairie Cord Grass. A small genus of grasses of which *S. pectinata* 'Aureomarginata' is sometimes grown in gardens. They can be increased by division in spring. The straight species can also be grown from seed sown in spring. Plant out in a moist soil in sun, but beware of its invasiveness. (Seed not generally available, although plants are commercially obtainable.)

Speirantha (Convallariaceae/Liliaceae). A monotypic relation of Lily-of-the-Valley (*Convallaria*) likewise best propagated by dividing its creeping rootstock in autumn or spring after flowering. It can also be grown from seed sown when fresh. Plant out in a woodland-type soil in light shade. (Seed not generally available.)

Sphaeralcea (Malvaceae). Globe Mallow. A medium-sized genus of increasing interest, with several plants in cultivation, although it can only be grown in warmer areas. Can be grown from seeds sown in spring, although seed is not frequently set in cultivation (possibly needs more than one clone to set viable seed). They will also increase from young cuttings taken in spring. Plant out in a warm, sunny spot, in a well-drained soil. (Seed not generally available, but plants can increasingly be found.)

Spigelia (Loganaceae). Pinkroot. A medium-sized genus of annuals, perennials and subshrubs for warmer areas. The perennials can be increased from seed sown in spring or division at the same time of year. Seed of some species may benefit from a period of pre-chilling. Plant out in woodland soil in a light shade; will tolerate full sun if soil kept moist. (Seed not generally available but may be found in US seed exchanges.)

Stachys (Labiatae). Betony, Woundwort. A large genus of creeping or clump forming species easily divided in spring. Some, such as *S. byzantina* (*S. lanata*), need dividing every year or so to prevent the clump dying out in the middle and looking ragged. Alternatively they can be increased from basal cuttings made from young growth in spring. Most can also be increased from seed sown in spring, but named forms and other good forms are unlikely to come true. Many will self-sow. Plant out in a well-drained soil in sun. (Seed available from specialist commercial sources and from HPS and other seed exchanges.)

Stanleya (Cruciferae). Prince's Plume. A small genus of American plants of which *S. pinnatifida* is sometimes grown. Like most crucifers this comes readily from seed and can be sown in spring. It can also be divided in spring. Plant out in a well-drained, sunny position. (Seed not generally available, but plants can be found in some nurseries.)

Statice (Plumbaginaceae). See **Limonium**

Stellaria (Caryophyllaceae). Stitchworts. A large genus of plants normally considered weeds although a couple are grown, particularly wild gardens. They can be increased either by seed sown in spring or by division of existing plants. Plant in any soil in sun or light shade. (Seed available from some specialist seed companies, particularly those dealing with wild flowers.)

Stenanthium (Melanthiaceae/Liliaceae). Featherbells. A small genus of North American plants easily propagated by division of the bulbous clumps in spring. They can also be grown from seed sown fresh or in spring. Plant out in a moisture-retentive soil in light shade or sun. (Seed not generally available but may occasionally be found in alpine and USA exchanges.)

Sternbergia (Amaryllidaceae). Bulbous plants of which *S. lutea* is grown as a border plant. Propagation is generally by division, preferably when the bulb is still in leaf in spring ('in the green' as with *Galanthus*), or in late summer and early autumn, before growth starts. They can also be increased by cutting up the bulbs, providing each piece contains part of the basal plate from which root will grow (see p. 69). They can also be grown from seed, but as with most bulbs this may take several years to produce flowering plants. Plant out in a well-drained, sunny position. (Seed available from alpine seed exchanges.)

Stipa (Gramineae). Feather Grass. A large genus of clump-forming grasses that can be increased by division in spring. The species can also be grown from seed sown in spring. Plant out in any good garden soil in sun. (Seed available from some specialist commercial sources and seed exchanges.)

Stokesia (Compositae). A monotypic genus represented by *S. laevis*, which a very easy plant to increase. Seed can be sown fresh or in spring. It will also come very easily by division in spring, even small slips readily establishing themselves in open ground. If these two methods are not enough, it will also come from root cuttings taken in late autumn. Plant out in any good, well-drained soil in full sun. (Seed available from commercial sources as well as HPS and other seed exchanges.)

Stratiotes (Hydrocharitaceae). Water Soldier. A monotypic genus represented by *S. aloides*. This is a floating water plant that produces plantlets on the end of vigorous stolons. These can be removed and potted up, keeping the pots under water, or replanting direct into the bottom of the pond. They may need anchoring to prevent them floating away. It can also be propagated by dividing the plant in early spring, ensuring that each piece includes a dormant bud. Seed is occasionally set. Sow when fresh in a moist compost and stand the seed pan in a tray of water. Plant out in shallow water. (Seed not generally available but plants can be purchased.)

Streptopus (Convallariaceae/Liliaceae). A small genus of woodland plants akin to *Polygonatum*. It has the same creeping habit and can thus be easily divided in spring. The species can also be grown from seed, which should be sown fresh. Plant out in a woodland-type soil in light shade. (Seed only available from one commercial source and only rarely occurs in seed exchange lists, mainly USA ones.)

Strobilanthus (Acanthaceae). A large genus of mainly tropical plants although one, *S. atropurpureus*, is grown in gardens. This plant can best be increased by dividing the bushy clumps in spring. It can also be grown from seed by sowing in spring. (Seed available from one specialist seed merchant and from the HPS seed exchange.)

Stylophorum (Papaveraceae). A small genus of woodland species best increased from seed as long as it is sown as soon as it is harvested or in the open ground in late spring. With a bit of care the crowns can be divided in spring or autumn. Plant out in a cool, woodland-type soil in light shade. (Seed available from specialist seed merchants and the HPS and other seed exchanges.)

Succisa (Dipsacaceae). A small genus with affinities with *Scabiosa*. Increase can be effected by dividing the short rhizomes in spring or by taking cuttings at the same time of year. Can also be grown from seed sown in spring. Plant out in a moist or even boggy soil in full sun. (Seed not generally available, although it does occur in the HPS seed list.)

Swertia (Gentianaceae). A large genus of moisture-loving annuals and perennial plants of which a few are in cultivation. Both can be grown from seed sown preferably when fresh. Prick out when small and plant out as soon as possible as they resent root disturbance. Perennials can also be increased by division in spring. Plant out in a moist soil in sun or light shade. (Seed available from one specialist commercial seed merchant and from alpine seed exchanges.)

Symphyandra (Campanulaceae). A small genus closely related to the *Campanula*. The most common way of increase is from seed sown in spring. Most will self-sow giving more than enough plants for most uses. They tend to be short-lived or biennial so it is best to sow new plants every year to ensure continuance. Vegetative increase is very difficult although division can be attempted with care. Alternatively cuttings can be tried in spring. Plant out in a sunny position in a well-drained soil. (Seed available from specialist commercial sources and seed exchanges.)

Symphytum (Boraginaceae). Comfrey. One of the easiest of genera to propagate, indeed once obtained it is difficult to eradicate. It is a rapidly-spreading plant and is very easy to divide up in spring or autumn. Will also come very readily from root cuttings, which should be taken in winter, as anyone will know who has attempted to remove a plant but has left fragments of root behind. Will also come readily from seed and does seed itself around, but this is not a good method for special colour forms nor for variegated cultivars. Plant out in a rich soil in sun or light shade. (Seed available from specialist commercial sources and seed exchanges.)

Symplocarpus (Araceae). Skunk Cabbage. A single species genus represented by *S. foetidus*. The plant has thick rhizomes which, with care, can be divided in winter or early spring just before the flowers appear. Division can be difficult and an alternative is to remove the seed from their fleshy fruit and sow as soon as they are ripe. Plant out in a moist or boggy ground in sun. (Seed not generally available but plants can be purchased.)

Synthyris (Scrophulariaceae). A small genus of woodland plants suitable for the peat garden. They are clump forming and can be divided in autumn or spring after flowering. They resent disturbance and so may take a little time to resettle, perhaps making it preferable to grow them from seed sown in spring. Plant out in a cool, woodland-type soil in light shade. (Seed not available from commercial sources but can be found in alpine seed exchange lists.)

Tanacetum (Compositae). Pyrethrum, Tansy. A medium-sized genus that has recently had an influx of new species from *Chrysanthemum* and *Pyrethrum*. Like most of their close allies, these are best increased vegetatively. This can be easily achieved by either dividing the plant in autumn or spring, or by taking basal cuttings from the young growth in spring. They can also be grown from seed and this is the best way for some of the bedding-plant strains developed by seed merchants. These are best sown under gentle heat in spring, whereas the species can be sown in autumn or spring and left outside. Plant out in any good garden soil in full sun. (Seed available from most commercial sources and from the HPS and other seed exchanges.)

Tanakaea (Saxifragaceae). A single species genus represented by *T. radicans*, a Japanese woodlander. Like many woodlanders it has a creeping habit, which makes it easy to divide in early spring or autumn. It can also be grown from seed sown in spring. Plant out in a cool, woodland-type soil in light shade. (Seed not generally available, although it can occasionally be found in alpine seed exchanges.)

Telekia (Compositae). See **Buphthalmum**

Telesonix (Saxifragaceae). (See also *Boykinia*.) A monotypic genus with one species, *T. jamesii*, which used to belong to *Boykinia*. Easily increased either by division of the older clumps or sowing seed in spring. Plant out in a well-drained, humus rich soil, preferably in partial shade. (Seed available from exchanges, especially the alpine garden exchanges. Occasionally available from commercial sources.)

Tellima (Saxifragaceae). Fringecup. A single species genus represented by *T. grandiflora*, a spreading plant easily divided in spring. It can also be grown from seed sown in spring. It self-sows, which can save a lot of trouble in raising plants. Plant out in a woodland-type soil in light shade. (Seed available from specialist commercial sources and from HPS and other seed exchanges.)

Teucrium (Labiatae). Germander. A large genus of sun-loving plants of which only a few are suitable for the perennial border, although quite a number appear on the rock garden. The clump-forming and spreading species that can be divided in spring. They can be increased from cuttings taken in spring or late summer, the latter useful for overwintering the more tender species. They can also be grown from seed, either sown fresh or in spring. Plant out in a well-drained soil in a warm sunny position. (Seed available from specialist commercial sources and seed exchanges.)

Thalictrum (Ranunculaceae). Meadow Rue. A surprisingly large genus (130 species) many of which are suitable for the garden. Except for cultivars, most can be easily raised from seed. This should preferably, as with all Ranunculaceae, be sown fresh but it can be sown in spring if necessary. Some, *T. aquilegiifolium* being a good example, self-sow and produce enough offspring for most uses. Many clump up or spread and can be easily divided. *T. delavayi* 'Hewitt's Double' is always considered difficult but can easily be increased by lifting the cylindrical rootstock in March and cutting vertically down through it. This can be further sectionalized, creating up to eight thin sections that can be potted up. There is no need to have visible buds at the top of each section as these will quickly form. Plants can be planted out in August in a rich, moisture-retentive soil in sun. (Seed available from commercial sources and from HPS and other seed exchanges.)

Thelypteris (Polypodiaceae). A very large genus of ferns of which a few are in cultivation. They mainly have creeping rhizomes and can be increased by division in spring or by sowing the spore when ripe. Plant out in a moist soil in sun or light shade. (Spore may be available from pteridological societies.)

Thermopsis (Leguminosae). A small genus of lupin-like plants. They can be grown from seed sown in autumn or spring with the resulting seedlings being planted out in autumn with as little disturbance as possible. Like most legumes, a soaking overnight in warm water may be beneficial. In colder areas germinate under glass. It is a spreading plant, which makes division in the autumn or spring easy. It can also be increased by taking basal cuttings in spring. Plant out into a well-drained, moisture-retentive soil in full sun. (Seed not generally available commercially except from USA native plant merchants; available from HPS and other seed exchanges.)

Thladiantha (Curcubitaceae). A small genus of herbaceous climbing plants. They can easily be increased from seed sown in spring under glass in gentle heat. The plants are dioecious and therefore both male and female plants will be required to produce seed. They can also be increased by division of the tuberous rootstock. Plant out in any good soil in a warm sunny position, preferably against a wall. (Seed not generally available and plants are equally difficult to obtain.)

Thymus (Labiatae). Thyme. Although these are shrubby plants, they are often grown on the edge of borders or in walls. They can most easily be increased by taking cuttings in late spring. Many of the prostrate shoots bear roots and can be either treated as a rooted cutting or as a division. As will be seen in any garden that grows them, they will also grow from seed, but this is not a suitable method for the many cultivars. Plant out in a well-drained soil in a sunny position. (Seed available from commercial sources and seed exchanges.)

Tiarella (Saxifragaceae). Foamflower. A small genus of plants that, as with so many woodlanders, has a creeping habit. This makes it an easy genus to divide in either autumn or spring. They can also be grown from seed sown, preferably, when fresh although it can be delayed until spring. Plant out in a humus-rich, woodland-type soil in light shade. (Seed available from some specialist seed merchants and seed exchanges.)

Tigridia (Iridaceae). A small genus of bulbous plants for the warmer areas. They can easily be increased by dividing the offsets in autumn. They can also be grown from seed sown in the autumn or spring; maintaining a minimum night-time temperature of 13°C (55°F). Plant out in April or May in a well-drained but moisture-retentive soil in a sunny position. (Seed available from some specialist commercial sources and from seed exchanges.)

Tofieldia (Melanthiaceae/Liliaceae). A small genus of plants for a wet or boggy area. They can easily be divided in spring or can be sown from seed either fresh or in spring. Plant out in a moist acid soil in sun or light shade. (Seed not commercially available but occasionally occurs in seed exchange lists.)

Tolmiea (Saxifragaceae). Pickaback Plant, Piggy-back Plant, Youth on Age. A monotypic genus represented by *T. menziesii*. This is a spreading woodland plant that can easily be divided in spring. It also produces gemmaceous plantlets, that is plants that appear at the base of the leaf blades. These can be potted up and will readily root. If a further method were needed it is also possible to grow them from seed sown in spring. Plant out in a moist, woodland-type soil in light shade. (Seed available from some specialist seed merchants and occasionally from seed exchanges.)

Tovara (Polygonaceae). See *Persicaria*

Trachystemon (Boraginaceae). A two species genus of which one, *T. orientalis*, is in cultivation. It is an invasive plant that can easily be divided to provide more plants. This should be done in autumn or spring. It can also be grown from seed sown in spring. Plant out the young plants in any good garden soil in sun or light shade. (Seed not generally available but does occasionally crop up in seed exchanges. Plants, however, are available.)

Tradescantia (Commelinaceae). Spiderwort. A medium genus with a few hardy or near-hardy plants for the border. They are spreading plants that form clumps that can be easily divided in spring or autumn to provide propagation material. The species can also be grown from seed sown in spring. They happily self-sow providing sufficient plants for most uses. Plant out in any good garden soil in full sun. (Seed available from some specialist commercial sources as well as seed exchanges.)

Trapa (Trapaceae). Water Chestnut. A small genus of floating water plants. The species most commonly grown is *T. natans*, which is in fact an annual. It produces seed that overwinters at the bottom of the pond before germinating in spring. Seed should be collected and kept underwater or in wet sphagnum moss until required for germination. If the seed dries out it dies. The self-sown seed usually provides enough spare plants. (Seed not generally available, but plants can be purchased.)

Tricyrtis (Convallariaceae/Liliaceae). Toad Lilies. These are rhizomatous plants that can easily be increased by division. This is best done while the plants are dormant, in early spring before growth starts. They will also come readily from seed, preferably sown fresh. Some species flower in late autumn and so seed is not always available except in favourable years. Plant out in spring in a shady position with woodland soil. *Tricyrtis* have also been increased by stalk cuttings; a leaf with a piece of stalk is placed in a warm, moist propagating frame in late summer. The dormant buds in the leaves' axils produce new plantlets. Since other methods produce excellent results for most needs, this method is really for those who want to experiment, or make rapid increased from one plant. (Seed available from HPS, RHS and alpine seed exchanges and specialist commercial sources.)

Trientalis (Primulaceae). A small genus of two species, *TT. borealis* and *europaea*. They grow in pine forests with a running habit, which makes them easy to divide in spring. They can also be grown from seed, which is best sown fresh. Plant out in a woodland-type soil in light shade. (Seed not available commercially but is occasionally available from alpine seed exchanges. Plants commercially obtainable.)

Trifolium (Leguminosae). Clovers. A large genus of which only a few are in cultivation. The easiest method of increase is by sowing seed in spring. Many are spreading plants and in spite of their deep tap roots can be divided. The procumbent stems of many species root as they spread. These can be divided off and used as rooted cuttings or as divisions. Plant out in any garden soil in sun. (Seed available from specialist sources, including wildflower suppliers, and from seed exchanges.)

Trillium (Trilliaceae/Liliaceae). Wake Robin. A large genus of popular plants. Unfortunately they are not that easy to propagate either vegetatively or by seed. The former can be achieved by lifting the plant as soon after the flower has died down and by carefully removing the new shoot or bud at the tip of a rhizome. The trillium is then replanted. After another year the plant is again removed from the soil and offsets should have developed around the concave area where the shoot was removed. These can be removed and potted up singly. Flowering-sized plants should be achieved in another three years or so. Growing trillium from seed is a lengthy business, taking up to seven years to reach flowering size. The seed is best sown fresh; if stored it should never be allowed to dry out. It is double dormant. In the first instance, it needs a period of cold followed by a warm period. At this stage the root is put down but it is only after another period of cold and return to warmth (which break the second dormancy) do the leaves appear above the level of the soil. Thus all seed pans should be kept for at least two years if left outside. Two periods of artificial pre-chilling can help reduce the time taken. Plant out in a humus-rich, woodland-type soil in light shade. (Seed available from some seed merchants and most seed exchanges, especially alpine ones.)

Triosteum (Caprifoliaceae). Horse Gentian. A small genus of woodland plants often grown for their attractive drupes. Remove the flesh from these drupes and either sow the inner seed while fresh in autumn or store without allowing to dry out and sow in spring. They will self-sow and enough seedlings can be found around the plants for most purposes. They can also be increased vegetatively by division in spring. Plant out in a woodland-type soil in light shade. (Seed does not appear to be generally available but the North American species may be found in catalogues of native flowers in the USA. Some plants are, however, available.)

Tritelia (Alliaceae/Liliaceae). These are closely related to the *Brodiaea* and increased in a similar fashion, namely by regularly (every three to four years) dividing the clumps of bulbs during the autumn, or by sowing seed either fresh or in spring. Plant out in a well-drained soil in full sun. (Seed available from all seed exchanges and occasionally from commercial sources.)

Tritonia (Iridaceae). Plants very akin to the *Crocosmia*. Cormlets are found next to the main bulb and these can be detached during the dormant period after the foliage has died down. Unlike *Crocosmia*, only one species produces new corms on stolons. These can easily be used for propagation purposes. They will also come from seed sown in spring, but this is a longer process. Plant out in any well-drained soil in full sun. (Seed not generally available although it occasionally occurs in alpine exchanges.)

Trollius (Ranunculaceae). Globe Flowers. Since there are now several cultivars of the different species, the only general method of propagation is by division of the clumps. This can be done after flowering in spring or autumn. The species come readily from seed as long as it is sown fresh. It can be sown in spring but germination is erratic, although a period of pre-chilling may help. Plant out, preferably in autumn, in damp or moisture-retentive soil in sun or light shade. (Seed available from commercial sources and seed exchanges.)

Tropaeolum (Tropaeolaceae). Nasturtiums. They can all be propagated from seed sown fresh or in spring. They can also be propagated by division of their tuberous roots, but some, *T. polyphyllum* for example, delve very deep and can be very difficult to extract, the struggle often ending in the plant's demise. Others, like *T. speciosum*, resent disturbance. Some others, such as *TT. tuberosum* and *polyphyllum*, will respond to the taking of basal cuttings of the young growth in late spring. (Seed of the annual form, *T. majus*, very commonly available, others are carried by some specialist seed merchants and seed exchanges. Seed of exciting, new coloured and hardy forms has been recently introduced by seed-collecting expeditions.)

Tulbaghia (Alliaceae/Liliaceae). A small genus of bulbous plants, suitable only for warmer areas. The bulbs are clump forming and the easiest method of propagation is to lift and divide them. They will also come from seed sown fresh or in spring. The new variegated form, *T. violacea*, can only be increased by division. Plant out in any well-drained soil in a warm, sunny position. (Seed only available from specialist seed merchants and seed exchanges, especially alpine ones.)

Tulipa (Liliaceae). Tulips. A large genus of popular garden plants. The many cultivars can only be increased vegetatively, which means lifting and splitting off the offsets. *T. saxatilis* is a creeping tulip, producing new bulbs on extended stolons, which can be removed. Species and cultivars that are slow to increase can be multiplied by twin scaling (*see* p. 69). The species can be readily increased from seed, preferably sown fresh, but also in spring. Plant out in a well-drained soil in sun. (Seed available from specialist seed merchants and seed exchanges, especially alpine ones.)

Typha (Typhaceae). Reedmace, Bulrush. A small genus of marginal water plants. They increase naturally by a creeping rootstock that can easily be divided just before growth starts in spring. They can also be raised from seed sown either fresh or in spring. Germination is erratic. Plant out in shallow water. (Seed not generally available although it is stocked by at least one commercial source and also by firms specializing in wildflowers. Rarely seen in seed exchanges.)

Uvularia (Convallariaceae). A small genus of delightful woodland plants. Like most members of this family, they have a creeping, rhizomatous rootstock that readily allows increase by simple division, preferably in autumn or spring after flowering. They can also be increased from seed sown in autumn or spring. Plant out in a woodland-type soil in light shade. (Seed not generally available from commercial sources although it may be found on native North American seed lists. It also occurs in alpine seed exchange lists.)

Valeriana (Valerianaceae). Valerian. A large genus with only a few plants in cultivation. They can be grown from seed sown in spring. This should not be sown too deeply as they require light for germination. Many can also be divided in either autumn or spring. An alternative vegetative method is to take basal cuttings of the young growth in spring. Plant out in a moisture-retentive soil in light shade or sun. (Seed available from specialist seed sources and seed exchanges.)

Vancouveria (Berberidaceae). A small genus of three species closely akin to *Epimedium*. They are spreading plants that can be easily divided, preferably in autumn, but also in spring. The plants become terribly congested and should be separated out when dividing. They can also be grown from seed, if it is available, sown in spring. Plant out in a humus-rich, woodland-type soil in light shade. (Seed not generally available commercially, but can occasionally be found on seed exchange lists.)

Veltheimia (Hyacinthaceae/Liliaceae). A small genus of South African bulbous plants that can be grown in warmer districts. The simplest way to increase the population is to divide them in autumn. They can also be grown from seed sown either fresh or in spring. Plant out in a well-drained soil in a warm sunny spot. (Seed not generally available although at least one commercial source stocks some. They also occur in seed exchange lists. Plants available.)

Veratrum (Melanthiaceae/Liliaceae). False Helleborine. A small genus with thick rhizomatous, almost bulbous rootstock. They can be increased by sowing some of the copious amounts of seed produced, in spring. Growing plants from seed is a slow business as they can take seven or eight years to reach flowering size. The first season after germination is devoted to producing roots and nothing can be seen above ground until the second year, so do not prematurely throw away what appear to be empty seed pots. Leave the seedlings in their pots for at least a year after the first leaves have appeared before potting up or planting out in a nursery bed. Fortunately they do produce offsets that can be divided to form a speedier method of increase. The roots are very poisonous. Plant in a humus-rich woodland-type soil in light shade. (Seed available from at least one commercial source and usually occurs on all the main seed exchange lists.)

Verbascum (Scrophulariaceae). Mullein. A large genus of stately, biennial and perennial plants of which quite a number are in cultivation and even more have been produced by hybridization. They produce copious amounts of seed, which is easy to germinate. Sow it either fresh or in spring. Most will also self-sow, producing plenty of offspring. Some coloured strains have been developed by seed merchants and these can be sown in spring. However, vegetative means are required for the named forms and this can be achieved by carefully dividing off the secondary rosettes, if any exist, in spring, or earlier in the year by taking root cuttings. Plant out in a well-drained soil in full sun. (Seed generally available from most commercial sources, although seed exchanges are better for the species.)

Verbena (Verbenaceae). A large genus of plants many of which are in cultivation although most are tender and need winter protection. They are easy to increase by most of the main methods. Species can be sown from seed in spring, early spring if you are in a hurry as they are slow to germinate. Pre-chilling and gentle heat will speed up the process. Light may also be beneficial for most species. Some, such as *V. bonariensis*, will happily self-sow saving the grower the bother. Basal cuttings can be taken from the young growth in spring, but again many will root on their prostrate stems, providing sufficient rooted cuttings or divisions that can be taken at any time when the plant is in growth. Some should be taken in early autumn in case of plant losses during the winter. Plant out in a well-drained soil in full sun. (Seed available from commercial sources and seed exchanges.)

Verbesina (Compositae). Crown Beard. A large genus of yellow or white flowering plants occasionally seen in gardens. They can be grown from seed sown fresh in late autumn or spring. The perennials lend themselves to division, which should be carried out in spring. Plant out in any good garden soil (preferably in the wild garden) in sun. (Seed not generally available but may be found in North American native plant seed lists.)

Vernonia (Compositae). Ironweed. A very large genus of up to 1,000 species of which just a few have made it into cultivation. They will all grow from seed sown, preferably, in autumn, although it can be left until spring. They can also be increased vegetatively by being divided, again, during autumn or spring. Basal cuttings can be taken in spring. Plant out in any good garden soil in full sun. (Seed available from at least one commercial source and is occasionally seen in seed exchanges. Firms specializing in North American native plants may stock some of them.)

Veronica (Scrophulariaceae). Speedwells. A large genus with many interesting plants in cultivation. The species can be grown from seed sown in spring. The seeds require a certain amount of light in order to germinate, so do not cover them too deeply, just sufficiently to allow diffused light to penetrate. They can, of course, also be increased vegetatively. The majority are spreaders allowing easy increase by division, either in autumn or spring. They can also be propagated from cuttings taken, preferably, in spring, but also in summer. Plant out in a well-drained soil in full sun. (Seed available from commercial sources as well as seed exchanges.)

Veronicastrum (Scrophulariaceae). Culver's Physic. A small genus of two species that are very close to *Veronica* except in certain botanical variations and can be propagated by exactly the same methods. (Seed not generally available although it does occasionally occur in seed exchanges. Plants available.)

Vicia (Leguminosae). Vetch, Tare. A large genus of annuals and perennial climbing plants, few of which are considered garden-worthy. The easiest method of increase is from seed sown in spring. The seed may benefit from being soaked overnight in warm water before sowing. Some of the stoloniferous or spreading plants can be divided either in autumn or spring. Plant out in any well-drained garden soil in sun. (Seed not generally available although it occasionally occurs in seed exchanges. Can also be found in catalogues of wild-flower seed merchants.)

Vinca (Aponcynaceae). Periwinkles. A small genus of perennials and subshrubs. The main, and easiest, method of increase is vegetative. Its clumps can easily be divided and plantlets formed where the arching stems touch the soil can readily be detached and potted up or replanted. These two methods should be sufficient for most needs but, if necessary, summer cuttings can also be taken. The species will also come from seed, but it is not too easy to find. Plant out in any good garden soil in light shade or sun. (Seed not generally obtainable but plants are abundantly available.)

Viola (Violaceae). A very large genus of popular garden plants. All the species and seed merchant's strains can be easily grown from seed sown in the autumn or spring. Gentle heat can be used for the strains but do not exceed 24°C (75°F), most pansies prefer a much lower temperature. Violas sometimes have cleistogamous flowers, that is, flowers that pollinate themselves without opening, and thus seed seems to appear on plants that have not flowered, especially late in the season. This seed is perfectly viable. Do not pick any seed too soon; it should be brown and not green. Seed is ready for harvesting when the pod splits open to the gentlest of pressures from the fingers. Most violas will self-sow, although cultivars will not necessarily come true. The tufted forms of violas and violettas can be divided in autumn or spring. They can also be grown from cuttings. The best are young shoots, which can be promoted by shearing over the whole or part of the plant ten days before the cuttings are required. Plenty of good young growth will then appear. Many will also respond to being layered, indeed rooted shoots can often be found where they have layered naturally. The species are more difficult to increase vegetatively as they generally have one central root and are not easy to take cuttings. However some, *V. odorata* for example, have stolons that produce plantlets and these can be potted up or planted out. Plant out in a light shady position in a well-drained soil that does not become too dry, although many will also take full sun. (Seed generally available from most commercial sources, although the species are more likely to be obtained from seed exchanges, especially alpine ones.)

Viscaria (Caryophyllaceae). See **Lychnis**

Wachendorfia (Haemodoraceae). A small genus of bulbous plants for warmer areas. The easiest method of increase, as with most bulbs, is simple division during the dormant period. Alternatively, they can be grown from seed sown in spring. Plant out in a warm sunny position in any good garden soil. (Seed available from at least one commercial supplier and occasionally occurs in seed exchanges. Bulbs can be purchased.)

Wahlenbergia (Campanulaceae). A large genus of plants closely allied to *Campanula*. All can be grown from seed sown in spring. Many have a spreading habit and can easily be divided either in autumn or spring. Plant out in a well-drained soil in a sunny position. (Seed available from at least one commercial source and seed exchanges, especially alpine ones.)

Waldsteinia (Rosaceae). A small genus of rhizomatous woodland plants. Their creeping habit makes them easy to divide in either autumn or spring. They can also be increased from seed sown in spring. Plant out in a woodland-type soil in light shade. (Seed not commonly available but can be found in at least one commercial list and occasionally in seed exchanges. Plants widely available.)

Watsonia (Iridaceae). A medium-sized genus of bulbous plants, mainly for warmer areas. The easiest method of increase is to detach the new corms that are formed each year on the parent. This should be done when the plant is dormant. The species can also be grown from seed sown in spring, although there will be variation in the resulting colours. It will take at least three years to reach flowering size. Plant out in a well-drained, yet moisture-retentive soil, in a warm, sunny position. (Seed available from at least one seed merchant and from seed exchanges.)

Weldenia (Commelinaceae). A single species genus represented by the beautiful *W. candida*. The normal method of increase is by sowing seed in spring. The seed may take a bit of finding as the seed capsule is buried deep in the rosette. Vegetatively they can be increased by root cuttings taken in winter. Plant out in well-drained soil in a warm sunny position. (Seed not available commercially but does occur on seed exchange lists.)

Woodsia (Aspleniaceae). A medium-sized genus of ferns. All will come from spore sown when ripe. Some are rhizomatous and can be increased by division in spring. Plant out in a well-drained soil in light shade or sun. (Spores may be obtainable from pteridological societies.)

Woodwardia (Blechnaceae). Chain Fern. A small genus of ferns most of which are too tender for the open garden. As with most ferns, they can be increased by sowing spore when it is ripe. They can also be increased by dividing the plants in spring. *W. radicans* can be increased from bulbils found on some fronds. Peg down such fronds in autumn and keep moist until the bulbils have put down roots, then pot up individually. Plant out in a moist soil in light shade. (Spore may be obtainable from pteridological societies.)

Wulfenia (Scrophulariaceae). A small genus of tufted, rhizomatous plants. They can be vegetatively propagated in autumn or by division in spring. They can also be grown from seed sown in spring. Plant out in a moisture-retentive soil in sun. (Seed available from at least one commercial source and from seed exchange lists.)

Xerophyllum (Phormiaceae/Liliaceae). Bear Grass. A two species genus, both of which are quite difficult to cultivate. The easiest method of increase is from seed, if it can be found. It will take up to seven years to reach flowering size. The grasslike clumps can also be divided with care. Plant out in a lime-free, moisture-retentive, almost boggy, soil in full sun. (Seed not commonly available but occasionally may be found in seed exchanges or native plant seed lists.)

Yucca (Agavaceae). Adam's Needle, Palm Lily, Spanish Dagger. Easily grown from seed. No pretreatment, but it does need a temperature of 20–30°C (68–86°F) for successful germination. Hand pollination is usually needed away from American gardens to produce seed. They can also be propagated from root cuttings. Suckering species, such as *YY. flaccida* and *filamentosa*, can be propagated by division in spring or by making stem cuttings from the side shoots in autumn. Plant out in a well-drained soil in a warm, sunny position. (Seed available from specialist commercial sources, seed exchanges, and native plant lists.)

Zantedeschia (Araceae). Arum Lily, Calla Lily, Lily-of-the-Nile. A small genus of plants for warmer areas. The plants form large clumps, which can be divided in early spring or while the plants are dormant. Alternatively, root cuttings can be taken from the fleshy roots in winter. They will also come from seed sown in spring, although the cultivars will not, of course, remain true. Plant out in a moisture-retentive soil or in shallow water. (Seed available commercially and from seed exchanges.)

Zauschneria (Onagraceae). California Fuchsia. We all have at least one plant name that we refuse to change and this is mine. Strictly speaking this is now classified under *Epilobium*. A small genus of woody perennials easily raised from cuttings taken in spring or summer. With care they can also be divided in spring. It can also be increased from seed, although colour forms will not come true. Seed should be sown in spring, possibly with a little gentle heat. Plant out in a well-drained soil in a warm, sunny position. (Seed not generally available commercially but does occur in seed exchange lists often under *Epilobium canum*.)

Zephyranthes (Amaryllidaceae). A medium-sized genus of bulbous plants easily propagated from the many offsets produced. These can be lifted and separated in autumn or spring. They can also be grown from seed sown in spring, possibly using a little gentle heat. The seed seem to appreciate light for germination. Plant out in a well-drained but moisture-retentive soil in sun. (Seed not available commercially but does appear on seed exchange lists.)

Zigadenus (Melanthiaceae/Liliaceae). A small genus of bulbous plants best increased by division in spring. They can also be grown from seed sown in spring. The whole plant is extremely poisonous so care should be taken. Plant out in a well-drained soil in full sun. (Seed not generally available from commercial sources but is widely available from seed exchange lists.)

Zizania (Gramineae). A small genus of annual and aquatic grasses. The usual method of increase is by division in spring. They can also be increased by seed (essential for annual species) but this rarely sets in northern climates so imported seed must be relied upon. Plant out in shallow water or boggy ground. (Seed not generally available except from specialist sources. Plants obtainable.)

APPENDIX 1

Sources of Seed

Societies

Generally only members of a society can use its seed exchange. Since most societies are run on a voluntary basis, addresses are likely to change. If there are any difficulties in contacting them check with either the Royal Horticultural Society or the American Horticultural Society, both of which keep a register of current addresses.

American Hemerocallis Society, 1454 Rebel Drive, Jackson, MS 39211, US
American Herb Association, PO Box 353, Rescue, CA 95672, US
American Horticultural Society, 7931 East Boulevard Drive, Alexandria, Virginia 22308, US
American Hosta Society, 5206 Hawksbury Lane, Raleigh, NC 27606, US
American Iris Society, (Carol Ramsey), 6518 Beachy Avenue, Wichita, KS 67206, US
American Penstemon Society, 1569 S. Holland Court, Lakewood, CO 80226, US
American Primrose Society, (Brian Skidmore), 6750 W. Mercer Way, Mercer Island, WA 98040, US
British Hosta and Hemerocallis Society, (R. Bowden), Cleeve House, Sticklepath, Oakhampton, Devon, EX20 2NN, UK
British Iris Society, (Mrs E. M. Wise), 197 The Parkway, Iver Heath, Buckinghamshire, SL0 0RQ, UK
Cottage Garden Society, (Mrs C. Tordoff), 5 Nixon Close, Thornhill, Dewsbury, West Yorkshire, WF12 OJA, UK
Cyclamen Society, (Peter Moore), Tile Barn House, Standen Green, Iden Green, Beneden, Kent, TN17 4LB, UK
Hardy Plant Society, (Tricia King), Bank Cottage, Great Comberton, Nr Pershore, Worcs, WR10 0HT, UK
Hardy Plant Society of Oregon, 33530 SE Bluff Road, Boring, OR97009, US
Perennial Plant Association, 3383 Schirtzinger Road, Columbus, OH 43026, US
Royal Horticultural Society, Vincent Square, London, SW1P 2PE, UK

Commercial firms

Many nurseries besides selling plants also sell seed from their stock plants. These are obviously far too numerous to list. A listing here is no guarantee that the firm is still trading.

Albion Seed, PO Box 492, Bolton, Ontario, L0R 4A2, Canada

Apache Seeds, 10136–149 Street, Edmonton, Alberta, T5P 1L1, Canada

Applewood Seed Company, 5380 Vivian Street, Arvada, CO 80002, US

Arthur Yates & Co., PO Box 940, Auckland, New Zealand

Bamert Seed Co., Route 3, Box 192, Muleshoe, TX 79347, US

J. W. Boyce, Bush Pasture, Lowercarter Street, Fordham, Ely, Cambridgeshire, CB7 5JU, UK

D. T. Brown & Co., Station Road, Poulton-le-Fylde, Blackpool, FY6 7HZ, UK

Buckerfield's Ltd, 1640 Boundary Road, PO Box 7000, Vancouver, BC V6B 4E1, Canada

Burpee Seeds, 300 Park Avenue, Warminster, PA 18991, US

Chelsea Choice Seeds, Regal Road, Wisbech, Cambridgeshire, PE13 2RF, UK

Chiltern Seeds, Bortree Stile, Ulverston, Cumbria, LA12 7PB, UK

Botanic Garden Seed Co., 9 Wyckoff Street, Brooklyn, NY 11201, US

Clyde Robin Seed Co., PO Box 2855, Castro Valley, CA 94546, US

F. Copper Ltd., PO Box 12–347, Penrose, Auckland 1135, New Zealand

Country Garden, Route 2, Box 455A, Crivitz, WI 54114, US

Eden Seeds, The Finch Family, MS 316, Gympie, Queensland 4570 Australia

Environmental Seed Producers, PO Box 5904, El Monte, CA 91734, US

Gruydt-hoeck, Postbus 1414, Groningen, Holland

Harris Moran Seed Co., 3670 Buffalo Road, Rochester, NY 14624, US

C. C. Hart Seed Co., PO Box 9169, Wethgersfield, CT 06109, US

J. L. Hudson, PO Box 1058, Redwood City, CA 94064, US

Jack Drake, Inshriach Nursery, Aviemore, Inverness-shire, Scotland PH22 1QS, UK

John Chambers, 15 Westleigh Road, Barton Seagrave, Kettering, Northamptonshire, NN15 5AG, UK

Izard Ozark Native Seeds, PO Box 454, Mountain View, AR 72560, US

L. Kreeger, 91 Newton Wood Road, Ashtead, Surrey, KT21 1NN, UK

Lindy Emmett, MS 1197, Cooloolabin, Via Nambour, Queensland 4560, Australia

Lofts Inc, Chimney Rock, Road Bound Brook, NJ 08805, US

McFayden, Box 1800, Brandon, Manitoba, R7A 6N4, Canada

Maver Rare Perennials, Route 2, Box 265B, Asheville, NC 28805, US

Midwest Wildflowers, PO Box 643, Rockton, IL 61072, US

Moon Mountain Wildflowers, PO Box 34, Morro Bay, CA 93442, US

Mr Fothergill's Seeds, Gazeley Road, Kentford, Newmarket, Suffolk, CB8 7QB, UK

S. E. Marshall & Co., Wisbech, Cambridgeshire, PE13 2RF, UK

Native Plants Inc, PO Box 177, Leigh, UT 84043, US

Native Seed Inc, 114590 Triadelphia Mill Road, Dayton, MD 21036, US

Nichols Garden, 1190 N. Pacific Highway, Albany, OR 14240, US

North Australian Plant Exports Pty Ltd., 247 Tower Road, Suite 12, Montgomery House, Casuarina, NT 5792, Australia

L. L. Olds Seed Co., 2901 Packers Ave., PO Box 7790, Madison, WI 53707, US

Ontario Seed Co., 16 King Street South, Waterloo, Ontario, N2J 3Z9, Canada

D. Orriell, 11.10 Golfview Street, Nr Yokine, Western Australia 6060, Australia

Park Seeds, Highway 254 N., Greenwood, SC 29647, US

W. H. Perron & Co., 515 Labelle Boulevard, Chomedey, Laval, PQ, H7V 2T3, Canada
Phoenix Seeds, PO Box 9, Stanley, Tasmania
Plant World, St Marychurch Road, Newton Abbot, Devon, UK
Prairie Seed Source, PO Box 83, North Lake WI 53064, US
Robertson-Pike, PO Box 20000, Edmonton, Alberta, T5J 3M3, Canada
Robinett Bulb Farm, PO Box 1306, Sebastopol, CA 95473, US
S & R Seed Co., Box 86, Cass Lake, MN 56633, US
S & S Seeds, PO Box 1275, Carpenteria, CA 93013, US
Samuel Dobie & Son, Broomhill Way, Torquay, Devon, TQ2 7QW, UK
Seed Centre Ltd., Box 3867, Station D, Edmonton, Alberta, T51 4K1, Canada
Seed House, 9A Widley Road, Cosham, Portsmouth, PO6 2DS, UK
Southern Cross Seeds, Templestowe Road, Lower Templestowe, Victoria 3107, Australia
Speciality Seeds, PO Box 34, Hawksburn, Victoria 3142, Australia
Stock Seed Farms Inc, Route 1, Box 112, Murdoch, NE 68407, US
Stokes Seeds Ltd., PO Box 10, St Catharine's, Ontario, L2R 6R6, Canada
Suffolk Herbs, Sawyer's Farm, Little Cornard, Sudbury, Suffolk, CO10 0NY, UK
Sunshine Seed Co., Route 2, Box 176, Wyoming, IL 61491, US
Suttons Seeds, Hele Road, Torquay, Devon, TQ2 7JQ, UK
Thomas Butcher, 60 Wickham Road, Shirley, Croydon, Surrey, CR9 8AG, UK
Thompson and Morgan Inc., PO Box 1308, Jackson, New Jersey, 08527, US
Thompson and Morgan Inc., 132 James Avenue East, Winnepeg, Manitoba R3B ON8, Canada
Thompson and Morgan Ltd, London Road, Ipswich, Suffolk, IP2 0BA, UK
Thompson and Morgan, Erica Vale, Australia Pty Ltd, PO Box, 50 Jannali, New South Wales 2226, Australia
T & T Seeds Ltd, PO Box 1710, Winnepeg, Manitoba R3C 3P6, Canada
Unwins Seeds, Histon, Cambridge, CB4 4ZZ, UK
Vermont Wildflower Farm, Route 7, Box 5, Charlotte, VT 05445, US
Wehr Nature Center, 9701 W. College Avenue, Franklin, WI 53132, US
Wildseed Inc., 16810 Barker Springs, Suite 21B, Houston, TX 77084, US
William Dan Seeds Ltd., West Hamboro, Ontario, L0R 4A2, Canada
Windrift Prairie Shop, Route 2, Oregon, IL 61061, US

Seed-collecting expeditions

Jim and Jenny Archibald, Bryn Collen, Ffostrasol, Llandysul, Dyfed, SA44 5SB, Wales, UK
Chris Chadwell, 81 Parlaunt Road, Slough, Berks, SL3 8BE, UK
Euroseeds, PO Box 95, 741 01 Novy Jicin, Czechoslovakia
Northside Seeds, Ludlow House, 12 Kingsley Avenue, Kettering, Northants, NN16 9EU, UK
John Watson, 24 Kingsway, Petts Wood, Orpington, Kent BR5 1PR, UK

APPENDIX 2

Bibliography

Armitage, Allan M. *Herbaceous perennial plants*. Varsity Press (Georgia), 1989

Bird, Richard, *Border pinks*. Batsford (London), 1993

Bird, Richard, *Complete book of hardy perennials*. Ward Lock (London), 1993

Bird, Richard, *Lilies*. Apple Press (London), 1991

Bird, Richard, *Woodland gardening*. Souvenir Press (London), 1992

Clausen, Ruth Rogers, and Ekstrom, Nicolas H., *Perennials for American gardens*. Random House (New York), 1989

Cobb, James L. S., *Meconopsis*. Helm/Batsford (London), 1989

Cribb, Phillip and Bailes, Christopher, *Hardy orchids*. Helm/Batsford (London), 1989

Grenfell, Diana, *Hosta*, Batsford (London), 1990

Grounds, Roger, *Ornamental grasses*. Helm/Batsford (London), 1989

Growing from seed. Thompson & Morgan (Ipswich, Suffolk & Jackson, N.J.), quarterly, 1986–1991

Jellito, Leo and Schacht, Wilhelm, *Hardy herbaceous perennials*. 2 vols. Batsford (London), Timber Press (Portland), 1990

Lewis, Peter and Lynch, Margaret, *Campanulas*. Helm/Batsford (London), 1989

Lloyd, Christopher, *The well-tempered garden*. Collins (London), 1970

Mathew, Brian, *Hellebores*. Alpine Garden Society (Pershore), 1989

Mathew, Brian, *The Iris*. Batsford (London), 1981

Perry, Frances, *Collins guide to border plants*. Collins (London), 1957

Pesch, Barbara, *Perennials: a nursery source manual*. Brooklyn Botanic Gardens (Brooklyn), 1989

Phillips, Roger and Rix, Martyn, *Perennials* 2 vols, Pan (London), 1991

The Plant Finder. Headmain (Whitbourne), annual

The Plantsman. Royal Horticultural Society (London), quarterly

Swindells, Philip and Mason, David, *The complete book of the water garden*. Ward Lock (London), 1989

Thomas, Graham Stuart, *Perennial garden plants*. 3rd ed. Dent, 1990

Yeo, Peter, *Hardy geraniums*. Helm/Batsford (London), 1985

Young, James A. and Young, Cheryl G., *Collecting, processing and germinating seed of wildland plants*. Timber Press (Portland), 1986

General Index

Page numbers in **bold** refer to the illustrations

Index of Common Names